INVENTIONS OF A BARBAROUS AGE

POETRY FROM CONCEPTUALISM TO RHYME

Robert Archambeau

MadHat Press
Asheville, North Carolina

MadHat Press
MadHat Incorporated
PO Box 8364, Asheville, NC 28814

Copyright © 2016 Robert Archambeau
All rights reserved

The Library of Congress has assigned
this edition a Control Number of
2016914696

ISBN 978-1-941196-35-9 (paperback)

Cover art and design by Marc Vincenz
Book design by MadHat Press

www.madhat-press.com

First Printing

*In memory of Ron Ellingson and the Aspidistra Bookshop,
both of them gone and always with me.*

Table of Contents

Introduction   vii

I. The Future, The Present

You Will Object: Four Futures for Poetry	3
Who is a Contemporary Poet?	9
The Future of Genius	16
Invitation to the Voyage: Notes on the Trajectory of the Poetic Image	23
Charmless and Interesting: The Conceptual Moment in Poetry	31
Inventions of a Barbarous Age: Contemporary Rhyme in Poetry	41

II. Poetry and Community

When Poetry Mattered	65
The Disinheritance of the Poets	71
In Solitude, In Multitude: Crowds and Poetry	81
Between Facebook and Montparnasse: Poetry's Lonely Time	96
Proud Men in Their Studies: On Mark Scroggins	101
So a Poet Walks into a Bar: Notes on Poetry Readings	105

III. Mystics and Gnostics

A Stranger from the Sky: Sun Ra as Poet and Alien	117
The Open Word: An Essay and a Letter for Peter O'Leary	124
A Scribe and His Ghosts: The Poetry of Norman Finkelstein	133
"That's a Real Angel You're Talking To": Robert Duncan and Mythological Consciousness	140
Kenneth Rexroth's Other Worlds	145
A Strange and Quiet Fullness: The Uncanny Charles Simic	150
John Crowe Ransom's Quarrel with God	157
History, Totality, Silence	167

IV. Others

An ABC of Gertrude Stein	177
The American Poet as European, or: Egon Schiele's Ladder	185
Poetry Ha Ha	190
Camping Modernism: Timothy Yu's Chinese Silences	204
Ambiguous Pronouns are Hot: On Rae Armantrout	213
If I Were A Freudian This Essay Would Be Called "The Mother's Penis": A Note on Daisy Fried	219
Poetics of Embodiment	223

V. On Criticism

Hating the Other Kind of Poetry	231
The Work of Criticism in the Age of Mechanical Recommendation	240
The Avant-Garde in Babel	245
Fanaticism! Intolerance! Disinterest! Toward an Aesthetics of Camp	252
The Abject Sublime, or: Jean Genet's Vaseline	264

VI. Afterword

Death of a Bookseller	273

Acknowledgments	278
About the Author	280

Introduction

When Milton set out to defend *Paradise Lost* against potential critics, he anticipated resistance to the fact that the poem did not rhyme. "The measure," he wrote,

> ... is English heroic verse without rime, as that of Homer in Greek, and of Virgil in Latin—rime being no necessary adjunct or true ornament of poem or good verse, in longer works especially, but the invention of a barbarous age, to set off wretched matter and lame meter; graced indeed since by the use of some famous modern poets, carried away by custom, but much to their own vexation, hindrance, and constraint to express many things otherwise, and for the most part worse, than else they would have expressed them. Not without cause therefore some both Italian and Spanish poets of prime note have rejected rime both in longer and shorter works, as have also long since our best English tragedies, as a thing of itself, to all judicious ears, trivial and of no true musical delight ...

How to claim legitimacy for his unrhymed lines? By attacking the legitimacy of rhyme itself. Nothing, with the possible exception of the Bible, could be more legitimate than the classics, so an appeal to the authority of the unrhymed masters of Greek and Latin was in order, an appeal supplemented by the suggestion that English rhymesters were retrograde, falling behind Continental peers who have already abandoned the barbaric invention that is rhyme.

I am as besotted with Milton's poetry as any other ink-stained pedant with tenure in an English department, but I rankle at the example this passage of his prose sets for the discussion of poetry. It's the notion that legitimating one's own style requires the de-legitimation of other styles that strikes me as pernicious, and as much a feature of contemporary discourse about poetry as it was in Milton's day. The poet's will to push his or her own work forward, to establish the taste by which that work will be judged, is of course understandable. And if one is a critic, rather than a poet, the will to impose one's own tastes and convictions on those who read and those who write alike is likewise understandable. But to operate always within the penumbra of one's existing sympathies is an inherently limiting enterprise. One way to treat an encounter with poems that leave you cold, or even repel you, is to stand in judgment over them, but another is to examine the nature of the missed connection, to try to understand what it is about the text, and what it is about your own expectations, that keeps the two from playing well together. This, however poorly realized, has been my goal as a reader of poetry, and that goal has resulted in what seem to me to be two features that inform this collection of otherwise disparate essays.

The first of these features is a refusal to commit, at least consciously, to partisanship for anything other than stylistic pluralism. I do not maintain that if John Crowe Ransom or R.S. Gwynn were right to write the way they have written, Gertrude Stein or Rae Armantrout or Sun Ra must be wrong. Barbarous our age may be, in a thousand ways, but I won't dismiss any poetic inventions deployed in our time as trivial or offering no delight. The subtitle of this book, "Poetry from Conceptualism to Rhyme," seeks to give some sense of the range of poetic practice in our moment, and if the reversal of the expected progression from the established conventions of rhyme to the *arriviste* techniques of Conceptualism seems mannered, my hope is that it avoids the pitfall of offering a vision of poetry as progressing from obsolete forms to the new and improved.

The second feature informing many of the essays gathered hear is what I can only describe as an interest in the contexts giving rise to particular kinds and conventions of poetry. This can be a matter of institutions, such as the poetry reading, or of historical moments, such as the strange geographic dispersion of poets during the early decades of their mass entry into the academy, before the rise of convenient technologies for maintaining community. It can also be a matter of identity, of sexuality, say, or (this is, after all, America) of race. One way or another, many of the essays here seek to understand poetry as a symptom of its originating conditions, although not only as that: an attempt at explaining a poem in terms of its social or psychological origin need not be the same thing as attempting to explain that poem away.

One result of looking to the forces conditioning and giving rise to the creative work of others is the creeping sense that one's own structures of thought, response, and feeling are also contingent on a thousand factors, that one's critical practices are socially located and far from absolute. This makes arguing for the legitimacy of one's tastes harder to do, and even undesirable. But it does give one cause to reflect on the nature of criticism, and to ask about our categories of analysis: hence the inclusion in this book of a number of essays about the practice of criticism. Another result has been, almost by accident, to find myself considering the trajectory of poetry through time, and sometimes to speculate (a foolish but fascinating activity) on the future of poetry, and of the ideas we use to understand it. I await and welcome the rebuke of future history for anything I have written in this vein.

Looking over the table of contents for this book, I'm surprised by how much I have been drawn to two themes in particular: poetry and community, and poetry connected, however tenuously, to mystical experience. All I can say by way of explanation is that I have long felt the presence of Karl Marx over one shoulder, urging me to look to the social sphere, and St. Francis over the other, pointing toward some elusive and otherworldly elsewhere. I have been grateful for the guiding presence of both figures while examining a range of poetic invention.

I
The Future, The Present

You Will Object:

Four Futures of Poetry

As a coward and an academic, if that is not redundant, I must begin with a caveat: the future is hard to predict. But with that out of the way, let me say this about the future of poetry—two things are certain: it will be ubiquitous, and it will rhyme. And I'm not just talking about subtle rhyme, or 'background rhyme,' to steal a term from Stephen Burt's essay "Cornucopia, or, Contemporary American Rhyme"—not just the kind of rhyme that, in modern poems like Auden's "Musée des Beaux Arts" or Larkin's "Mr. Bleaney" "would not usually draw more attention to itself than other aspects of the verse." I'm talking about rhyme that pushes itself to the foreground, rhyme that sets out to showcase virtuosity.

Almost any respectable contemporary American poet you're likely to be thinking of eschews this sort of rhyme on all but the rarest of occasions, and for good reason. As Anthony Madrid puts it in his history of the topic, *The Warrant for Rhyme*:

> The vast majority of perfect rhymes in English are in very heavy rotation during the many centuries of English rhyming. In order to fetch a rhyme pair that would in any way be novel in itself, a poet ... would have to travel a great distance—and the resulting rhyme would very likely have the character of a stunt.

But stunts—amazing stunts, comic stunts, aggressive stunts—are exactly what the most prominent practitioners of rhymed verse in America want, and achieve. Consider, for example, the words of Clipse:

> All the snow on the timepiece confusin' 'em
> All the snow on the concrete Peruvian
> I flew it in, it ruined men, I'm through with them
> Blamed for misguiding their life

> So go and sue me then

Or those of Jay-Z:

> Rollin' in the Rolls-Royce Corniche
> Only the doctors got this, I'm hidin' from police
> Cocaine seats
> All white like I got the whole thing bleached
> Drug dealer chic
> I'm wonderin' if a thug's prayers reach
> Is Pious pious cause god loves pious?
> Socrates asks, "whose bias do y'all seek?"
> All for Plato, screech.
> I'm out here ballin', I know y'all hear my sneaks
> Jesus was a carpenter, Yeezy laid beats
> Hova flow the holy ghost, get the hell up out your seats,
> Preach.

These are, of course, the words of rappers. And their rhymed verse is ubiquitous in our culture, and certain to continue to be so well into the future.

But you object! Perhaps you're thinking "that's not poetry, that's *rhymed verse*" and using one or another of the arguments made to disentangle the two (I like Wordsworth's, from the "Preface" to *Lyrical Ballads*, but Milton's attack on rhyme is good, too). In any case, you feel there's been some kind of sleight of hand—and since I'm nothing if not accommodating, let me allow the objection, and change my thesis.

*

So this: it's difficult to predict the future of poetry, but two things are certain: it will be ubiquitous, and it will be so delicately suggestive and allusive that we would be forgiven for thinking it comes straight out of Mallarmé's symbolist playbook. Consider what Mallarmé said when, in 1891, he condescended to an interview with *L'Echo de Paris*:

... there must only be allusion. The contemplation of objects, the images that soar from the reveries they have induced, constitute the song. The Parnassians, who take the object in its entirety and show it, lack mystery.... the enjoyment of the poem ... derives from the pleasure of step-by-step discovery; to suggest, that is the dream.

This is ordinary enough as a statement of French symbolist poetics: Paul Verlaine makes much the same point in his poem "Art Poétique," when he declaims "... nothing but nuance! / Only nuance affiances / Dream to dream and the flute to the horn!" But is this sort of thing really ubiquitous in America? And is it our future (as opposed to the French past)? Yes!

Symbolist poetics are everywhere. They might even be in your pocket, if you're one of that dying breed of people who still uses a Blackberry to check email and make calls. Consider the name of that device—the people who named it certainly did. When the marketing people at Research in Motion (Blackberry's parent company) approached David Placek of the publicity firm Lexicon with the device, they wanted to call it the "Mail Merge." Placek and his team hated the name, for much the same reason that Mallarmé hated the flat-footed poems of the Parnassians: because it offered nothing but accurate description. What was wanted was nuance, allusion, connotation—and so we got "Blackberry," a one-word symbolist poem of great intensity. Think of it! Of how the word "Blackberry" brings to mind the seriousness and the sleekness of high technology associated with 'black' and the fun, happiness, and freshness associated with 'berry.' It also brings about another association with fruit, which in the context of information technology invokes Apple, and therefore alludes to ideas of innovation, high standards, and the David who challenges Microsoft's stodgy Goliath.

If the Blackberry is dead or dying, it is by no means the fault of the gizmo's name. We've become used to product names concocted in this way, so it's difficult for us to grasp how this means of creating brand names is specific to an advanced state of the consumer economy. The naming conventions that gave us "Blackberry" represent a real departure from earlier naming conventions. "Blackberry" is not a brand name like those of the earlier industrial period, when a product was called "Murphy Oil Soap" because it was oil soap sold by Murphy. New products don't have names like "Heinz Tomato Ketchup," they have names like "Swiffer," or "Dasani"—also products of the good people at Lexicon. Advertisers have systematized symbolist poetics, and placed them all around us, in a manner that only promises to become more intense and all-saturating in the market-researched future.

But you object! You object, perhaps because the notion that Mallarmé has been kidnapped by Pepsico is too sad to bear. Or maybe because you wanted to hear about art poetry—the stuff people in the poetry biz think of as poetry. And since I'm nothing if not accommodating, let me allow the objection, and change my thesis.

*

So this: it is difficult to predict the future of poetry, but two things are certain: it will be marginal, and it will become increasingly about itself. Consider the trajectory of American poetry from the Puritans, through the Fireside Poets of the mid and late nineteenth century, on through modernism and beyond. If we compress that whole history into a few sentences, what we get is this. We begin with religious tracts in verse, produced with less concern for the art of language than with the work of saving souls. By the time we get to the Fireside poets, we see American poetry even more popular, with no respectable household lacking its book of verse. But it wasn't the art that put those books into those households so much as it was the respectability: those poets were figures who gave voice to the middle class's values. The poetry was at the service of expressing and upholding those values, and treasured for that reason. Then things got strange. Poetry became much less about popular public morality, and more about things particular to itself. With the more radical elements of modernism, and the tradition stretching on to the Language Poets, we see poetry that foregrounds language for its own sake—something that becomes so commonplace in poetry that, by the middle of the century, the linguist Roman Jakobson calls it "the poetic function," treating something particular to our peculiar circumstances as a transhistorical norm.

The movement from poetry as a popular means of soul-saving and public morality to poetry as a kind of special use of language for its own sake runs concurrently with the growth of a subculture specific to poetry (journals consisting of nothing but poetry and poetry reviews, academics hired to be poets, degrees in poetry writing, and so forth). And the trajectory toward specialization continues, with a movement away from language and toward commentaries on the subculture of poetry itself. This is, after all, a major topic of Conceptualism, the movement making considerable waves in the tiny teacup of poetry culture, if nowhere else. Consider, for example, Vanessa Place's chapbook titled *$20*, which consists of twenty one-dollar bills stitched together, presented under her signature, and sold for $50 each. It's a commentary on cultural capital and on what happens when something becomes designated "poetry." It's also a lot more specialized than the poems of the Puritans, in that it means most to those equipped to see it as part of, and a commentary on, the little demimonde of the poetry world (a world which did not exist in the America of the seventeenth or eighteenth century, nor, arguably, in the nineteenth, in anything like the current form or scale).

But you object! That movement into linguistic and institutional self-refection may be one future for poetry, but surely it isn't the whole future, or even the whole of the past! Robert Frost, for example, who was the exact contemporary of Gertrude Stein, carried something like the Fireside Poet tradition function into the modern period, and Robert Pinsky has carried it into the present (making him, I should note, a very good graduation speaker, as I can verify from personal experience). So you object. Very well, and since I'm nothing if not accommodating, I will change my thesis: but I warn you, this is the last time.

*

So this: it is difficult to predict the future of poetry, but two things are certain: it will be marginal, and it will be everywhere. This sounds contradictory, but only until one accepts what demographers (and, especially, marketing firms) have come to accept as fact: there is no mainstream America, not anymore. There are only margins, or identity groups—and each identity group has its politics. And along with these identity politics come a myriad of identity poetics: poetry that sets out to articulate ethnic identity, gender identity, racial identity, disability identity, generational identity, regional identity, or even professional identity (consider cowboy poetry). Sometimes this poetry remains invisible outside of its micro-community, sometimes it is taken up by and celebrated in the institutions of the poetry world. The critic David Kellogg once demonstrated that Adrienne Rich was the identity poet *par excellence*, since she "participates in, or is read as participating in, the social claims" of multiple identities. This kind of poetry promises to grow with the increasing diversity of America, and the need for new groups to claim their place and articulate their values. It is a far cry from art for its own sake, this identity-articulation, and in some sense more vital for having greater reach: one is reminded of what Arthur Henry Hallam once said about his friend Tennyson, who grew popular for articulating the ideology of the rising English bourgeoisie: "whatever is mixed up with art … is always more favorably regarded than art free and unalloyed." So if you didn't like my earlier claim about the increasing specialization of poetry and the increasing centrality of language-as-language, let this latest thesis about the future of poetry warm your heart.

*

Of course my four theses—which amount to eight certainties, if my math holds—are not mutually exclusive. In fact, each one of them refers to an element of poetry's present, and to contemporary activities that draw on different elements of the past (rhyme, French symbolism, aesthetic autonomy, identity politics). And one thing is certain: in the future, poets will continue to find things in the past worth reviving. Which things, we can't say for sure, because it's hard to predict the past.

Who is a Contemporary Poet?

What does it mean to be a contemporary poet? It's a trickier question than it seems, and not just because of the difficulty in defining poetry. In fact, the greater part of the difficulty may come in defining the nature of the contemporary.

I'm no stranger to arguments about the meaning of the term. In 2011, for example, the conceptual poet Kenneth Goldsmith and I had a bit of a disagreement that, at root, was a disagreement about the meaning of the contemporary. He had said something about how writers who respond to their times will of necessity be innovative and relevant, and had pointed to those who engage the vast changes wrought by electronic communications as an example of this. I had objected, saying:

> To dismiss all that writing by saying that people who are not engaged in a particular practice are not "relevant" or not "responding to their time" … is to argue that there is only one way to respond to our times—which is patently false. I mean, crawling into a cave and trying to write runic poetry on stones, if one did it now, would be a response to our times, since the imaginative rejection of the present moment is a very powerful and critical way of responding to that moment (think of all the Victorian medievalism of guys like William Morris: it was a radical response to the industrial moment).

Goldsmith was kind enough to respond, saying, *à propos* those poets who make an art out of the electronic appropriation of existing textual archives (often of great scale) that theirs is "the most relevant, contemporary, and engaged response" to our moment.

Our dispute was based on two different senses of the meaning of the contemporary. My own sense, which could charitably be described as expansive, and uncharitably described as ploddingly commonsensical, was that anything produced in our time was, by definition, contemporary. Our moment produces everything in it—and in poetic terms, that includes everything from traditional odes and sonnets to free-verse lyrics to emulations of classical epic to surrealism to things that could have appeared in the first issue of $L=A=N=G=U=A=G=E$ to the kind of textual appropriations Goldsmith admires, and much else besides. In the view I was espousing back in 2011, to elide any of that was to lie about our moment, to reduce something heterodox and complex to something much simpler. Goldsmith's sense, which could charitably be described as precise, and uncharitably be described as narrow, was rather different. The category of the contemporary wasn't a grab bag into which anything coming into being at the moment must be stuffed. It was more like a Platonic form, which could be approached with various degrees of perfection: some things were more contemporary than others, and at the time of his argument Goldsmith considered works of conceptual appropriation the "most … contemporary." I inferred from this that what made one thing more contemporary than another, for Goldsmith, was the degree to which it engaged with the features of our moment that, in his estimate, set us apart from the past. A love sonnet might still be made, but it didn't address what made our age different from Shakespeare's age. But works that made use of, and depended on, the textual conditions created by new media were more contemporary that those that did not.

Neither my own definition nor Goldsmith's seems adequate to me now. My definition was too breezily commonsensical, too free of any careful attempt to understand the meaning of the term. Goldsmith's, too, left too much unexamined and unarticulated: indeed, I've had to infer a lot in order to make sense of it, and those inferences may or may not connect to what he had in mind, most of which he kept in his mind. So, in quest of something more refined than what either I or Goldsmith offered, I've gone to Giorgio Agamben, the Italian philosopher whose many works include the elegant little essay "What is the Contemporary?" If we follow his line of reasoning, we come up with something subtler than the blunt instruments Goldsmith and I had at our disposal.

There are five points to Agamben's concept of the contemporary. He derives the first of them from Nietzsche—or, to be precise, from an observation Roland Barthes once made about Nietzsche's *Untimely Meditations* during a lecture at the Collège de France: "the contemporary," said Barthes, "is the untimely." In this view, to be contemporary is to be a little at out of phase with one's own time. Nietzsche called his thinking "untimely" because, as he put it, it sought "to understand as an illness, a disability, and a defect" the kind of consciousness that his age took pride in. To share the general way of thinking of your time may seem like the most contemporary thing possible, but not for Nietzsche, and not for Agamben, who follows him. In Agamben's view, "Those who are truly contemporary … are those who neither perfectly coincide with it nor adjust themselves to its demands." It is their out-of-jointness with their moment that renders them "more capable than others of perceiving and grasping their own time." Those who fit in with their times too easily simply lack the distance to see those times. They embody their moment, but cannot understand it—indeed, they probably feel no need to understand it, understanding being the fruit of alienation.

The second component of Agamben's idea of contemporaneity has to do with the nature of the understanding that comes to those who are out-of-joint with their times. "The contemporary," says Agamben, "is he who firmly holds his gaze on his own time so as to perceive not its light, but rather its darkness." This isn't a matter of seeing only the evil or unpleasant side of the moment, or its injustices. The darkness is not so much ethical as epistemological: the truly contemporary person sees the time in which he or she lives not in its own terms, but in terms that reveal things about the time that those who live in it comfortably do not see. Agamben doesn't provide an example, but we might think of Freud as a true contemporary thinker of the late nineteenth and early twentieth centuries. In an era that still thought in terms of progress, he was a great revealer of the primitive, the animalistic and the atavistic. Where others saw rational motives, he saw the irrational at work. His thinking seemed utterly counter-intuitive to many, and his notions of the eroticized family drama are still disconcerting to many. If, as Agamben says, "the contemporaries are only those who do not allow themselves to be blinded by the lights of a century, and so manage to get a glimpse of the shadows in those lights," Freud was surely one of them.

Knowledge is insufficient for true contemporaneity, though, or so Agamben asserts in the third moment of his thinking about the issue. For Agamben, the contemporary person (who, as you have no doubt noted, is quite rare) is in agreement with Marx when, in the "Theses on Feuerbach," he maintained that interpreting the world is inadequate and said "the point is to change it." In Agamben's thinking, the contemporary "working within chronological time, urges, presses, and transforms it."

The final two components of Agamben's theory of the contemporary concern the connection of the present with other periods of time, especially the past. Firstly, the contemporary sees the living power of the past within the present:

> Contemporariness inscribes itself in the present by marking it above all as archaic. Only he who perceives the indices and signatures of the archaic in the most modern and recent can be contemporary. 'Archaic' means close to the *arkhé*, that is to say, the origin. But the origin is not only situated in the chronological past: it is contemporary with historical becoming and does not cease to operate within it, just as the embryo continues to be active in the tissues of the mature organism, and the child in the psychic life of the adult.

In any given period, most people are unaware of the presence of the past in their everyday life: it is part of the darkness of their era, the darkness that only the true contemporary sees. This isn't an obscure point, though it may sound like one. Almost no speakers of English, for example, give any thought to the fact that the words they speak are a living example of particular historical events. The Battle of Hastings in 1066 led to the domination of the Anglo-Saxons by a French-speaking elite, and the language we speak was forged in that crucible of conquest, where French and Anglo-Saxon melted together, giving us the rich and redundant (Anglo-Saxon "underwater" and

French-derived "submarine") vocabulary we use. 1066 *happens* in every sentence spoken in English, it *lives* in every sentence, though the speakers of the language tend to have no notion of it whatsoever. And this lack of awareness, this darkness, means that most people don't fully live vast portions of the things that live in them: that is, they don't grasp, and never come into conscious contact with, the things that make them who they are. As Agamben puts it, "The present is nothing other than this unlived element in everything that is lived.... The attention to this 'unlived' is the life of the contemporary."

Finally, Agamben tells us that the true contemporary, in seeing the dark or unlived parts of his or her time, doesn't just work to change that time: the contemporary changes the nature of the past as well. St. Paul, says Agamben, was a contemporary, because he saw in the Old Testament prefigurations of the moment of Christ: Adam became something new, a figure for and even a promise of Christ. The capacity to re-see the entire past in relation to elements of the present that the majority do not see is of central importance to the contemporary: "the contemporary is not only the one who, perceiving the darkness of the present, grasps a light ... he is also the one who, dividing and interpolating time, is capable of transforming it and putting it into relation with other times." This needn't be conscious: indeed, it ought not to be something one tries to do: for the true contemporary, it arises spontaneously, as "he is able to read history in unforeseen ways, to 'cite it' according to a necessity that does not arise in any way from his will, but from an exigency to which he cannot not respond."

So a true contemporary is out of joint with the times, and this alienation gives a perspective from which he sees the time in ways the time does not see itself. He sees, in particular, the persistence of the past in the present, and wishes to change or modify the present in ways that also reconfigure how we feel about the past. It's a tall order, and contemporaries are rare. I've mentioned Freud. Marx seems like another figure who lived his times as a true contemporary—discontented, seeing forces at play in the world that others could not see, seeing the persistence of the past in the social order and wishing it away, and providing us with a way of seeing that re-scripted all of history from a tale of battles and kings to a tale of economic forces, and all of this not chosen as an academic project but coming about as a result of social injustices he could not abide.

But what about the question we started with? What about the contemporary poet? If we view the contemporary as Agamben does, we find ourselves looking for poets surprisingly similar to those described in T.S. Eliot's essay "Tradition and the Individual Talent." What, after all, is Agamben's notion of the contemporary's sense of the living nature of the archaic but an extrapolation, beyond poems, of Eliot's assertion that "we shall often find that not only the best, but the most individual parts of [a poet's] work may be those in which the dead poets, his ancestors, assert their immortality most vigorously"? What is the conscious awareness of the often-darkened past than Eliot's "historical sense," which "involves a perception, not only of the pastness of the past, but of its presence" and which compels the poet to write "not merely with his own generation in his bones, but with a feeling that the whole of the literature of Europe" is present? And what is Agamben's sense that the true contemporary reconfigures the past but Eliot's notion that the monuments of the tradition "form an ideal order among themselves that is modified by the introduction of the new (the really new) work of art among them"?

An Agambenian contemporary poet, then, is much like an Eliotic one. Dante, surely, was a contemporary poet by this definition: aware of the presence of the classical past, deeply critical of his own era's failings, writing with those things in his bones, and compelled to re-present the past as a mere prelude to the Christian order of the present (Dante's Virgil, we must recall, was his necessary guide to the underworld, but was unable to enter the territory of the *Paradiso*).

If to be a contemporary were merely to be fashionable—to be up to date in terms of style and technique—then all one would need to do to be a contemporary poet would be to read "The Moves," an essay outlining various elliptical and post-elliptical poetic techniques by Elissa Gabbert. But to be a contemporary poet in an Agambenian sense is altogether more demanding. One would have to know those poetic moves, but also see their limits, their historical genesis, and the reasons for their prominence, and to be dissatisfied with the state of affairs they represent. One would have to write with an animus toward those moves, and to draw on unexpected elements of the literary past in ways that make us reconceptualize our relation to that past. It's easy to be a fashionable poet, but hardly any poets can be contemporary.

Seen from the perspective of Agamben's theory, my old definition of the contemporary appears naïve, and Goldsmith's is hardly any better, depending as it does on the poet's engagement not with things about our time that most of us do not see, but with the most obvious manifestations of our time: new communications technologies. Goldsmith, though, has always been more interesting than his ideas. When, for example, he was invited to read poetry at the White House, he presented his own work *Traffic*—a verbatim transcription of New York traffic reports, including reports for travel over the Brooklyn Bridge—alongside poetry about that bridge by Walt Whitman and Hart Crane. In drawing his work into overt relation to a literary past, he took a step toward the kind of awareness of, and critical relation to, the past that was so important to Eliot, and is so important to Agamben. In short, he proved that he may become a contemporary poet yet—one of the few. But if he does, it will be despite his theory of contemporaneity, not because of it.

The Future of Genius

If one were to shout the question "Who is a literary genius?" in the general direction of a gaggle of young men in Warby Parker glasses and Chuck Taylor sneakers, the air would likely resound with shouts of "David Foster Wallace!" much to the chagrin of Jonathan Franzen, should he skulk within earshot. But what is meant by the term *genius*? And how much longer will it be with us? The term, after all, sits more easily with the Romantic poet in his garret than with the writer of our moment, recycling found text on her Twitter account, and thinkers and artists from Walter Benjamin to Damien Hirst have sought to consign the term to the dustbin of critical history. Indeed, should you punch the word into Google's Ngram Viewer, you'll see a slow decline in frequency of usage since 1800, with a steepish drop between 1970 and 1980 before a more recent leveling-off. One wonders, then: does genius have a future in our understanding of literature? Or is the genius to be taken to Roland Barthes' graveyard and buried in state, next to his less-distinguished peer, the author?

*

To understand the possible death of the genius, we need first to go back to the circumstances of his birth. The idea of genius, of course, has been with us since long before 1800: the Romans used the word to refer to a tutelary spirit attendant upon a birth or creation, the guiding force of a life, institution, or nation. In the Renaissance, the notion was revived in a less supernatural sense, and used to refer to someone's disposition or personality. By the seventeenth century, it had come to refer to one's capacities or capabilities, but it lacked the sense of uniqueness and creativity that it was to take on a century later, when it became the subject of intense theorizing. In the middle of the eighteenth century we find Samuel Johnson arguing in *The Rambler* to the effect that genius was nothing but hard work, a property of all who would earn their laurels by the sweat of their brows. But as with so many of Johnson's efforts, this was a rearguard action: a new genius, shimmering with glamor, was about to be born, Johnson's reservations notwithstanding.

While the creation of the modern genius was a group effort, it was preeminently Kant who shaped the contours of the idea. Echoing the ancients with their tutelary spirits, Kant saw genius as something with which one was born, not something gained through efforts and exertions. He also saw it as something that could not be governed by rules: "no definite rule can be given beforehand the products of genius," he writes in *Critique of Judgment*, "originality must be its first property." Indeed, the genius feels the force of original perception thrusting itself upon him, beyond any idea he may have had about good taste or fine art: he "does not know himself how the ideas come to him, and also does not have it in his power to think up such things at will or according to plan, and to communicate to others precepts that would put them in a position to produce similar products." Despite this inability to lay down rules, genius demands posterity. It's not that the work of a genius is not to be imitated, not exactly, but that it calls out the genius in others, "whom it awakens to a feeling of their own originality and whom it stirs to exercise art in freedom from the constraint of rules."

The Kantian idea of genius has resonated down the centuries: John Stuart Mill, for example, sings a Kantian tune to a Victorian liberal beat when, in *On Liberty*, he describes the "necessity of allowing it [genius] to unfold freely both in thought and practice," away from rules, and grants genius the capacity to give those who appreciate it "a chance of being themselves original." Closer to our own time, Michel Foucault sounds the Kantian note when, in "What is an Author?" he describes the "founders of discursivity" as "not just the authors of their own works" but the makers of possibilities for new creation by others, including marked departures from their own works. "Freud," says Foucault, "is not just the author of *The Interpretation of Dreams* or *Jokes in Their Relation to the Unconscious*; Marx is not just the author of the *Communist Manifesto* or *Das Kapital*: they both have established an endless possibility of discourse" including divergences from their own writing. Geniuses like Freud and Marx have a fecund posterity, inspiring not only imitators but the original genius of others.

Foucault, it is true, flinches at the possibility of extending his concept to literary writing, seeing the conventions established by a literary innovator as too prescriptive, a matter of rules rather than new possibilities:

> Ann Radcliffe's texts opened the way for a certain number of resemblances and analogies which have their model or principle in her work. The latter contains characteristic signs, figures, relationships, and structures that could be reused by others. In other words, to say that Ann Radcliffe founded the Gothic horror novel means that in the nineteenth-century Gothic novel one will find, as in Ann Radcliffe's works, the theme of the heroine caught in the trap of her own innocence, the hidden castle, the character of the black, cursed hero devoted to making the world expiate the evil done to him, and all the rest of it. On the other hand, when I speak of Marx or Freud as founders of discursivity, I mean that they made possible not only a certain number of analogies but also (and equally important) a certain number of differences. They have created a possibility for something other than their discourse, yet something belonging to what they founded.

Foucault's refusal to see Radcliffe in the company of Freud and Marx may simply stem from ignorance, though: who among the viewers of *Buffy the Vampire Slayer* can say that Radcliffe's gothic novels haven't led to something other than her own discourse, yet still belonging to that which she founded?

Along with its inborn quality, its rule-breaking, and its inspiring of future originality, genius has another element: autonomy vis-a-vis the needs of its immediate audience. Saint-Lambert, writing for Diderot's *Encylopédie*, tells us that genius cannot be bound by the taste of an audience:

For something to be beautiful according to the rules of taste, it must be elegant, polished, wrought without the appearance of labor: to be a work of genius it must sometimes be careless, must have an appearance of irregularity, roughness, wildness. Sublimity and genius shine in Shakespeare like lightening in a long night, while Racine is always beautiful: Homer is full of genius, and Virgil full of elegance.

Mill puts the matter a bit more bluntly. People will nod and agree that genius is a good thing until they actually encounter it, when "nearly all, at heart, think that they can do very well without it." Sad though this is, it should, he continues, come as no surprise, since "originality is the one thing which unoriginal minds cannot feel the use of." From where Mill sat when he wrote these lines in *On Liberty* we can take in a historical vista including several generations of bohemian artists, whose freedom from conventional taste is matched only by their belief in posthumous appreciation, and by the desperation of their material poverty. The desire to offend established taste with newness continues to our own day, too, not only in obvious ways, but in ways that could only come out of the long history of the idea of the originality of the genius. What is the Conceptualist "unoriginal genius" of a writer like Kenneth Goldsmith—who seeks to present unmodified existing texts under his own name—but an attempt to shock the taste of a public long accustomed to originality? Rule-breaking remains the currency by which certain ambitious writers seek to claim the prized title of genius—all that has changed are the rules of the moment, waiting to be broken.

*

Why, we may ask, was our particular notion of the genius born in the eighteenth century, and why didn't it die there? The answer, or much of it, is simple: the genius had a friend, far less glamorous but in a historical sense far more consequential: that drab hero of history, the hardy, stolid bourgeois. Just as the genius was to break the rule-bound aesthetic conventions of the court (whose great icon must be Nicolas Boileau-Despréaux, Louis XIV's arbiter of taste), the bourgeois set out to break the norms of aristocratic behavior and the aristocratic stranglehold on the economy. Both genius and the bourgeoisie hold up the free individual as an ideal, and overlap so strongly in disposition that the literary historian Alfred Optiz would declare "genius is the elevation of the free bourgeois individual." He glosses his thesis by saying that genius offers

> ... an image of man that proclaims the creative freedom and unlimited possibilities of the outstanding individual. The figure of the artist or scientist of genius displays the same features as that of the dynamic entrepreneur of original accumulation which entered upon an expansive phase in France during the seventeenth and eighteenth centuries with the growth of manufacturing and overseas trade. Where the artist of genius demands freedom from censorship and emancipation from restrictive institutional rules or intellectual prejudices, the entrepreneur calls for economic freedom of trade and the abolition of the guild system.

Rule-wreckers, born to remake the world in their image rather than to bow and scrape to the court on its own terms—such are the geniuses, and such are the members of the bourgeoisie. Is it any surprise that Romanticism, the first truly bourgeois literary movement, puffed itself up on the idea of genius? And it didn't just do this in literary manifestoes: it did it in the realm of the law. The very notion of copyright was invented with reference to the idea of a genius' unique style making his writings more than a mere restatement of commonly known facts. The need to protect the genius' claim on his work into the future was born out of the sense that only in posterity would his work become recognized, accepted ... and profitable. Indeed, the legal writings of Thomas Noon Talfourd, the great nineteenth-century English advocate of copyright, are peppered with phrases from Wordsworth, especially the quip that "every great and original writer in proportion as he is great and original, must himself create the taste by which he is to be relished." The genius and the creator of intellectual property law stand as unlikely, but vital, allies.

Genius, though, is an unreliable ally, and is at least as much an anti-bourgeois force as it is an emanation of bourgeois civilization. When the great theorist of the avant-garde, Peter Bürger, turned his gaze to the question of genius, he concluded that the questioning of rule-driven aesthetics was integral to the rejection of bourgeois rationality. Commitment to genius, that inexplicable, indefinable gift from beyond, was part of an irrationalist rebellion against the quantification, commodification, and disenchantment of the world, a rebellion breaking out worldwide from Romanticism to Surrealism and beyond. Historian Darrin McMahon expands on this idea, seeing the idea of the genius as a way of preserving the idea of the divinely touched prophet in a secularized age. He also sees in the ideal of genius a rejection of bourgeois egalitarianism: in the age of democracy, when we are taught that all men are created equal, the genius gives those who crave it someone to believe in as a glamorous superior, an *übermensch* Zarathustra in a world gone grey with disappointing sameness.

The genius, like Barthes' author, is very much a modern figure, produced (as Barthes out it) as our society "discovered the prestige of the individual," and in good measure the result of capitalism, with its emphasis on the individual over the collective, its contempt for old rules and love of "creative destruction," and its emphasis on everything—even individual style—as a kind of property. But is it likely to remain with us?

The important thing to remember, when asking about the future of genius, is that the authority of genius is charismatic: it derives from an individual's exemplary status, his or her ethos, rather than any external force. No institution bestows it; nor is it legitimated by a religion, by credentials, or by state ideology. It is no coincidence that the genius is born when literature enters its un-institutionalized phase: it comes into being when the writer ceases to subsist on court patronage, basking in an authority that radiates out from the prince or monarch. It is the child of an era when literature is subject to fickle market forces, and must accommodate itself to them (via copyright and other measures) or defend itself against them (by claiming the autonomy of genius, a self-affirming rejection of market values). The novel is a child of this era, whereas poetry is flung into it kicking and screaming and nostalgic for lost status, but both genres are equally without external sanction. The authority of the writer must be charismatic, since (a very few knighthoods and laureateships notwithstanding) there is precious little institutional authority on offer.

But what now, when much of literature (especially literature that sees itself as *literary*) has entered the academy, not only as the site of interpretation and evaluation but as the site of creation? For those who make their way in creative writing programs, authority is, for most practical purposes, a matter of credentials and institutional position. In this academic context, the term "genius" has come to seem quaint as a way of describing literary glamor—and how could it not? If, as Marx has it, our social being determines our consciousness, a life led in a context of institutionally sanctioned authority will sap one's faith in charismatic forms of power. One of academe's contributions to the dip in the Google ngram ranking of the word "genius" in the 1970s stems from how critical thinking, in that period, followed Barthes' cue to direct critical thinking away from the individual and toward large-scale processes of signification. But the failure of the term to revive since then owes something to another side of academe, with offices across the corridor from the critical theorists: the institutionalized, even industrialized, creative writing program.

The literary genius may be languishing among the academics, but he still breathes in non-institutional contexts, among those Brooklyn-and-Portland-dwelling wearers of Chuck Taylors and Warby Parker glasses, where the dream, or myth, of the unique, free, rule-breaking original genius, unbeholden to any authority beyond his own charisma, lives on, and inspires. And as we enter a crisis of the academic humanities, with its attendant undermining of institutional literary authority, we may be seeing history breathe new life into the body of the literary genius.

INVITATION TO THE VOYAGE:

Notes on the Trajectory of the Poetic Image

"Invitation to the Voyage," the dark jewel in the crown of Baudelaire's prose poems, is many things. For me, it has become a touchstone for understanding what is modern—and, for that matter, postmodern—in poetry. The modern quality of Baudelaire's prose poem shows best when we hold it up in contrast against its most significant background: Dante's *Vita Nuova*. Both "Invitation to the Voyage" and the mixed prose and poetry of the *Vita Nuova* are drenched in yearning for a woman who is more than just a woman: she is also a gateway to something infinite and eternal. But the differences between Baudelaire's eternity and Dante's are striking, and go beyond matters of religious doctrine to the far more serious issue of the nature of the literary image. To look at the differences between Baudelaire and Dante is to see the trajectory of the poetic image through time, and perhaps to better understand the nature of that image today.

Aesthete that he is, Baudelaire gives us, in "Invitation to the Voyage," an image of a place that is somehow the antithesis of the ordinary world—a place that isn't described in isolation, but through contrast to our busy, vulgar world. It shines in the beyond, this better place where "slower hours" than ours "contain more thoughts, where clocks strike happiness with a deeper and more significant solemnity." The nature of the place isn't defined with any exactness, but evoked by a series of images—tall windows divided into leaded glass panes, a bright, shining array of kitchen copper, the light of sunsets settling richly on the walls. Is it an aesthetic place? A place of interiors and artifice? A place of order? Of dignified domesticity? It's hard to say, exactly, except that there's a mood of quiet and order and timelessness. It isn't just an indefinite place, though: it is also an impossible one, or contradictory: it might, says Baudelaire, be called "the China of Europe."

If anything is certain about this place to which Baudelaire would flee, it is that it is a country made in the image of his beloved—a point on which he insists. Everything made in the country, he tells her, "is made in your image"—indeed, it is a country entirely "in your image." As the prose poem reaches its climax, we read "These treasures, this furniture, this luxury, this order, these perfumes, these miraculous flowers, are you. They are you, too, these great rivers and these quiet canals." The beloved is this escapist paradise, into which Baudelaire himself enters in his mind. Continuing with his image of rivers and canals, he writes, "these vast ships that drift down them, laden with riches, and from whose decks rise the monotonous songs of laboring sailors, they are my thoughts which slumber or rise and fall on your breast." It is the beloved who, in embodying or signifying the better, purer, more timeless place, brings Baudelaire away from this world and toward the eternal: she leads his river-faring thoughts "gently toward the sea, which is infinite." This infinity isn't the beloved, exactly, though: it is a place the poet reaches via love for her, a place where his thoughts can stay only for a while before they weary of it, and "now enriched ... return to you from the infinite."

The debt Baudelaire owes to Dante is profound. Firstly, there is the way the beloved woman connects to the other, better world. The best way to describe the relationship of the two in "Invitation to the Voyage" is to lift a passage on the *Vita Nuova* from the scholar and translator Barbara Reynolds, who says Dante writes of Beatrice in a manner that represents "not personification or symbolism, but the perception that actual persons can be images of qualities beyond themselves." That is: a real person, rather than an allegorical figure, an imaginary metaphor, or a symbolic creature is the image and pathway to a world better than the one around us. The concept is new with Dante, and ranks among his greatest inventions. It is a concept very much alive in contemporary poetry, as we see, for example in Lorenzo Thomas' poem "God Sends Love Disguised as Ordinary People," where we needn't go further than the title to see the notion that real individuals in our lives represent something greater and more eternal than themselves.

What is more, the specific qualities of the world Baudelaire associates with the beloved hold much in common with the world to which Dante ascends via Beatrice. For both poets, the beloved is the gateway to a love not only of the beloved herself, but of eternity. Dante's initial love for Beatrice in the *Vita Nuova* begins with the senses, with his glimpse of her on the street. The book recounts the transformations of this love: from a love governed by the sensual attraction, to a love of the poetry of love, to a despair of love at the death of Beatrice, to an abortive revival of earthly love for "Lady Pitiful," the woman who looks on him compassionately in his bereavement. Had Dante allowed this new love to flower, the *Vita Nuova* would have been a startlingly secular book, one in which the pleasures of this life follow upon one another cyclically, one dying love leading to another. But the new secular love, a "little spirit, newly sent by Love," that "Its longings and desires before me brings" is banished. Dante tells of how, before this little spirit could grow, his "heart began to repent sorrowfully of the desire by which it had so basely allowed itself to be possessed for some days." Instead, he turns his gaze upwards, to love Beatrice in Heaven—and this brings about the final, most profound transformation of his love. His love becomes "a pilgrim spirit" and "ascends into the heavens." The final poem of *Vita Nuova* traces the journey:

> Beyond the widest of the circling spheres
> A sigh which leaves my heart aspires to move.
> A new celestial influence which Love
> Bestows by virtue of its tears
> Impels it ever upwards.

Just as Baudelaire's voyage on the river of the beloved guides him to the infinite sea, Dante's quest for Beatrice guides him away from the moral to the eternal.

Of course Dante's eternity is specifically Christian—indeed, when he depicts Beatrice following one Giovanna (the Italian feminine of John) he makes her a female Christ, appearing after John the Baptist, and his association of her with the number nine (the age at which he first saw her, among other things) underlines her specifically Christian perfection, since nine is the square, or perfection, of the trinity's three. This is one key difference between Dante and Baudelaire: Baudelaire's infinity is indefinite and visited only momentarily—it lies outside of any particular doctrine or orthodoxy. In contrast, Dante takes pains to affiliate his sense of the infinite with specifically Christian iconography and dogma.

The pains Dante takes to specify the nature of the eternity to which he ascends are at least as important in differentiating him from Baudelaire as is the Christian nature of his eternity. Not only does he work with Biblical allusion, Christian numerology, and other semiotic systems to control the way the poems of *Vita Nuova* are read: he structures the book in such a way that most of the poems are sandwiched between contextualizing prose passages and little critical interpretations of their meaning—including helpful indications of what he meant in each part of the poem, and where exactly the parts should be divided. Moreover, he makes his wishes for hermeneutic clarity explicit, writing that poets must be able to "justify what they say," for "it would be a disgrace if someone composing in rhyme introduced a figure of speech or rhetorical ornament, and then on being asked could not divest his words of such covering so as to reveal a true meaning." "My most intimate friend and I," Dante adds, "know a number who compose rhymes in this stupid manner."

Dante is, indeed, very clear about the way the love that begins with the senses directed at a woman can lead to a love of the divine (or, one should add, for a woman's sense-based love of a man to do so—Dante allows for both forms of heterosexual desire, although his views of same-sex desire were less tolerant, as readers of *The Inferno* know). So very clear is Dante about the relation of earthly to divine love that his views, announced at the end of the thirteenth century, endure and become a doctrine, still articulated in full force more than two centuries later in Castiglione's *Book of the Courtier*. In Castiglione they appear as part of the ideological equipment of all civilized gentlemen:

... speaking of the beauty we have in mind, which is that which is seen in bodies and especially in faces, and which excites this ardent desire that we call love,—we will say that it is an effluence of divine goodness, and that although it is diffused like the sun's light upon all created things, yet when it finds a face well proportioned and framed with a certain pleasant harmony of various colors embellished by lights and shadows and by an orderly distance and limit of outlines, it infuses itself therein and appears most beautiful ... like a sunbeam falling upon a beautiful vase of polished gold set with precious gems. Thus it agreeably attracts the eyes of men, and entering thereby, it impresses itself upon the soul, and stirs and delights her with a new sweetness throughout, and by kindling her divine goodness excites in her a desire for its own self.... Love gives the soul a greater felicity; for just as from the particular beauty of one body it guides her to the universal beauty of all bodies, so in the highest stage of perfection it guides her from the particular to the universal intellect. Hence the soul, kindled by the most sacred fire of true divine love, flies to unite herself with the angelic nature, and not only quite forsakes sense ...

The attempt to delimit specific meaning and to control it is central in Dante and, as the legacy of European literature demonstrates, largely successful. It is also entirely understandable for someone who wrote about eternity in a time when religious orthodoxy was enforced at the end of pikes and halberds. And this is by no means something limited to Catholicism or to the Middle Ages: in the seventeenth century, the great English Protestant writer John Bunyan prefaced his *Pilgrim's Progress* with a poetic "Apology" in which he goes to pains to prove that his allegory contains nothing but "sound and honest gospel strains," perhaps like those sung by Cromwell's soldiers on their way to behead that Catholic sympathizer, Charles the First.

Here, in the insistence on a clearly defined meaning, we see the principal point of difference between Dante and Baudelaire, and the point at which we can begin to understand what is modern about the latter poet. Baudelaire's prose poem is suggestive, not definitive.

It evokes meanings, but does not delimit a specific meaning. Baudelaire was not the first to work with elusive poetic images: indeed, he draws upon a rich Romantic heritage, including the works of Coleridge, whose theory of the symbol (as opposed to the allegory) can serve almost as a statement of poetics for Baudelaire and his kin. Coleridge uses the term "symbol" inconsistently over the course of his career, but it is his sense of the word in *The Statesman's Manual* that is important here. In that work Coleridge tells us that, unlike the allegorical figure, the symbol is characterized "above all by the translucence of the eternal through and in the temporal." It connects us to the ever-changing yet timeless eternity that Coleridge calls "the infinite I AM." As the scholar James C. McKusick puts it, with Coleridgean symbol,

> the form of the sign is determined by the form of the referent"— and when the ultimate referent is the infinite I AM, as it must at some level be in true works of imagination, the form will, like its referent, be dialectical, a process of coming together and diffusing."

That is, with symbols, we never come to a definite meaning, but watch as meanings come together and fall apart, watch as they are evoked and dismissed and replaced continuously in the rapt mind of the reader. We're pretty far from Dante's ideal situation, in which the meaning of the poetic image can—indeed must—be paraphrased by any poet aspiring to a state beyond stupidity.

The emphasis on an ultimately elusive poetic image grows over the course of the nineteenth century, reaching a kind of apogee in the works of the French symbolists of the *fin de siècle*. Mallarmé, for example, tells us that the poem ought to present an array of "resonant meanings and associations" rather than specific referents. This art of suggestion rather than delimitation is at the very heart of the symbolist enterprise: Paul Verlaine insists, for example, that the poet "must not / select [his] words without some vagueness."

In the early twentieth century the notion of the modern poetic image as suggestive rather than definitive becomes codified by that great tribe of rationalizers of the irrational, the Surrealists. André Breton cites Baudelaire as an inspiration in the *First Manifesto of Surrealism*, where he proclaims that the most powerful poetic image is that which presents the greatest degree of arbitrariness; that

> which takes the longest to translate into everyday language, either because it contains an immense amount of apparent contradiction; or because one of its terms is strangely hidden; or because proclaiming its sensational nature, it has the appearance of ending weakly ... or because it is of a hallucinatory nature ...

He then cites examples, including Lautréamont's "the ruby of Champagne," Louis Aragon's "the frosted gleam of freedom's disturbances" and his own "on the bridge the dew with a she-cat's head rocks itself to sleep." The grand point of such images is not that they communicate a meaning already determined by the poet, but that the mind, "at first confining itself to submitting to them, soon perceives that they stimulate its powers of reason ... it goes onward, borne by these images which delight it." The dark night through which such obscure images take us is, for Breton, the confusion that leads us to discovery, to new and unpredictable insights, and so it becomes "the most beautiful night of all, the night of the lightning-flash: day, compared to it, is night."

Après les Surréalistes, le déluge: the decades between the *First Surrealist Manifesto* and the present brim over with poetic language and images that cultivate the indefinite, that seek by their strange beauty to refute Dante's assertion that the poet ought to be able to write a clear prose summary of his meaning. From the New Critical heresy of paraphrase to the midcentury American "deep image," from the drifting syntax of John Ashbery to the elliptical juxtapositions of Anne Carson or Graham Foust, to Michael Stipe's ambiguous lyrics (styled after Patti Smith, herself a student in the school of Baudelaire and Rimbaud) our proximate heritage consists of a thousand versions of the poetics of evocation, rather than definiteness. It is a tradition inviting us to discovery rather than educating us in dogma, and in that sense the modern poetic image is not an illustration of an idea, but something altogether different: it is an invitation to the voyage.

Charmless and Interesting:
The Conceptual Moment in Poetry

Fourteen months after reading at the White House, Kenneth Goldsmith found himself in the real center of American power: cable television. His July 2013 appearance on *The Colbert Report*, though, coincided not with a general celebration of the conceptual poetics with which he is associated, but with two stinging attacks on such poetics: one by the young poet Amy King in *The Rumpus*, and another by the esteemed poet-critic Calvin Bedient in *Boston Review*. King's criticism revolved around the idea of conceptualism as an in-group phenomenon, and on the hypocrisy of conceptual poets striking anti-establishment poses while simultaneously seeking, and beginning to find, such laurels as the established institutions of American poetry have to offer. Bedient's article criticized conceptualism for a lack of concern with emotion and affect, which he linked with both a truncating of poetry's possibilities and a kind of reactionary political stance. People's responses to these criticisms, to judge by the emails, texts, phone calls, and Facebook messages I received, were passionate—half of my friends in the little world of poetry expressed delight that the horrible careerist bastards were finally getting called out for their sins, while the other half spluttered in outrage at those who dared try to quench the glorious yet fragile flames of poetic innovation.

What we saw, then, was a moment for an assessment of the virtues and vices of conceptual poetry. What does conceptual poetry lack, compared to other poetries, and what does it have to offer? Any brief answer will, of course, be too general, but we can begin to sketch things out with reference to two aesthetic categories: the charming and the interesting. Whatever else conceptualism has got going for it, it lacks—at least in its pure form—the former. And whether one likes conceptualism or not, anyone who has engaged with it has found that it has, wonderfully or frustratingly, got plenty of the latter.

The Charmlessness of Pure Conceptualism

To begin, then, with definitions: what is meant, in aesthetics, by this thing called charm? In Kantian thinking about aesthetics, charm is the appeal made by the material, or the medium, of the work of art: the timbre in music, the color in painting, the words themselves in poetry. The material appeals to the senses, and is agreeable to them. The appeal is also pre-conscious: "we linger on charm," writes Kant, "the mind all the while remaining passive." Charm, for Kant, is minor stuff, and doesn't play a part in what he takes to be a true judgment of beauty, which has much more to do with structure, form, and pattern ("purposiveness without purpose," he says) than with materials—indeed, Kant refers to taste that depends to any degree on charm as "barbaric." There's a real downplaying of the value of the senses in this view, with charm being a "merely empirical delight." "Mere," as we'll soon see, is a word also often attached to the other aesthetic category we'll be mentioning in detail, the interesting—but the past denigration of these categories is not necessarily just or relevant. I use the terms here in a descriptive, not a judgmental, manner.

Conceptual poetry is charmless. Immediately upon making this statement, I want to offer two qualifications: firstly, this is true only of a certain kind of conceptual poetry, the kind Vanessa Place and Robert Fitterman refer to as "pure conceptualism"; secondly, this is not a criticism, but an observation. It is no more a criticism to say that conceptual poetry of a certain kind lacks charm than it would be to say that paintings lack sound. The attraction of the art comes elsewhere.

What, then, is "pure conceptualism," and from what other conceptualisms is it distinguished? "Pure conceptualism," write Place and Fitterman in *Notes on Conceptualisms*, "negates the need for reading in the traditional textual sense—one does not need to 'read' the work as much as think about the idea of the work." The purely conceptual poem does not necessitate the direct experience of the words: this is about as radical a claim for something calling itself poetry as anyone has made in the present century, and perhaps in the prior one. That the idea of pure conceptualism is radical in the field of poetry speaks volumes of the relative conservatism of poetry compared to some other arts, though, since it was being bandied about in the realm of visual art at least as far back as the 1960s (and, arguably, earlier, in the provocations of Marcel Duchamp). Consider the words of artist Sol LeWitt, who argued more than a generation ago in his "Paragraphs on Conceptual Art" that "in conceptual art the idea or concept is the most important aspect of the work.... What the work of art looks like isn't too important." This takes Kantian disdain for the charm of material media to a new level, denying almost entirely the importance of the physical embodiment of the artwork. LeWitt dreamed of an art free of charm, and pure conceptualism brings that dream into the field of poetry.

The most direct transmission of LeWitt's ideas into poetry—one can hardly imagine a more direct one—came in Kenneth Goldsmith's 2005 "Sentences on Conceptual Writing," which reproduces LeWitt's text almost verbatim, adding only a few modifications to change the subject from visual to written art (specifically, Goldsmith's "uncreative writing"). So we find, in Goldsmith's text, statements like "Literature that is meant for the sensation of the ear primarily would be called aural rather than uncreative. This would include most poetry and certain strains of fiction." Goldsmith's kind of writing turns against the aural charms of words, what Ezra Pound would call their melopoeia, and seeks to give satisfaction elsewhere, at the level of the concept.

Goldsmith returns to the relative unimportance of the actual embodiment of the poem in words again and again, making it the foundation for his notion that the conceptual poem need not be read, but considered in the abstract, thought about, and discussed. Here's a representative statement, from an interview with Goldsmith called "Against Expression":

> The best thing about conceptual poetry is that it doesn't need to be read. You don't have to read it. As a matter of fact, you can write books, and you don't even have to read them. My books, for example, are unreadable. All you need to know is the concept

behind them. Here's every word I spoke for a week. Here's a year's worth of weather reports ... and without ever having to read these things, you understand them.

So, in a weird way, if you get the concept—which should be put out in front of the book—then you get the book, and you don't even have to read it. They're better to talk about than they are to read.

If there is any charm to the words of a purely conceptual poem as Goldsmith describes it, that charm is incidental, not an essential part of the art. So keen is he to downplay the charm of the particular words (whether it be a matter of *melopoeia*, the play of associations, the visual organization of the words upon the page, or any other beauty derived from the words *qua* words) that, in "Conceptual Poetics," he downplays the very idea of readership:

Conceptual writing is more interested in a *thinkership* rather than a readership. Readability is the last thing on this poetry's mind. Conceptual writing is good only when the idea is good; often, the idea is much more interesting than the resultant texts.

There's a great reversal, in pure conceptualism, of Mallarmé's point in his famous exchange with Degas, in which the painter, saying he had many ideas for poems, was rebuked by the poet, who said *"ce n'est point avec des idées que l'on fait des vers.... C'est avec des mots"* ("you can't make a poem with ideas ... you make them with words"). Pure conceptualism sides with Degas.

Even readers sympathetic to Goldsmith can find the actual experience of reading some of his works to be charmless. Sianne Ngai, for example, writing about Goldsmith's *Fidget*, describes it in terms that hardly invite a slow, luxuriant lingering over the words:

Goldsmith's deliberately stupefying poems relentlessly focus on the tedium of the ordinary ... the movements of a body not doing anything in particular. Simultaneously astonishing and boring, the experiment in 'duration' is taken ... to a structural extreme ...

Goldsmith's *Fidget* documents the writer's impossible project of recording every single bodily movement made in a twenty-four-hour period.

Stupefying to read, but interesting (to Ngai, and to others) to think about: Goldsmith's art is, to use his own terms, thinkership-friendly, readership-unfriendly.

I have tried to be scrupulous in describing only pure conceptualism as charmless, because there are other kinds of poetry that are, in one quarter or another, called conceptual, and that do depend on a reading of the actual text. These are conceptualisms that call for a readership, or in some cases a viewership, rather than a thinkership. When, for example, Elizabeth Clark erases all of Raymond Roussel's *Nouvelles Impressions d'Afrique* except for its quotation marks, she creates a work from which someone looking at the pages can derive considerable (albeit austere) visual charm. And the Steinian verbal play of, say, Craig Dworkin's *Mote* is very much a poetry of verbal charm. Indeed, Marjorie Perloff has written about a genre, or sub-genre, she calls "the conceptual lyric." How these phenomena are related to pure conceptualism, and whether the relation is more than a matter of institution and affiliation is a large and question, well worth pursuing, and a question beyond my scope here. So, too, is the question of the relation of purely conceptual poetry to the longer tradition of poetry, which is very much a tradition devoted to readership, and to the charm of the particular word. In what sense is pure conceptualism poetry, beyond the institutional sense of being distributed and considered through the channels by which poetry is distributed and considered? It's a question worth asking, given the radical nature of the break with the past. I do not propose an answer. Not today.

Those who feel that conceptualism is a malevolent phenomenon have, thus far, concentrated on institutional, political, and affective matters (and, more recently, on the racial politics of certain works by Place and Goldsmith, addressed by Cathy Park Hong better than I feel myself capable). It would be of considerable interest to see what would result from the critics of conceptualism pursuing in greater detail the notion of the charmlessness of pure conceptualism, since some argue that the particularity of words as a medium of art isn't just a matter of agreeable sensations (Kant's role for charm). When Ruth Padel, for example, writes in "Reading a Poem," about the *resistance* offered by particular words, or particular arrangements of words, to reduction to concept, she implies that there are important hermeneutic and ethical possibilities that an inattention to these qualities would truncate:

> J.H. Prynne's word 'resistance': *that* is what is truly traditional; what creative readers value in all poems, from the past or from the present. One aspect of it is the subtlety which lets meaning be found through pattern. Not necessarily a rhyming or a regular pattern; any in which words make relationships with each other through sound, through their tactile being, as well as in all the meanings that can be woken from them. In resistance, words become, as Coleridge put it, hooked atoms. They mesh and cross-mesh with all the other words in the language-net of the poem.

Meaning, in this view, is infinitely enriched by the qualities of the particular words, their irreducibility as individual entities and their irreducibility in their particular relationships to the surrounding words. The invocation of J.H. Prynne is important here, since his work depends on the particularity of words, their etymologies, the history of their usage, and their many subtleties. In Prynne's works an ethics, a critique of the Enlightenment's emphasis on concepts, and, some argue, a politics, depend upon the particularity of words. A Prynnian critique of pure conceptualism would, one imagines, be withering. The pluralist, of course, is likely to believe the world is large enough to contain both Prynne and Goldsmith, though pluralists, among whom I number, are quite open to the charge (rooted in Hegel's sense of the "end of art") that they lack both conviction and a sense of the importance of art.

The Interest of Conceptualism

"It was interesting," we say, of certain films or books or artworks—or, perhaps we say it a little differently, with a slight hesitation and a bit of emphasis: "It was ... *interesting.*" The pause is significant, I think, in part because the hesitation indicates an uncertainty about how the work in question would fit into any other aesthetic category. "Interesting," in general usage, often implies a certain indefinableness of the qualities of the object in question, an expression of approval, perhaps hesitant approval, or perhaps even of qualified disapproval, without a firm grasp on the exact nature of the qualities we describe. This is appropriate, because the interesting is the aesthetic category least tied to the specific qualities of the text or art object in itself, and the most dependent on context.

Sianne Ngai, whose seminal 2008 article in *Critical Inquiry*, "Merely Interesting," is essential reading on the topic, describes this context-dependence precisely. In ordinary, unselfconscious conversation, she maintains, we tend to use aesthetic categories as ways of referring to properties inherent in the object itself, with the cute referring to things small, soft, and non-angular; the gaudy referring to bright things with intense color, and so forth. The interesting, though, is different, and makes us a little uneasy—a fact that the word's frequent pairing with the adjective "merely" underscores. Interest, says Ngai, is "bound up with the perception of novelty" and is therefore "much more radically dependent on context than features [of the object] such as round or bright." Since the interesting is so context-dependent, "no particular kind of evidence [for an object or text's interestingness] will ever seem ... finally convincing."

Novelty is now so thoroughly established as an aesthetic virtue with us that "innovative," "experimental," "fresh," "original," and the like are all terms of praise. It was not ever thus: in the eighteenth century, Lord Shaftesbury could write about beauty as a timeless, natural harmony, and condemn innovations in the arts such as Orientalism or the Gothic with the then-negative epithet "novel." Even as late as the Romantic period, when the concept of originality or novelty was gaining philosophical ground, it could still be looked upon with suspicion. German idealists contrasted the new or *intéressante* with the classical or eternal *schöne*, often to the disadvantage of the new. Much of the suspicion had to do with whether the new kind of art would be of lasting interest. In fact, this sense of the moment-bound nature of the interesting has continued down to our own time, although without the accompanying suspicion. As affect theorist Silvan Tomkins put it, "in contrast to the once-and-for-allness of our experience of, say, the sublime, the object we find interesting is one we tend to come back to, asking to verify that it is *still* interesting."

The interesting, then, is modern in a broad sense of the term (that is: post-Romantic); it is bound to its context more thoroughly than other types of aesthetic appeal; and it is less dependent on the qualities of the object or text itself than are other aesthetic categories. "With the exception of its special relationship to novelty (or more exactly because of it)" writes Ngai, "the interesting could ... be described as an aesthetic *without content* and, as such, one ideally suited to the historical emergence of the modern subject as a reflective, radically detached, or ironic ego."

Pure conceptualism's downplaying of the reader's experience of the text allies it with the notion of the non-content-dependent category of the interesting, as opposed to the charming. Moreover, Kenneth Goldsmith has insisted on conceptualism as "a poetics of the moment." In a response to some comments of mine, Goldsmith, in his essay "You'd Better Start Swimmin' or You'll Sink Like a Stone," described conceptualism as "the most relevant, contemporary, and engaged response" to our particular technological moment. "Conceptual Poetics," Goldsmith's presentation at the University of Arizona's conference on "Conceptual Poetry and Its Others," elaborates on the idea of conceptualism as depending on the specific, novel, and transient technological norms of the moment, such as current technologies of "information management, word processing, databasing" and the like. What is more, the alienation of the conceptualist poet from his or her material—material that is generally found or systemically generated rather than presented as an expression of the poet's unique and sincere subjective affect—is very much a product of "the modern subject as a reflective, radically detached, or ironic ego." Consider another passage from Goldsmith's Arizona presentation, in which he describes the language of conceptualism in terms of:

> Language as junk, language as detritus. Nutritionless language, meaningless language, unloved language ... Obsessive archiving & cataloging, the debased language of media & advertising; language more concerned with quantity than quality.

He continues by describing the relations of the conceptual writer to his or her text:

> In their self-reflexive use of appropriated language, conceptual writers embrace the inherent and inherited politics of the borrowed words: far be it from conceptual writers to morally or politically dictate words that aren't theirs. The choice or machine that makes the poem sets the political agenda in motion, which is oftentimes morally or politically reprehensible to the author.

One can hardly imagine a more detached and ironic ego than that of the Goldsmithian conceptualist. Such a figure may shy away from charm or traditional forms of the beautiful or sublime—but his or her detachment and irony connect quite readily with the idea of the interesting.

Related to the novelty or moment-specific nature of conceptualism is another quality associated with the interesting: controversy. As Ralph Barber Perry put it in his *General Theory of Value*, interest has a "disposition of favor or disfavor" for us. Things we find interesting, much more than things we find beautiful or cute or gaudy or charming, invite and demand us to be with them or against them. And here we find further explanation for the hesitation in that frequently heard phrase "it was ... interesting." The pause can function as a moment of indecision, in which we try to decide where we stand on the thing: are we pro-, or are we contra-? The interesting courts controversy, not necessarily through its contents or any polemical position about which it tries to be didactic, but through the way in which it collides with the expectations of the moment.

The criticisms of conceptualism by people like Amy King and Calvin Bedient, whatever their merits on their own terms, stand as testimony to conceptualism's interest—and in this sense affirm conceptualism's success on its own terms. Charmless pure conceptualism may well be, but it is hard to deny its interest. You may not be reading much conceptualism, and you may well be very much against it, but you're thinking about it right now, as am I. And whatever else we may think about it, however else we may judge it, we most definitely find it ... *interesting*.

Inventions of a Barbarous Age:
Contemporary Rhyme in Poetry

Rhyme, argued Milton, defending the blank verse of *Paradise Lost*, is "no necessary adjunct or true ornament of a poem ... but the invention of a barbarous age," and the poet's freedom from rhyme is "an ancient liberty recovered ... from the troublesome modern bondage of rhyming." Times have changed: try thinking of a contemporary poet who has felt the need to defend the lack of rhyme in his or her poetry and odds are pretty strong you'll come up blank. Indeed, it's the rhymers who are more likely to feel the need for a defense. The best defense, of course, is a good poem in rhyme—and if we look, we begin to find these in many different quadrants of the poetry world.

But there are rhymes and there are rhymes, and it's worthwhile considering what some of the recent scholarship has to say about the differences between them, especially if we hope to understand the various ends to which contemporary poets have put rhyme. Perhaps it's not coincidental that the most provocative critical thoughts about rhyme in recent years have come from poets, notably Stephen Burt and Anthony Madrid.

Burt looks at rhyme primarily in terms of its function, making a general distinction between what he calls "background" and "foreground" rhymes. For most of the history of rhymed poetry in English, argues Burt in his essay "Cornucopia, or Contemporary American Rhyme," rhymes were not meant to pull focus away from other elements of the poem. Rhyme was one element in the "metrical contract," an agreement between poets and readers that poems would be more tightly organized and musical than prose. Individual rhymes, though, "would not usually draw more attention than other aspects of the verse." Indeed: they were part of a norm—a background—against which deviations or less usual effects became more visible. They were the settings in which verbal gems were placed, not the gems themselves. When they were too ingenious—or, alternately, too worn and cloying—they became too noticeable, and failed to serve their vital if unglamorous function. Burt cites Robert Graves' analogy between good rhymes and good servants as an example of this theory of rhyme's function: good rhymes, says Graves, "are the good servants whose presence at the dinner-table gives the guest a sense of opulent security; never awkward or over-clever ... You can trust them not to interrupt the conversation." Rhyming "moon" with "June," in this view, is much like spilling a bowl of soup in a diner's lap; while rhyming "intellectual" with "hen-pecked you all" is more a matter of spending far too long explaining the choice of appetizer, or making an unctuous compliment about the diner's choice of necktie.

When rhyme forces itself onto our attention, it pushes itself into the foreground. The move may be propelled by all sorts of different fuel: rhymes may jump forward "because they are polysyllabic, because they employ proper nouns ... because the words they use are the oddest in their respective lines" or for any number of other reasons. What matters is that it demands attention: rather than being a part of an accepted contract, it comes across as a violation of some kind, making the verse seem "consciously artificial—ornamental, or antiquary, or ironic (even sarcastic), or willed, or faux-naïve." Most of you wouldn't want this kind of rhyme serving you dinner on a big night out, though you'd probably enjoy it as a cabaret performer.

A contract, of course, has two parties, and Burt's theory of rhyme isn't so much about the qualities of rhymes in isolation, but about the way they interact with readerships. The percentage of published American poems that rhyme is smaller than it was even a few decades ago, fewer and fewer readers take rhyme as a norm—with the result that it is harder and harder for rhyme to fulfill a background function. "Foreground rhyme," therefore, "has become, for *most* American poets now, the only kind that we can use: its possibilities have expanded immensely, while background rhyme has become, though not unheard of, scarce, and extremely hard to use well."

While Burt focuses on the function of rhyme in a shifting context, Anthony Madrid gives us a bold, broad history of English rhyme. In *Warrant for Rhyme* he tells a story of rhyme's transformation from the Renaissance to the present day, centering on a "rhyme shift" that quietly remade English poetry over the course of the seventeenth century. Before this shift, we find a much greater emphasis on rhymes that bear a sematic resemblance as well as a sonic one: 'cherry' and 'berry,' for example, or 'mother' and 'brother." After the shift, though, such rhymes occur with greatly reduced frequency. By 1660 or so, Madrid argues,

> ... serious poets unconsciously resisted using rhyme pairs wherein the two words bore to each other any strong and essential semantic link. This resistance sometimes reached a pitch of utter exclusion in cases where the words in the rhyme pair were perceived on some level as participating in a semantic algebra of equivalence or opposition ... whole categories of rhyme were decommissioned. In particular, rhyme pairs wherein the words are near-synonyms or near-antonyms were to be avoided. Thus, {*moan* | *groan*} would have been counterintuitive to an Augustan poet, because the two terms are near-synonyms. {*Sad* | *glad*} would have seemed undesirable because the words are opposites.

Since the move away from semantic/sonic combinations in rhyme happens in poetic practice without ever becoming the subject of a manifesto-like polemical essay in the period, the rationale remains evasive, although Madrid advances a hypothesis that we might take as a description of the birth of what Burt calls background rhyme. "The implied purpose of rhyme" after the shift, says Madrid, "was to affect the audience in the same way that music does: not by encoding information, but by manipulating the sensual apparatus of the body." The hypothesis, then, is that poets sought "to exclude rhymes they expected would call attention to themselves, thus disturbing the operation of the music."

For Madrid, this system began to break down in the nineteenth century, beginning with the comic masterpieces of Lord Byron. In Byron we see the first poet to work, not intermittently or marginally, but in his great works quite consistently, with rhymes that willfully violate the norms of decorum. He does so not by turning back the clock to the Renaissance emphasis on semantically significant rhymes, but by turning to a kind of rhyme that insistently "demonstrates inventiveness and originality."

This turn to eccentricity prepared the ground for the diminished role of rhyme in modern poetry. The flashy virtuosity of Byronic rhyme inevitably led the reader to ask "Are not all these crazy rhymes a joke on poetry itself?" The ultimate effect of Byron and those he influenced was to help undermine the old contract about rhyme between poet and reader, giving us a "demotion of rhyme from an effect that characterized a given poem as a whole to a local and unpredictable effect whose pretensions to power were sharply limited." We find ourselves in the world of Burt's foreground rhymers, with rhyme coming across as artificial, ornamental, willed, ironic, or faux-naïve. Madrid laments this situation more than does the even-handed Burt, claiming that while rhyme culture never disappeared among songwriters, "in literary poetry ... rhyme will," in the absence of some champion, a Moses of rhymes, "languish in a perpetual catarrh, and students of English poetry will have to strain hard to lend half of our greatest poets the sympathetic ear they deserve." When, oh when, Madrid calls out in the wilderness, will the covenant be revived?

One answer to Madrid's question is that the old metrical contract, in which rhyme draws no more focus than any other element of a poem, has never gone away—for a minority. It is from this minority that R.S. Gwynn rises, and to this minority that he, for the most part, speaks. Make no mistake about it: when it comes to meter, to rhyme, and to the traditional classical and Christian codes once all-but universally familiar to the readers of literary poetry in English, Gwynn is a master. He knows the functions of the traditional forms and modes—the sonnet, the ballad, the elegy, the satire. He respects them, as a true craftsman will, and he turns them to their time-hallowed purposes. And yet there are quadrants on the map of American poetry where his work struggles to be taken seriously—in no small measure, one suspects, because he writes for those who take the old "metrical contract" for granted, for those who do not rankle at an un-ironic, non-faux-naïve rhyming of "all," and "call"—the first rhyming couplet in his latest collection, *Dogwatch*.

Indeed, when we look at where many of the poems in *Dogwatch* have appeared—in such traditional rhyme-and-meter friendly journals as *Able Muse, The Hudson Review, Light Quarterly, The Sewanee Review*, and *Measure*—we get confirmation that Gwynn's primary audience is more predisposed to recognize the old style "metrical contract" than is the American poetry world as a whole. Indeed, Gwynn is a habitué of the West Chester Poetry Conference, where formalist poets congregate, and was one of the 25 poets collected in *Rebel Angels*, the anthology with which Mark Jarman and David Mason brought the New Formalist movement in poetry to the attention of the public. He moves within a world well-primed to appreciate his considerable skill with traditional forms: with the sonnet, the ballade, with the jazzed-up pantoum and with terza rima (a particular favorite of Gwynn's, sometimes spiced up with other formal gestures or patterns).

Gwynn is very good at letting traditional forms do what they do best—the voltas in his sonnets turn on a dime—but is can be inventive with form, too, as in the poem "348 S. Hamilton, 27288." The poem, which begins with the single-line stanza "Here is a life to clear away," tells the story, through the enumeration of objects in the house of someone who has died, of the growth and decline of a family's life at a particular address. There is a simple anaphoric technique at play (Here is this, here is that ...) but we also see stanzas, each with a single end-rhyme, grow: a couplet, a tercet, a quatrain, up to a sestet, and then begin to shrink down again until we arrive at the single line "Here is a life to clear away." We arrive at our beginning, changed by the journey.

In addition to his sure hand with traditional meter and rhyme, Gwynn has a fine and easy grasp of the traditional classical and Christian codes that were once considered standard equipment for any poet. He puts the old traditions to good use: in the sonnet sequence "Afterwords," for example, he lets the women of classical myth, and legend—Galatea, Leda, Eurydice, Helen, Calyspso, Psyche—express their dismay at their lots. In "Something of a Saint" takes a passage about St. Joseph from the Gnostic Gospel of Philip and retells the incidents in such a down-to-earth way one is reminded of the treatment of Christ's childhood in Millais' painting *Christ in the House of His Parents*. While Millais' straightforwardness offended the Victorian audience by its refusal of pomp and grandeur, one suspects some readers might rankle at Gwynn's poem for its refusal of irony or pastiche: there is a piety to the poem that brings it close to the realm of the devotional.

There is a plainspokenness to Gwynn's poetry that goes hand in hand with his preference for rhymes that the intended audience will hear as "background" rhyme—indeed, one of the poems, "On the Lea, April, 1621," takes this plainspokenness as a theme, juxtaposing it to an altogether more flashy style. The poem invokes Izaak Walton, author of the mixed prose and verse classic *The Compleat Angler*, beginning with a scene that reminds us of Izaak's limited sympathy for fly fishing (Thomas Barker contributed the fly-fishing passages of the original *Compleat Angler*):

> Honest Izaak, angling with a worm,
> Knows the duration of each fish's term
> Upon these waters, and he rests content
> With the plain species which God solely meant
> For table—pickerel, barbel, tench and loach—
> Paying small heed when forward spring's approach
> Moves the great salmon. Let more zealous men
> Clamber from rock to rock with feverish ken,
> Fanning with eager arms an inward fire
> To catch the phantoms of their souls' desire;
> Beguiled by shadows which their tippets seek
> They shower disdain upon the plaice and bleak—
> Or such as Izaak, who rely on bait
> To grant them ease merely to stand and wait.

We're talking about fishing, here, but we're talking about more than that. The two types of fishing—silent standing and fervid fly-casting—stand for two different kinds of writing, and two different approaches to things spiritual. The "more zealous" fly fishers wave their arms about and, "beguiled by shadows," chase elusive visions. Izaak and his low-key ilk "merely stand and wait"—the resonance with the end line of Milton's sonnet "On His Blindness" underlines the assertion that this less-showy activity is also a true form of devotion.

Later in the poem we're told that Walton "represents the character named *prose*," while "A hundred rods upstream—and more *Poetic*" stands another figure:

> The vicar of St. Dunstan's, Dr. Donne,
> Flailing the air with rhythms that no one
> But the man and his Maker understand,
> Senses the presence with a tremulous hand
> Of some great thing now barely out of reach.

Yes, it's *that* Dr. Donne, here pictured as a fly-fisher. He is also the writer of more obscure and tangled lines than Walton, and the seeker after mystical visions that he almost, but never quite, manages to catch.

If Gwynn's rhyming couplets have a neo-Augustan quality, reminiscent of Pope, so too does his clarity, his embrace of what Robert Pinsky once called "the prose virtues" of poetry: "Clarity, Flexibility, Efficiency, Cohesiveness." While much contemporary poetry aims to be "free-playing, elusive, more fresh than earnest, more eager to surprise than to tell," we can lose sight of how the prose virtues can be "not merely the poem's minimum requirement, but the poetic essence." It is significant that, while Donne is respected, it is Walton who emerges as the superior figure here, patient and serene in his fishing, quiet and sincere in his devotions: he may be the figure of prose, but he is a better emblem of Gwynn's poetry than is the flailing and flashy Donne, chasing shadows and disdaining other fare.

This is the point for full disclosure, and I will give it: the opening poem of *Dogwatch*, "God's Secretary," is dedicated to me. The dedication is a sign of Gwynn's considerable generosity of spirit, since it came about as the concluding gesture in a brief correspondence I had with Gwynn after I'd written about how I could see the fine technique of his poem, but nevertheless found it unappealing. The poem, an Italian sonnet, opens with this stanza:

> Her e-mail inbox always overflows.
> Her outbox doesn't get much use at all.
> She puts on hold the umpteen-billionth call
> As music oozes forth to placate those
> Who wait, then disconnect. Outside, wind blows,
> Scything pale leaves. She sees a sparrow fall
> Fluttering to a claw-catch on a wall.
> Will He be in today? God only knows.

The iambic pentameter is varied just enough to avoid a sense of the metronome, and the rhymes are softened, here and there, by enjambment—although they are so full and frequent that those unwilling to sign the old metrical contract may rankle, as I did at first. This, of course, tells us more about contemporary taste than about the poem itself, which is nicely balances: an interrogative breaks up the series of declaratives, and the quotidian images counterbalance the divine subject matter. The sparrow is an allusion to Pope, who wrote about how God "sees with equal eye, as God of all, / A hero perish or a sparrow fall," and beyond Pope, an allusion to the Bible. There's a lot to admire, here, but what chafed me, when I first read the poem, was the sensibleness, the down-to-earthness, of it, especially given that it dealt with something as sublime and ineffable as the divine. We might say, thinking of "On the Lea, April, 1621," that the poem was written under the aegis of Izaak Walton, not John Donne. The Donne of that poem spurns common things in pursuit of "some great thing now barely out of reach," but Gwynn himself does so only rarely—in, for example, "Being and Nothingness," an elegiac sonnet for his father, in which some meaning or truth of great significance is uncannily present and evasive at the same time, a condition captured in a refrain, "sometimes I feel so close," in which the object of the closeness remains unspecified.

Dogwatch is divided into four sections: "Tribes," concerning family and community; "Scribes," which features all manner of references to other writers (tributes, adaptations, translations, anecdotes), "Vibes," where the primary modes are elegiac, or concerned with the failings of the flesh, and "Gibes," where Gwynn proves himself as fine a satirist as any Augustan, and where his formal gifts shine in a tribute to southern cuisine in a pastiche of Hopkins, "Fried Beauty." Throughout, his work is accomplished, and his dedication to ways of writing unfashionable since the decline of the metrical contract shows both mastery and modesty: uncommon virtues in the American poetic scene.

Michael Robbins, like R.S. Gwynn, has many poetic virtues, but modesty is not among them—it is as alien to his persona as it is to his rhymes. In both of these, Robbins is neo-Byronic rather than neo-Augustan. The figure Robbins cuts in his poetry and his critical prose alike is that of the bad boy, a rebel armed with ego but not idealism, an iconoclast who has, as a saving grace, the capacity for ironizing himself: a kind of postmodern amalgam of Byron's disdainful Childe Harold and his often-hapless or deflated Don Juan. W.H. Auden, writing on the kind of comic rhyme we find in Byron's *Don Juan*, makes an observation as true of the Edward Lear limerick he quotes as it is of Byron and, frequently, of Robbins:

> ... the words, on the basis of an auditory friendship, had taken charge of the situation, as if, instead of an event requiring words to describe it, words had the power to create events. Reading the lines "There was an Old Man of Whitehaven / Who danced a quadrille with a raven" one cannot help noticing upon reflection that, had the old gentleman lived in Ceylon, he would have had to dance with a swan ...

Stephen Burt says, *à propos* this kind of rhyme, that it gives the sense that "words, not events, are in charge, and all rhymes do not seem to have arisen (as if naturally) from the other aspects of the poem." The rhymes force themselves into the foreground—they aren't good servants, they're insolent waiters. Or better yet, they're rap battlers, seeking to outdo all comers through novelty and surprise, and willing to bend the story to fit the snazzy rhyme.

Consider "Springtime in Chicago in November," the poem that opens Robbins' second collection, *The Second Sex*. The opening stanza is all persona and no rhyme:

> Springtime in Chicago in November.
> My forty-first year to heaven.
> My left hand wants to know
> what my right hand is doing.
> Oh. Sorry I asked.

We begin with a disunified self. The opening line seems to promise hope in a grim time, an impression not entirely incongruent with the statement of the second line, where Robbins pairs a sense of the end of youth with a subtle expectation of salvation. But then in the next three lines we get a twist on the old cliché about the left hand not knowing what the right hand is doing, a twist that implies the right hand does something a bit shameful—the primary implication is masturbation, but one might also sense a suggestion that it might involve the writing cynical poetry. The slightly-hopeful, ever-so-slightly sentimental persona of the opening lines is undermined by the implied of lust and the overt shame: it's a move straight out of Byron's *Don Juan*, where the title character's noblest aspirations are constantly trumped by sexual disgrace.

Rhyme kicks in with the second stanza, and is decidedly foregrounded:

> First comes love, which I disparage.
> I blight with plagues a baby carriage.
> Green means go and red means red.
> *Now* we're cooking with Sudafed.

The stanza is a kind of exhibit of the varieties of foreground rhyme. The first rhyme, disparage/carriage, actually involves a third term, "marriage," which does not appear except in the mind of the reader—all but the dullest native speaker will hear the old schoolyard rhyme beginning "first comes love, second comes marriage, then comes [the name of whichever unfortunate boy has been picked out of the scrum at recess] pushing a baby carriage." Much ink has been spilled trying to define the kind of rhyme that involves a word alluded to, but not actually appearing in a poem. My preference is to call it crypted rhyme, since a word unspoken in a poem but invoked by allusion has been called a crypt word, but not wanting to contribute to the critical tower of Babel I will not insist. The point is that the first rhyme we come across in *The Second Sex* is a kind of stunt: a seemingly simple couplet that is in reality a triplet, depending on an allusion to a children's rhyme. And the allusion itself is sort of clever, since on the one hand it makes us juxtapose the campy cynicism of the stanza's content with the naiveté or innocence of childhood, but on the other hand it represents a continuation, and amplification, of the childhood rhyme's sentiment that marriage and parenthood are conditions upon which to cast aspersions. Is the opening couplet of the stanza at war with itself or not? Is it about the loss of innocence in cynicism, or is it about the continuation of childish attitudes, taking them to their logical conclusion? There's no way to tell.

The second rhyme in the stanza—red/red/Sudafed—confronts us with the blunt no-no of word rhyming with itself, a kind of taboo clumsily broken and thrown in our faces. The red/Sudafed rhyme gives us a truly dark sense of the speaker, since "now we're cooking" implies enthusiasm, but "cooking with Sudafed" implies the making of methamphetamine. And the rhyme seems to come from nowhere—the auditory friendship of the rhyming words having taken charge of the situation in the manner described by Auden. Perhaps, for those who don't take the old metrical contract for granted, this is the only way too rhyme. If a simple moon/June, *sans* allusion, slant, irony, or other complication, is ruled out, aren't we left with the condition Anthony Madrid describes when he writes:

... the vast majority of perfect rhymes in English are in fact in very heavy rotation during the many centuries of English rhyming. In order to fetch a rhyme pair that would in any way be novel in itself, a poet (then as now) would have to travel a great distance—and the resulting rhyme would very likely have the character of a stunt.

"Stunt" is one way to put it, though another, offered by a more enthusiastic reader, might be "virtuosic." The rhymes in the final stanzas of "Springtime in Chicago in November" certainly zing with stunts and/or virtuosity:

> Steer by, deerfly. I hereby declare
> the deer tick on my derriere
> a heretic. Derelict, hunker down.
> Get the Led out, Goodman Brown.
>
> Get thee behind me, Nathan.
> Horseman, ramble on.
> Springtime snows white hairs on me.
> Green means go and go means gone.

The nexus of by/deerfly, declare/derriere, tick/heretic/derelict cries out to be noticed, by its density of sound if nothing else, but the real action is to be found in the crypted rhyme. The crypt phrase "Get thee behind me, Satan"—Christ's response when tempted by the devil—manifests as the slant-rhyming "Get thee behind me, Nathan," where the context of *Young Goodman Brown* invites us to think of Nathan as Nathaniel Hawthorne. But what Satanic temptation does Hawthorne offer? Well, *Young Goodman Brown* gives us a world depraved except for the predestined few, a world where self-examination harms more than it helps. The crypted rhyme, then, implies a speaker seeking to escape from cynicism and resignation to fate in a sinful world.

The allusions to Led Zeppelin work well here: "Get the Led out," invoking as it does "get the lead out," gives us a speaker who fears he is slowing down, and does so by invoking an increasingly geriatric set of rockers. "Horseman, ramble on" combines a reference to Yeats' grave (and therefore death) with the Led Zeppelin hit "Ramble On," a song full of autumnal imagery, but one that ultimately urges us to persevere. When we come to the end of the poem, where "go means gone," we have a sense of despair: to continue is to continue only to death. But behind that injunction we have the resistance to Hawthorne's despair, and the Led Zeppelin lyrics urging us forward even in an entropic world. If we dispense with the allusions and crypted rhymes, we find ourselves in a world of infertility and disillusion. But if we trace the allusions (often made via rhyme) we can find—just—a narrow path of hope. Many have noted Robbins' debt to Frederick Seidel (the acid attitude, the chiming rhymes), but we mustn't overlook Robbins' more profound debt, especially in *The Second Sex*, to the Eliot of *The Wasteland*. The fisher king lives on.

Crypted rhyme may just be the signature move of *The Second Sex*: it occurs time and again, notably at the end of the second of three "Sonnets for Edward Snowden":

> So ferry cross New Jersey
> I'm a black kid in a hoodie
> This land's the place I love. Et odi.

Jersey/hoodie/odi—there's a fourth rhyming word waiting to be added, from the title of the old Gerry and the Pacemakers song "Ferry cross the Mersey." That song, devoted to the river running through the band's native Liverpool, speaks of divided hearts, but of a desire, nevertheless, to stay in the beloved home place, "the place I love." In the Snowden sonnet, the crypt rhyme is the key to understanding the sentiment of the poem. We're not in Liverpool, but in a distinctly American setting: New Jersey, sure, but also the Florida where Trayvon Martin was slain by a racist. The sonnet, taken as a whole, seems angry at America—and the final two words give us what seems like pure anger: they are Latin for "and I hate." But this hate is balanced by the love and feeling for native places conjured up by "Ferry Cross the Mersey," and by another allusion—"Et odi" comes from a live by Catullus reading "et odi et amori," meaning "I love and

I hate." Robbins' love for his country, like that of Edward Snowden, is a complicated one, rooted in a hatred of injustices perpetuated in his country's name. Perhaps that's why another allusion in the final line—to Woody Guthrie's "This land is your land"—fits so well. The poem is a marvel of compressed and complicated feeling, and crypted rhyme is central to its technique.

The poems of *The Second Sex* fall into two main categories: those, like the second Snowden sonnet, in which mixed feelings find some resolution via allusion, in a manner that ought to please any surviving New Critics; and those, like "Springtime in Chicago in November," that refuse to reduce to any resolution. If Keats were around, and had a good internet connection to look up the post-Romantic allusions, he'd call them poems of negative capability. But my sense of *The Second Sex* is that it doesn't rest, ultimately, on irresolution. In a move much at odds with most poets of his generation, Robbins seems poised to turn toward an ethos grounded in Christian faith. Hints may be found throughout the collection, but in the following stanza, the end lines of "Sweat, Piss, Jizz, & Blood," the religious sentiment becomes overt:

> You say that this is all there is:
> sweat and piss and blood and jizz.
> But I'm from wheat and dust and flat,
> and I was born to marvel at
> the Jayhawks in 2008.
> I don't believe you: God is great.

It is worth noting, in this context, that in recent months Michael Robbins has published both prose and poetry—including "Springtime in Chicago in November"—in the Catholic magazine *Commonweal*. Following the implications of his allusions and crypted rhymes helps give us a sense of why.

Robbins has been among the best-selling poets of our time, making a particular splash with younger readers of poetry. It stands to reason, then, that he'd have an influence on an emerging generation of poets—

an influence we can already see at work in Amanda Smeltz's debut collection *Imperial Bender*. Gwynn's *Dogwatch* touched on themes typical of a man deep in middle age—elegy and the unreliability of the flesh. Robbins' *The Second Sex* gave us early middle age, in all of its disillusion and gropings after meaning. And Smeltz's *Imperial Bender*, the poems of which were written while Smeltz was in her twenties, quite rightly give us the themes of youth: desire, waywardness, and friendship. The sense of camaraderie is palpable: a number of the poems are epistolary, and others drop the names of Smeltz's peers, as well as that of her teacher, the poet Paul Violi. There is often a sense of warfare in the margins—a friend's brother has seen atrocities in the Middle East, a cousin disembarks on native soil after a deployment to Afghanistan—but it never takes center stage. This feeling of strife simultaneously close to home and far away is, sadly, familiar to several generations of Americans.

Despite the distant rumble of war, the general impression of *Imperial Bender* is one of buoyancy, of parties and romances and exuberance in the big city. Combined with the frequency of proper names, this makes for something of a New York School vibe, albeit with an intermittent sense of belatedness, as in these lines from the suitably autumnal "October Poem":

> New York like it might've been:
> SPAGHETTI 30¢ and *womp womp*
> on the trombone
> New York like it is:
> Baby boutiques   pruned shivering
> dogs   food blogs and matching bracelets

The poems of the first third of the book are written in free verse, or, as in the case of "October Poem," in a loosely Black Mountain open-field style. In the latter parts of the book, though, Smeltz turns increasingly to rhyme. "Fête des Fous," for example, takes on one Smeltz's typical themes—indulgence—with an irregular, internal rhyme:

> Take the funnel cake and fashachts and the glow of Paris
>   swelter. Cram 'em down
> your gullet! Feels good to mirth and sloth, doesn't it? You
>   look like the paunch of
> some gilded Saturn's gut. So what? Hike a thick leg up
>   onstage, gloat in mourvedre
> parade.

Mirth/sloth, gut/what, onstage/parade—the rhymes tend towards slant, and are buried away from the line breaks, as if to de-emphasize them.

In "Dance for the Morning After" the rhymes are more overt: mostly full, and coming in couplets. There's a slight campiness to the lines, though, which describe contemporary events with reference to nursery rhymes:

> Jack brought me back a whole barrel of sherry.
> His time in Seville was so merry.
> We'll swill oloroso with purple plum pie.
> Jack sticks a thumb in. Good boy! I cry.

The routing of daily life in New York through "Jack be Nimble" serves as a kind of authorization for the rhyme: it is allowed into the poem contingently, as part of a larger intertextual move.

There's no such demureness with the rhymes in *Imperial Bender*'s longer, more ambitious poems, though. After the first few lines of "Crown for a Natural Disaster," for example, the rhyme works as hard to be noticed as it did to remain innocuous in "Fête des Fous."

> Tonight I'm too stupid to write a poem
> Who knows what poetry is.
> I know:
> My voice is too pronounced.
> My personal I is a needless gnome.
> I fall asleep in the spelling quiz

and sink to the shipwrecks fathoms below.
On the Titanic mosses grow.
The moon has been renounced
and burning tigers pounce
right off the Gold Gate.
Your poetry must obfuscate
or end up middlebrow.
Madonna says take a bow.

Lines irregular in length, though generally short, without an attempt at regular meter, tend to make the erratically appearing rhymes more strident, especially when, as in the latter part of the above stanza, they come in the form of couplets. These are rhymes that want to be noticed as rhymes. What is more, they follow the pattern outlined by Auden, and dictate, rather than serve, the sense of the poem. The seeming arbitrariness of the poem's structure is actually a part of the point: "Crown for a Natural Disaster" begins with self-deprecation and a sense that the lyric I is somehow grotesque, a "needless gnome." As the poem develops, though, the seemingly arbitrary elements generated by the quest for rhyme words are recycled, moved around, and have variations worked upon them, until we get a sense of the poet as someone with craft, turning volatile elements into something approaching order.

The emergence of order over the course of the ten pages of "Crown for a Natural Disaster" is not the sort of thing that can be demonstrated with brief quotations. But another characteristic of the poem—the influence of Michael Robbins—can be. Consider these lines:

> Tonight I'm too stupid to fight
> any angels. I'm erudite,
> but I don't want to wrestle.
> Tonight I cook meth with a mortar and pestle.

Coleridge once said, when shown Wordsworth's poem "There

was a Boy," "had I met these lines running wild in the deserts of Arabia, I should have instantly screamed out 'Wordsworth'!" Were I to meet these lines of Smeltz's wandering in the same deserts, I would instantly scream out "*Now* we're cooking with Sudafed!"

Influence is a complicated thing to trace, and sometimes it is hard to tell where Smeltz is rhyming like Robbins, and where she, like Robbins, draws on the foregrounded rhymes of Frederick Seidel. Certainly Seidel lurks in these pages: the final poem tips its hat to Seidel's famous love of red Ducati racing motorcycles: it is a variant on the rhyming violette form, titled "My Moped Burns the Red, Red Roads."

Ben Mazer is also a poet open to influence—indeed, he is a very literary poet, even an aesthete, whose vocabulary, characteristic gestures, and turns of phrase emerge from a life spent rambling among endless shelves of poetry: Auden, Marlowe, Hart Crane, Robert Lowell, and Keith Douglas seem to number among his favorites, as do Frederick Goddard Tuckerman, John Crowe Ransom, and Landis Everson, whose poems Mazer has edited. It is an idiosyncratic curriculum, and Mazer is an idiosyncratic poet. More often than not his poems rhyme, but despite the presence in *New Poems* of the long, loosely constructed sonnet sequence, "The King," we don't find a love of formal construction such as we find with R.S. Gwynn. Nor do we find rhymes that seek to dazzle with Byronic novelty, and there's nothing like the allusive crypt-rhyming we get with Michael Robbins. More than any contemporary poet of whom I know, Mazer is committed to the idea that a poem is not so much a well-wrought thing as it is something that comes to the poet's ear, and emerges without much intervention of his will. Rhyme, for him, is a fundamental part of this mode of composition. As he puts it,

> I do not think about rhyme or plan it: it comes when the expression of meaning of emotion calls for it. Rhyme, seen or understood in this way, is not an artificial contrivance meant to keep some arbitrary system or standard: it comes as easily as leaves to a tree in the unconscious mind....

The allusion to Keats' famous dictum that "if Poetry comes not as naturally as the leaves to a tree it had better not come at all" is indicative both of Mazer's commitment to poetry that emerges from the unconscious, and of the way his mind is conditioned by literary sources. It should come as no surprise, really, that the spontaneous language of Mazer's poetry is frequently a language of rhymed couplets.

One of the major influences on Mazer seems to be John Ashbery. We see it in the combination of high and popular culture (Hildegaard of Bingen rubs shoulders with Archie & Jughead) and in the elliptical pseudo-narratives that create moods but refuse clearly-defined resolution. We see it, too, in the way the poems revel aesthetic escapism, a turning from the world of power to the world of beauty. Consider these lines from "Dinner Conversation":

> "I have to work." The ruling class
> wishes to suffer. The poor sit on their ass.
> History and archaeology revive
> fear of the gods, the instinct to take a wife.
> A rich man's daughters are posted to inventories.
> The visiting statesman approves of the lawn frieze.
> The Botticelli bursts another spring.
> It is of Florentine silks that I shall sing.
> This rough and tumble clan
> will expire in madness to a man.
> Ah, to be mad, that must be truly glorious,
> to see each word as a sign and write in prose.

Wealth, dynasties, politics, class conflict are all here, as is the use of art in the creation of prestige—but the loved world is one of art for its own sake. What should a poem praise? Florentine silk. And what is prose for? The mad pursuit of endless signs. Aesthetic pursuits raise us above mundane concerns, and rhyme comes in as a sign of the poem's status as an aesthetic rather than a utilitarian object. In fact, the only resolution the poem finds, in its evocative wanderings, is an aesthetic one, where we shift from couplets to an ABAXB pattern, marking closure in terms of form if not in terms of narrative:

> In my dream they thought I had stolen clothes
> (books I had borrowed from the library)
> The horizon is never permitted to doze.
> The real shipment of gold
> is emblazoned in flames for all to see.

The ethos or sensibility is clear enough: alienation from forms of power and authority (from those who see the speaker as a thief, from librarians, even); and a sense that real wealth is not the gold in vaults, but the gold emblazoned in the sky at sunset. Mazer is a Bohemian aesthete, and his rhymes here indicate a love of sound, and of the gesture of closure.

The rhyming couplets "Poem for the First Day of Spring" give us, as do many of Mazer's poems, a kind of elliptical meditation on the nature of the aesthetic.

> The vampire's coffin in Los Angeles
> is kept company by an ape named Barabas.
> Sunlight through the basement windows all day
> projects dust motes where the ape and the coffin play.
> This shadow was once a movie star, this grave
> is a science experiment that the last actors crave.
> Whoever comes here, Thelma or Clara or Theda,
> will go in silence, paying homage to Rita.
> Children come home from school, but that is all.
> The lawn is trimmed, and the slate arches pall.

The opening couplet hints that the vampire as a kind of Christ figure—dead but ready to rise, and accompanied by an ape whose name evokes the man intended for crucifixion next to Jesus, but released at the behest of Pontius Pilate. He was once a film star, and is still important to other film stars (the catalog of women's names gestures toward Thelma Todd, Clara Bow, Theda Bara, and Rita Hayworth—all the but last from the silent film era). But is he important to those who did not participate in the art? The world beyond seems orderly but indifferent: new generations are unconcerned, and the ending landscape seems very much like a cemetery. The poem is more pregnant with possible meaning than it is overtly meaningful, but one of the interpretive possibilities is certainly connected to the notion of an aging art-form, loved more by its practitioners than by the larger world, an art form removed from the busy world and preserved in formal beauty. It might very well be the art of poetry—especially of poetry in rhyme—that awaits rebirth, here, in Mazer's couplets.

At times, Mazer turns his gaze onto the process of composition itself, as in "Avion, Gorrion." Here, the title words are poetic *donnée*, the gift-phrase that came unbidden to his ear. The rhyme comes first, a charm of sound, redolent of possible meaning. *Avion* is French for airplane, but it is also a boy's given name meaning, appropriately, gift of God; a gorrion is a term sometimes used for a specific kind of sparrow, and "*gorrión*" is the common Spanish word for sparrow, so already we sense rich possibilities having to do with imagination, flight, and the divine. The poem begins in wonder:

> Avion, Gorrion
> What does this mean?
> DC-3 divisible by three
> A bilingual entelechy.

One senses that the rhyme may be driving the sentence more than anything else, but the notion that the *donnée* is an entelechy—an essence that has fully realized itself, as an oak tree is the realized essence of an acorn—is intriguing.

The poem continues in long stanzas, each beginning with "And what of / avion, Gorrion" and threading bits of narrative about the moment when the phrase came to Mazer on a rainy street with speculations on how the phrase might generate meaning for him and for others. In the end, though, we come back to the sense of the *donnée* as an entelechy, as full in and of itself:

> Avion. Gorrion.
> Say it again, but do not understand
> the imprint of its meaning.
> ....
> There is no need to understand or visit
> what has been left behind, what cannot name itself
> for fear of belying its greater importance,
> stumbled on, perhaps, in the rain.

One is reminded of Wallace Stevens' "Of Mere Being," where we are confronted with "the palm at the end of the mind," where "A gold-feathered bird / Sings in the palm, without human meaning, / Without human feeling, a foreign song." For Stevens, it is an image that we find at the end of all interpretation, a fabulous bird whose "fire-fangled feathers dangle down." For Mazer, the irreducible experience is not an image: it is a rhyme.

The critic Robert Strong, speaking at the Midwest Modern Language Association convention in 2013, described several varieties of rhyme before raising his eyes up from the lectern, gazing out at the gathered scholars, and intoning "imagine that happening in poetry again." We are in the fortunate position, though, of not having to imagine: rhyme, in rich varieties, and deployed to a plethora of purposes, is happening, now, in American poetry.

II
Poetry and Community

When Poetry Mattered

Andrei Voznesensky, who died in 2010, was one of the best-loved Russian, or perhaps I should say Soviet, poets of a generation called "the children of the '60s." These were poets who came of age in the late '50s and early 1960s, the most famous of whom was Yevgeny Yevtushenko. Both Voznesenksy and Yevtushenko were born in 1933, and it was a good year for a Russian poet to be born. Not only were they too young to be sent to the horrible slaughter that was the Second World War in Russia, they began to come into their own as poets just in time for the Khrushchev Thaw, a relaxing of repression following the death of Stalin and the removal of much of the apparatus of the Stalinist police state. The period is also known as the False Spring, since it came to an abrupt end in 1963 and 1964, as Krushchev was replaced by that icon of dreary stagnation, Leonid Brezhnev.

During the brief thaw, though, it was good to be a poet in Russia, at least if you were the kind of poet who wanted attention. Readings in stadiums were commonplace, in a way they never have been in the United States. T.S. Eliot may once have delivered a lecture in a mid-sized university basketball arena, but these were actual poetry readings, in for-real stadiums: by 1962 Voznesensky was drawing crowds of 14,000 or more, and more than half a million people signed up to buy copies of his collection *An Achilles Heart* before it was published.

What accounted for this enormous interest, even mania, for poetry? I'm reminded of one of my critical touchstones, a passage from Declan Kiberd's *Inventing Ireland* where he speaks of the relative popularity of poetry in conditions of colonization and repression: when the national institutions don't represent the broadly-held values of a people, the people often turn to poetry as a vehicle for the articulation of those values. One can see why: if the theaters and newspapers and educational institutions are in the grip of oppressors, one can still take up a pen and write poems that say things unpalatable to the powers that be. And for a brief time in the Krushchev Thaw, poetry and other arts were liberated from the kinds of restrictions that still bound cultural institutions like museums and universities. You could go to a poetry reading—as so many did—and hear a version of things that rang truer than the official accounts. As my father, who studied Russian literature before becoming an artist, put it, "those readings in stadiums were the only places a Russian could go and not feel they were being bullshitted."

And what was it that Voznesensky had to say that didn't sound like bullshit to those crowds? Well, a lot of it was an affirmation of the individual conscience. In the 1959 poem "Who Are We?" for example, Voznesensky answers the title question by saying :

> Under the cold stars, I wander alive
> With you Vera, Vega, I am myself
> Among the avalanches, like the Abominable
> Snowman, absolutely elusive.

Against all the big, overwhelming forces, the little self remains, free and authentic to itself: there's a kind of individualistic sublime at work here. The poem wouldn't be a Big Statement in the United States of the 1950s, even though Senator McCarthy's reign of terror over the intellectuals had come to an end only two years earlier: the level of repression just wasn't comparable to what Russians had seen, and Cold War America always defined itself against Russia by emphasizing the ideology of individualism. But in Russia, where collectivism was an official ideology and individualism had been actively, and violently, discouraged, people heard in words like these a message of liberation.

It's no wonder that Voznesensky wrote the kind of individualistic poems for which people were thirsting: as a young man he was a disciple of Pasternak, having moved out to Peredelkino to be near the grand old man in his last days. Pasternak's *Dr. Zhivago*, the great testament of the individual conscience against Czar and Commissar, was a kind of sacred text for Voznesensky.

I sometimes wonder whether Voznesensky's individualism was made more palatable to the authorities by virtue of its being tempered with doses of nationalism. Voznesensky's most famous poem, "I am Goya," with which he used to begin all of his readings, is many things:

a harrowing picture of Russia during the Nazi invasion, a great piece of anaphoristic verse, a veiled remembrance of his father going off to war with a book of Goya reproductions in his backpack, an ekphrastic poem dealing with Goya's paintings of the Napoleonic invasion of Spain, and a testament to the achievement of the Russian people in throwing back the better-armed, better-fed, better-organized forces of Hitler's Germany. It ends like this:

> I am the gullet
> of a woman hanged whose body like a bell
> tolled over a blank square
> I am Goya
>
> O grapes of wrath!
> I have hurled westward
>   the ashes of the uninvited guest!
> and hammered stars into the unforgetting sky—like nails
> I am Goya

That last bit, about sending the Germans packing, or scattering their dead ashes on a wind that will take them back to whence they came: that's the kind of hard-core Russian patriotism that no General or Commissar could condemn, and no Russian of the war years could hear without a deep, heart-felt response. And the victory is portrayed as being as great, and as unlikely, as the hammering of stars into the sky. Great stuff!

    Even his patriotism couldn't really save Voznesensky when the False Spring came to an end. He was subjected to the fate of so many Russian liberals, from the Decemberists on, and sent into a kind of internal exile, wandering in the remoter provinces of the Soviet Union. His poems from this era take on a slightly different tone, emphasizing hope in the form of a kind of small, saving remnant of Russian society. Here's one I particularly like, "To B. Akhmadulina." It gives us a small group, on the move:

We are many. Four, perhaps, altogether,
spinning along in our car devil-may-care.
The girl at the wheel flaunts her orange hair,
the sleeves of her jacket yanked up to the elbow.

Ah, Bela, though your driving leaves me limp,
you look angelic, out of this world;
your marvelous porcelain profile
glows like a white lamp ...

In hell they bang their frying pans
and send scouts up to the gate to watch,
when you, as the speedometer runs wild,
lift both hands off the wheel to strike a match.

How I love it, when stepping on the gas
in your transparent tones you say,
"What a mess!
they've taken my license away ...

"I swear they've got me wrong!
   You'd think I was a reckless driver!
      Why! I was just poking along ..."

Forget it, Bela. To argue with a cop,
you know, is a losing proposition.
He can't appreciate your lyric speed—
it's past the power of his transmission.

A poet owes it to himself
not to be trapped in miles-per-hour;
let him resound at the speed of light
like angels choiring in the stratosphere.

No matter, taking light-years as our measure,

if we should vanish like a radiant star,
with not a creature left behind to earn the prize.
We were the first to crack the sound-barrier.

Step on it, Bela, heavenly friend!
Who cares if we're smashed to bits in the end?
Long live the speed of poetry,
the most lethal of all speeds!

What if the maps ahead are enigmatical?
We are only a few. Four, perhaps, altogether;
hurtling along—and you are a Goddess!
That makes a majority, after all.

We've got the exile's self-affirmation (no one will ever give us any recognition for breaking the sound barrier, but we recognize ourselves), and we've got a nice turn on the old trope of describing a woman as a goddess: here, her divinity makes the small group more than equal to any forces that oppose it. This would be mere sentimentality if it weren't balanced against the earlier assertion that there's no use arguing with a cop. Voznesensky is well aware that, in the realm of real power, he and his friends are no match for the authorities. But in the realm of art, they maintain a kind of freedom, where the police can't match their speed.

There are many things to admire in Voznesensky, including his revival of the Mayakovsky era breeziness and confidence that fell out of Russian poetry in the '30s and '40s. One of my favorite moments of this kind comes at the end of "Fire in the Architectural Institute." The poem is based on one of Voznesensky's experiences: he'd been an architecture student, and just before he was to defend his thesis the institute burned down, destroying all of his work. But like Mayakovsky, he's got a seemingly unlimited, irrepressible buoyancy: "Everything's gone up in smoke / and there's no end of people sighing," he writes, "It's the end? / It's only the beginning. / Let's go to the movies!"

But whatever his fine qualities as a poet may be, the reason

Robert Archambeau

Voznesensky mattered to most of his readers was that he spoke back to them their own values when those values weren't affirmed anywhere else. I think about this when I hear people say, of one or another contemporary American poet, "he deserves more readers," or "she deserves an audience." I think about it, too, when I hear suggestions about how to get more people interested in poetry (by adding music to readings, by putting little placards with stanzas on them in the subway, etc.) These are supply-side solutions to a demand-side problem. They try to make something available, in hopes that this availability will create demand. But if we really want giant audiences, stadium-filling audiences, we'd need social conditions that drive people to need what is on offer in poetry, and conditions that prevent it from being offered in other venues. History has been a bit too kind to us for that.

The Disinheritance of the Poets

I am, and will always be, a great lover of the poetry of W.H. Auden—and of his prose and plays, too. But any honest reader of Auden ought to ask two questions: why does W.H. Auden's early, English work read as if the most important events of the time all took place in an English boarding school? And why does his later, American period read as if it were inspired by the syllabus of a college course called, say, "Introduction to Western Civilization"? The answers to both questions come when we look at the social situation of Auden and the groups with which he associated in the English and American periods of his career. In each case, we're dealing with very particular kinds of disinheritance, and with poetics that speak to different kinds of disinherited people.

Many people have noted the fixation on schoolboy topics in Auden's early poetry: there is, most famously, *The Orators*, a send-up of prize day orations at English boarding schools; and the early poems are full of students-vs-elders conflict. It's not just Auden who writes this way. I remember first reading Christopher Isherwood's *Lions and Shadows*, and being astonished at what I took to be the narcissism of the piece: here was something claiming to be a novel that was really little more than a memoir of Isherwood's school days, with commonplace scenes laid out as if they were of the greatest significance. Edward Upward's fiction can have much the same quality; Graham Greene edited a collection of essays called *The Old School* (to which Auden contributed); and Cyril Connolly's *Enemies of Promise*, purportedly a book about what one must do to write a lasting piece of literature, consists for almost half of its length of recollections of Connolly's time at Eton. Why this obsessive emphasis on one's old school?

Connolly offers an answer that's at least half right. He writes, near the end of *Enemies of Promise*,

> ... were I to deduce any system from my feelings on leaving Eton, it might be called The Theory of Permanent Adolescence. It is the theory that the experiences undergone by boys at the great public

schools, their glories and their disappointments, are so intense as to dominate their lives and to arrest their development. From this it results that the greater part of the ruling class remains adolescent, school-minded, self-conscious ...

The passage goes on in this vein, and includes a bit about homosexuality that many would feel reflects poorly on Connolly. But for present purposes, the point is that the public schools (Americans would say private schools—both terms refer to schools paid for by individual fees, rather than by taxes) make a deep impression. No doubt this is true: such schools are about forming an elite, and they work hard to give their students a sense of status, with duties and privileges, and with a sense of obligation to the old school itself.

Connolly's theory of permanent adolescence, though, does not fully explain the school-obsession of the generation of English writers born between, say, 1902 and 1909. After all, other generations before them had gone through the intense experience of elite boarding schools without having their work deeply marked by specifically boarding school themes and imagery. What was so different about Auden's generation? The answer, I think, is disillusion and disinheritance. It's not just that they had intense experiences in school—it's that their experiences involved a terrible dissonance between the values and expectations of school and the reality into which the schoolboys entered. They were never able to fully rid themselves of school, because they were never able to fulfill the expectations the schools created for them.

Consider the timing of their births: Auden's generation came of age too late to participate in the First World War. They saw their elders at school—often their older brothers—go off to war, to face what Isherwood called "the test"—the battle in which one would prove one's value as a man, a leader, and a representative of one's elite training. The schools preached sacrifice and the military virtues, knowing that they were creating officers for a desperate struggle. Even a future skeptic of all things jingoistic, the 13-year-old Eric Blair (we know him as George Orwell) wrote poems in which he anticipated "the test." Here's the first stanza of one called "Awake! Young Men of England":

> Oh! Give me the strength of the lion
> The wisdom of Reynard the Fox,
> And I'll hurl troops at the Germans,
> And give them the hardest of knocks.

One could go on quoting the rest of it, but the point is already clear: one must muster one's courage and one's wisdom, appeal to one's God, and above all lead (it is the speaker who will, as an officer, hurl troops at the Germans). That the result of all this will be the giving of hard knocks is enough to show us the puerility of the poet: this is no Wilfred Owen writing, but a child whose sense of war comes from the old men teaching at his school and telling stories about Nelson and Wellington trouncing Napoleon, or quoting from the more heroic passages of Macauley's *Lays of Ancient Rome*.

We may well think that Auden's generation should be grateful for having missed the slaughter, and I'm sure in some sense they were. But in addition to a kind of survivor's guilt, there's a significant sense of not having been allowed to take the test for which one had prepared—a failure to fulfill one's set task. It's important not to underestimate the effect of this on a generation whose elite status was in large measure justified by the rhetoric of service through leadership. Many of Isherwood's travels and adventures, including his dangerous trip to China during the Sino-Japanese war, were in his own estimation attempts to take "the test" he'd missed. And Auden, the least militaristic of men, took an inordinate pride in his American major's uniform when, after the Second World War, he worked as part of a group surveying the psychological damage caused by bombing.

There was another role the boys at England's elite schools were meant to inherit, beyond that of military leadership: they were meant to rule over the greatest and most expansive economic empire the world had ever known. This empire, of course, was destroyed: war debt and the resulting taxation ruined the landed families, and the

Depression (or, in English terms, the Slump) ravaged the industrial economy. If you were a middle-class schoolboy, hoping to get ahead by your wits and your elite school credentials, you were in terrible trouble: of two million middle-class jobs in England during the Slump, some 400,000 disappeared. Joining the workforce when one in five of the positions you might have aspired to has disappeared is a terrible thing. One was meant to be a valiant leader at war and a prosperous leader at peace, and instead all of one's intense training and indoctrination at school led to ... well, to a sense of failure, and perhaps of betrayal. The arrested development and permanent adolescence of which Connolly speaks wasn't just the product of intense school experiences: it was the product of the failure to fulfill these experiences. It was a matter of disinheritance. And if you want to feel how powerful a sense of disinheritance can be, consider how largely the American Civil War looms in the consciousness of the southern states as compared to the states of the north. If we had to go by the numbers of war re-enactors, we'd think that the Confederates outnumbered the Union troops ten to one.

*

There is another disinheritance to consider here, also related to the Depression or Slump: the disinheritance of writers less privileged in background than Auden and company. W.H. Auden, Cyril Connolly, Stephen Spender, John Betjeman, Edward Upward, Cecil Day Lewis, Christopher Isherwood, Louis MacNeice, Evelyn Waugh, Graham Greene, George Orwell, Anthony Powell—the only real difference in their educational background (besides Orwell's refusal to go on to Oxbridge) was the degree of prestige associated with their respective public schools in the subtle hierarchy of English education. Not one was a grammar school boy. This, it should be noted, is an unusual state of affairs in English literature, one without precedent, and one not repeated in later generations. Consider the prominent writers active in England 1915, while the writers named above were still in school. Yeats, Conrad, Shaw, Joyce, Woolf, D.H. Lawrence, Wyndham Lewis, Pound, Eliot, H.G. Wells, Kipling—a few went to

English public schools (Ford, Kipling, Lewis for a time), but some (Conrad, Yeats, Pound, Eliot) were foreigners, others were from humbler backgrounds (notably Wells and Lawrence), some were both (Shaw, Joyce) and Woolf was excluded by gender from the schoolboy experience. Consider the prominent writers in England today, and the diversity is all the more striking.

Why, one wonders, was there such a concentration of public school old boys in the literary generation of the 1930s? What drove them to become writers at a higher rate than previous generations from similar backgrounds? Here we enter the realm of speculation. My sense of things is that there may be something akin to the nineteenth-century Parisian phenomenon at work. For much of the nineteenth century in France, the social and educational system produced far too much talent for the social system to absorb. Respectable professions such as the law, the clergy, finance, and politics couldn't take on all of the bright young men seeking places, and this contributed to the enormous growth in the field of culture—writing, the arts, and the bohemia that came along with them. In the England of the 1930s, the generation of public schoolboys faced a destroyed economy and much-reduced prospects. They were deprived of the areas of action and fulfillment available to previous generations with similar backgrounds. Along with this displacement came a sense of alienation from the ideology of leadership and service with which they had been instilled. They had, then, both motive and opportunity (or, shall we say, lack of opportunity) enough to become writers: critical of their time, needing to rethink the relation of self and society, equipped with exquisite educations, and unable to get traction in fields of social leadership, they took up their pens.

Of course there were many English writers of the time who did not come from the same sorts of school background as the Audens and Isherwoods. What of them? What of Julian Symons, Christopher Caudwell, Derek Savage, George Barker, and a host of others? One could make an argument along the lines of "well, they weren't as good, were they?" but this would be highly contentious. Read a few George Barker poems side by side with some of Spender's and tell me the case for the superiority of the public schoolboy remains clear. A more convincing case could be made for the relative lack of social capital among the non-public school set. That is: even though they may have been denied the easy entry into positions of security and authority that they had thought their birthright, the public schoolboys were still as a whole better connected socially, more financially secure, less burdened by family obligations, and held more impressive academic credentials than their peers from humbler backgrounds. Moreover, they had formed very close bonds with their peers at school—one of the main functions of prestigious boarding schools, and one that ensured the career-building value of the old school tie. This gave them a stronger starting position in the race for literary reputation.

Early advantages, as every investor knows, have a tendency to become still greater advantages as time goes by. If the public schoolboys entered the field of literature at an advantage over others, that advantage only increased as their concerns and stylistic ticks (such as the prevalence of public school imagery) became identified as the markings of a whole generation of writers—as part became taken for whole. This happened in the self-mythologizing of the public school writers, in their mutually-admiring critical writing, memoirs, and *romans-à-clef*, and it has continued to happen in the scholarly writing about the period. Here, for example, is the opening paragraph of Bernard Bergonzi's excellent study *Reading the Thirties*, which shows far more self-awareness about the process of taking part for whole than do most similar documents:

> This book is not about all of the literature written in England between 1930 and 1940. In the title, and throughout the book, I use the term 'the thirties' in the same deliberately selective fashion that made it possible for Edward Upward to give the all-embracing title *In the Thirties* to a retrospective novel about the progress of a young poet and schoolmaster from bourgeois individualism to the Communist Party which restricted itself to a dozen or so characters. Despite the narrowness of the range, Stephen Spender could still call Upward's novel 'the most truthful picture of life in that decade.' In

the present book I do not intend 'the thirties' to mean just a period, but also to refer generically to a group of writers and the work they produced in that decade, occasionally later. Indeed, "the thirties' in this sense largely corresponds to ... 'the Auden generation.'

I cherish the works of Auden, I read the works of Isherwood with a hearty appetite, I ransack Spender's journals for gems of gossip and social observation. But I try not to forget that both the achievement and the prominence of those writers rests on a bedrock of privilege, albeit of privilege displaced from the realm of power to the realm of art.

*

But what about Auden's American period, from 1939 on? After Auden settles in America, we find in his writing a marked turn away from psychological and Marxian terminology and a serious uptick in overt references to what we might call the classics of Western high culture. It's certainly true that his work appears in fewer political contexts and in more academic and cultural reviews. A quick survey of his bibliography reveals that about half of the appearances of his writings in journals during his English period appeared in politically oriented publications, while only about 15% of them did during his American period, which would make sense for a poet shifting from theory and politics to high culture. And there are certainly more poems like "The Fall of Rome," "The Shield of Achilles," "Voltaire at Ferney," and "At the Grave of Henry James"—that is, a lot more of the overtly high-culture-themed poems—in the work of the American Auden than in the English Auden. What explains this turn toward overt high-cultural references?

Once again, a certain kind of disinheritance comes into play. We can get at it by first considering some words Edmund Wilson wrote about Auden in 1954. Surveying Auden's *Collected Poems*, Wilson notes a difference between the English Auden and the American Auden. "He is no longer rebelling against British institutions," writes Wilson, he is dealing with a very different world, a hypermodern, industrialized, commercialized, materialistic and rootless world, and with "the problem of how to live in it ... to avoid being paralyzed or bought by it." Wilson continues:

> It may well be that this aspect of Auden is more intelligible to an American than an Englishman, for this feeling oneself a member of a determined resistant minority has been now for nearly a hundred years a typical situation [for cultivated humanistic writers] in America. Such people in the later nineteenth century were likely to be defeated or embittered. In our own, they have felt the backing of a partly inarticulate public who are not satisfied with the bilge that the popular media feed them in their movies and magazines, and who are grateful to anyone who will take a stand for that right to think for themselves which is supposed to be guaranteed us by the Bill of Rights and that right to a high level of culture which the framers of the Constitution—taking it so much for granted—would never have thought to include. These American writers of which I speak do not constitute a group, they do not frequent an official café; and on this account the visitor from Europe is likely to come to the conclusion that, except in universities, we have no intellectual life. He cannot conceive that the American writers are functioning in the crevices of cities, on the faculties of provincial colleges or scattered all over the country in the solitude of ranches and farms. This kind of life was now [since his arrival in 1939] to be Auden's lot....

Wilson describes a very real America, one dominated by the materialistic elite that displaced the old, cultivated elite best exemplified by the Boston Brahmins. It was an America from which Wilson, himself descended from the older and more cultivated elite, felt profoundly alienated. Here's something he wrote only two years after the piece on Auden, something about the destruction of the old elite by the new ruthlessly commercial and materialistic elite, and how that destruction affected his father's generation:

> The period after the Civil War—both banal in a bourgeois way and fantastic with giant fortunes—was a difficult one for Americans brought up in the old tradition.... They had been educated at Exeter and Andover and at an eighteenth-century Princeton, and had afterwards been trained ... for what had once been called the learned professions; but they had then to deal with a world in which this kind of education and the kind of ideals it served no longer really counted for much.... Of my father's close friends at college, but a single one was left by the time he was in his thirties; all the rest were dead—some had committed suicide. My father, though highly successful, cared nothing about making a fortune or keeping up with current standards of luxury, which in our part of the world were extravagant. Like many Americans who studied law, he had in his youth aimed at public life.... But he could not ... be induced to take part in the kind of political life that he knew at the end of the century....

The new America that arrived in the late nineteenth century was triumphant in the middle of the twentieth, and the disinherited class of people committed to high culture functioned, in mid-fifties America, as a kind of resistance to the dominant commercial culture. Its badge of membership came in the form of references to that culture. All this would change soon enough: generations that saw no conflict in citing Henry Adams and Mickey Mouse in the same novel or poem were on their way. But the view from Wilson's desk in 1954 was of a high culture that was a form of resistance to the values of commodity and commerce—the disdain for pop culture implicit in his statement about Auden rises almost to the level we find in Adorno. And there was a feeling among among a broader segment of the population that there was something to this sense of high culture as resistance: it's what sent the young Allen Ginsberg to the poems of Blake, for example, and caused him, in a poem written in the year between these two passages of Wilson's prose, to denounce America as "Moloch"—an ancient Ammanite god, and hardly a figure out of popular culture.

Auden was, of course, caught between the residual world of the American poet as highbrow or leftover Brahmin, and the then-incipient, now-dominant world of the American poet as academic (or, more precisely, as creative writing professor). His work wore the badge of the older, highbrow caste, and his poems provided something the caste, and those sympathetic to its resistance to commercial culture, needed: the *Collected Poems* that Wilson reviewed sold some 30,000 copies—a success even in the commercial terms that dominated, and still dominate, American life.

In Solitude, In Multitude:

Crowds and Poetry

Near the beginning of his strange, brilliant book *Crowds and Power*, the Bulgarian writer Elias Canetti claims that our most primal fear is the fear of being touched: the hand in the dark, something reaching out and grabbing hold of us. We only really lose this fear in crowds, says Canetti, since it is in crowds that we allow the boundaries of the self to melt away. We touch and are touched in the scrum and bustle of the crowd, but in the crowd we don't feel touch as a violation. It doesn't bother us, because we don't think of the crowd as other than ourselves: an angry mob, a multitude gathered in protest, a pack of like-minded sports fanatics surging back and forth and chanting in unison: when we're part of such groups, we don't experience the crowd as separate from ourselves: we're part of an *us*, and the only threat is from whomever we've collectively designated as *them*. From this Canetti builds a fascinating, and at times terrifying, theory of the crowd.

Poets, of course, have expressed revulsion from the crowd, but also felt the seductive bliss of immersion in the collective. Indeed, the two oldest and most revered modes of poetry—the lyric and the epic—respectively express the individualistic ethos of private emotion, and the collective ideals and aspirations of the group. But unless I miss my guess, it's really at the beginning of the nineteenth century that we see an uptick in the frequency with which poets consciously meditate on the meaning of the multitude. And this poetic examination of the relation of the individual to the crowd has continued up to the present.

Monstrous Ant Hills: The Crowd in Romanticism

Romanticism is a large and various literary movement, and it certainly has its moments of collectivism, especially in the more peripheral nations of Europe, where nationalist sentiment, even to the point of atavism, was an important part of the reaction to Enlightenment universalism and the spread of standardized, deracinated laws and customs under the banners of Napoleon's conquering armies. But the dominant reaction to the crowd in English Romanticism is certainly revulsion. Here's Wordsworth describing London in book seven of *The Prelude*:

> Rise up, thou monstrous ant-hill on the plain;
> Of a too busy world! Before me flow,
> Thou endless stream of men and moving things!
> Thy every-day appearance, as it strikes—
> With wonder heightened, or sublimed by awe—
> On strangers, of all ages; the quick dance
> Of colours, lights, and forms; the deafening din;
> The comers and the goers face to face,
> Face after face; the string of dazzling wares,
> Shop after shop, with symbols, blazoned names,
> And all the tradesman's honours overhead:
> Here, fronts of houses, like a title-page,
> With letters huge inscribed from top to toe ...

What really strikes Wordsworth about the crowded streets of London is the signage. It's hard for us to put ourselves in a state of mind where the presence of shop signs is a strange and alienating thing, but that's where Wordsworth is coming from. For him, the need of shops to spell out in gigantic letters the nature of their services indicates how impersonal a place the crowded city had become. In small villages such as those Wordsworth knew in the Lake District, one knew the individuals with whom one bartered, but in the city every shop needs to shout out its identity to a rushing crowd, lest it remain anonymous. No one really knows where they are or who they're with, not in the way the characters in, say, Wordsworth's "Michael" know each other. In "Michael," each little pile of stones has a story about the generations who lived around it, and all those stories are known to the locals. They know who they are and where they live in a way the inhabitants of the monstrous ant hill cannot.

Wordsworth is also a bit put off by the internationalized, multicultural space that London had already become. Here's a small piece of a long passage on a marketplace:

> ... another street
> Presents a company of dancing dogs,
> Or dromedary, with an antic pair
> Of monkeys on his back; a minstrel band
> Of Savoyards; or, single and alone,
> An English ballad-singer

Camels, monkeys, and Italian musicians from Savoy: the poor ballad-singer, a representative of indigenous culture, hardly stands a chance, surrounded as he is by a noisy array of exotics, including:

> ... every character of form and face:
> The Swede, the Russian; from the genial south,
> The Frenchman and the Spaniard; from remote
> America, the Hunter-Indian;
> Moors, Malays, Lascars, the Tartar, the Chinese,
> And Negro Ladies in white muslin gowns.

But what really throws Wordsworth off balance isn't anything so banal as the presence of the culturally different. It's a version of the anonymity and alienation that we saw earlier in the shop signs:

> How oft, amid those overflowing streets,
> Have I gone forward with the crowd, and said
> Unto myself, "The face of every one
> That passes by me is a mystery!"
> Thus have I looked, nor ceased to look, oppressed
> By thoughts of what and whither, when and how;
> Until the shapes before my eyes became
> A second-sight procession, such as glides

> Over still mountains, or appears in dreams;
> And once, far-travelled in such mood, beyond
> The reach of common indication, lost
> Amid the moving pageant, I was smitten
> Abruptly, with the view (a sight not rare)
> Of a blind Beggar, who, with upright face,
> Stood, propped against a wall, upon his chest
> Wearing a written paper, to explain
> His story, whence he came, and who he was.
> Caught by the spectacle my mind turned round
> As with the might of waters; and apt type
> This label seemed of the utmost we can know,
> Both of ourselves and of the universe;
> And, on the shape of that unmoving man,
> His steadfast face and sightless eyes, I gazed,
> As if admonished from another world.

The old blind beggar has no relation to the people swarming around him. In a village he'd be known to everyone, and they to him, and if it were his home village, he'd be connected to the community by webs of family obligation. His story would be well known, and he'd have a place. But here, in the crush of bodies pouring through the streets of London, he's no one at all. His only claim to any connection to others is through advertising his own story, in letters much like those of the shop signs we saw before. He has to assert his humanity and individuality and particularity, and in the passing rush this assertion takes on both pathos (he's so small, he's so vulnerable, he has so little claim on making us care) and sublimity (he's so small and vulnerable, yet he endures and is not destroyed, his small light held against the darkness). If you live in America, you've passed some homeless man, most likely a veteran in a wheelchair, and seen exactly this sort of life-story scrawled in marker on a piece of cardboard. I don't know what the sight made you feel, but Wordsworth would see in it "the utmost we can know / Both of ourselves and of the universe" — an emblem of our condition as little orphaned individuals in the largeness of space and time.

Crowds are, for Wordsworth, threats: threats to the dignity and rootedness of the individual. And he's not alone in his aversion to the crowd: Byron introduced us to Childe Harold (the Ziggy Stardust to Byron's Bowie) by saying:

> ... soon he knew himself the most unfit
> Of men to herd with Man; with whom he held
> Little in common; untaught to submit
> His thoughts to others, though his soul was quelled,
> In youth by his own thoughts; still uncompelled,
> He would not yield dominion of his mind
> To spirits against whom his own rebelled;
> Proud though in desolation; which could find
> A life within itself, to breathe without mankind.

To be with others in a crowd is to "herd"—to be subhuman, animalistic, erased as an individual. What a psychologist now might describe as the imperfect socialization of a severe narcissist, Byron sees with pride. Harold was "untaught to submit his thoughts to others"—he retains his swaggering individualism and independence, which gives him an isolation that is both a curse ("desolation") and a mark of specialness.

We find variations on the revulsion from crowds in all the major English Romantic poets, though in Coleridge it is tempered by a kind of nostalgia for a lost sense of community (the Ancient Mariner was only ever unselfconsciously part of a group before he killed the albatross, and at the end of the poem he preaches a gospel of community he cannot embody). In Shelley it is combined with a yearning for a small community of the likeminded (as we see in "Epipsychidion" and the deeply under-rated "Alastor," and in the pathos of "Lines Written Among the Euganean Hills").

I imagine the exalting of the individual, and the praising of the small community against the crowd, has to do with both the large-scale social conditions of the time, and with the particular circumstances of poets in the Romantic era. The French Revolution and the incipient industrial economy had uprooted the old social order. This both unleashed the power of the individual to find his or her own course through the world and bequeathed to those atomized individuals a host of anxieties about anonymity and dislocation. And poets, shut out of the old patronage networks and unaccommodated by the market, felt particularly out of place, alienated from (and therefore critical of) the dominant institutions of their age. They had their individual pride to fall back on, and dreams of happier days in closer communities.

The Poet as Flâneur in the City

Of course not all poets felt alienated from the crowds of the growing cities of the nineteenth century. As the century wore on, cities increasingly became the natural habitat of poets. How did these figures relate to the crush of bodies around them? Baudelaire, in "*Les Foules*" ("Crowds") admits to a taste for the multitude, but he begins by noting such a taste isn't for everyone:

> It is not given to every man to take a bath of multitude; enjoying a crowd is an art; and only he can relish a debauch of vitality at the expense of the human species, on whom, in his cradle, a fairy has bestowed the love of masks and masquerading, the hate of home, and the passion for roaming.

What makes it possible for Baudelaire to appreciate crowds? It's something having to do with imagination:

> Multitude, solitude: identical terms, and interchangeable by the active and fertile poet. The man who is unable to people his solitude is equally unable to be alone in a bustling crowd.

The poet enjoys the incomparable privilege of being able to be both himself and someone else, as he wishes. Like those wandering souls who go looking for a body, he enters as he likes into each man's personality. For him alone everything is vacant; and if certain places seem closed to him, it is only because in his eyes they are not worth visiting.

> The solitary and thoughtful stroller finds a singular intoxication in this universal communion. The man who loves to lose himself in a crowd enjoys feverish delights that the egoist locked up in himself as in a box, and the slothful man like a mollusk in his shell, will be eternally deprived of. He adopts as his own all the occupations, all the joys and all the sorrows that chance offers.
>
> What men call love is a very small, restricted, feeble thing compared with this ineffable orgy, this divine prostitution of the soul giving itself entire, all it poetry and all its charity, to the unexpected as it comes along, to the stranger as he passes.

For Baudelaire, the experience of the individual going out into the crowd is a matter of the individual more-or-less disappearing, becoming an egoless emptiness into which all passing things flow. It's much like what Emerson was getting at when he wrote "I become a transparent eyeball—I am nothing; I see all the currents of the Universal Being circulate through me," though Emerson was thinking about nature and wilderness, not the crush of humanity on the streets of Paris.

Baudelaire concludes by changing things up a bit. So far he's been following a kind of *via negativa*, an erasure of self in order to take in and become at one with all he encounters. Here, in the final paragraph of his prose poem, he compares this experience to that of a Moses-like figure who creates community around himself:

> It is a good thing sometimes to teach the fortunate of this world, if only to humble for an instant their foolish pride, that there are higher joys than theirs, finer and more uncircumscribed. The founders of colonies, shepherds of peoples, missionary priests exiled to the ends of the earth, doubtlessly know something of this

mysterious drunkenness; and in the midst of the vast family created by their genius, they must often laugh at those who pity them because of their troubled fortunes and chaste lives.

In the end, I suppose, there's not much to choose between the two paths: whether one's union with the crowd comes from self-erasure, or from the kind of assertive, paternal leadership of the "founders of colonies, shepherds of peoples," it all ends in the same place: blissful, promiscuous union in the crowd. Here, I think, is what Elias Canetti was getting at when he said that the crowd was the key to losing the fear of being touched: there is only touch, and no self to be touched from the outside.

Walt Whitman, another urban poet, takes a similar approach in "There was a Child Went Forth." The poem starts out with something like Baudelaire's self-loss in the encounter with the objects around one:

> There was a child went forth every day;
> And the first object he look'd upon, that object he became;
> And that object became part of him for the day, or a certain part of the day, or for many years, or stretching cycles of years....
> And the old drunkard staggering home from the out-house of the tavern, whence he had lately risen,
> And the school-mistress that pass'd on her way to the school,
> And the friendly boys that pass'd—and the quarrelsome boys,
> And the tidy and fresh-cheek'd girls—and the barefoot negro boy and girl,
> And all the changes of city and country, wherever he went.

Soon, though, we see that Whitman isn't giving us a self-erasure, but a kind of building up of the self: everything the child encounters enters into that child and "becomes part of him." That is, the child takes in and comprehends the world, digests it, and makes it part of an enduring and expanding self. All the people the child encounters "became part of that child who went forth every day," and if there's an encounter with the eternal, it isn't that the child enters a unity larger than himself. Rather, he gathers the passing faces of the crowd into himself, and it is there that they survive, as he "now goes, and will always go forth every day." Talk about the egotistical sublime!

What's striking about both Baudelaire and Whitman is the way there's a kind of meeting of the individual and the absolute through the medium of the crowd: the crowd is the way the self opens up to a connection with something like the infinite. It's a very abstract kind of community that's at stake here: not a matter of getting to know others as particular people, but of finding a mystical union between self and all. It may be profound, but it's hardly sociable. I doubt Wordsworth, who dreamed of communities where people knew one another's life-stories, would find it satisfactory. But it is a way to live in a city and find something other than horror and revulsion at the sight of the multitude.

Modern Ambivalence

Something about twentieth century experience in America seems to have made many of our best poets ambivalent about crowds. My great touchstone for this is William Carlos Williams' "At the Ballgame," which includes these lines:

> So in detail they, the crowd,
> are beautiful
> for this
> to be warned against
> saluted and defied—
> It is alive, venomous
> it smiles grimly
> its words cut—
> The flashy female with her
> mother, gets it—
> The Jew gets it straight— it
> is deadly, terrifying—
> It is the Inquisition, the

> Revolution
> It is beauty itself
> that lives
> day by day in them
> idly—
> This is
> the power of their faces
> It is summer, it is the solstice
> the crowd is
> cheering, the crowd is laughing
> in detail
> permanently, seriously
> without thought

The crowd is beautiful, happy, deeply rooted in the past of human experience (it's important, I think, that "it is the solstice," with all of the freight of pagan festivals that time of year carries). But then again, as Canetti knew, where there's an exalting us, there's also a threatened them. The flashy female is likely to find herself objectified—which is a form of not belonging, of being set apart. And the Jewish character has plenty of historical reason to distrust crowds as they thoughtlessly celebrate their oneness and togetherness.

George Oppen's *Of Being Numerous* presents another ambivalent meditation on the relation of solitude and multitude. Images of shipwreck and an isolated Crusoe figure haunt the 39-section poem from which the book draws its name. But no matter how deep Oppen's fears of isolation run, he remains committed to solidarity with others: "Obsessed, bewildered / By the shipwreck / Of the singular," he writes, "We have chosen the meaning / Of being numerous." Again, we see the desire to come together. But the urge for community is counterpoised to a skepticism about public platitudes: committed to concrete observation, Oppen cannot fathom those who, with such ease and abstraction, "talk / Distantly of 'The People.'"

The series ends with a quotation of a piece of Walt Whitman's prose, in which he looks on the capitol building rebuilt after the Civil War:

> The capitol grows upon one in time, especially as they have got the great figure on top of it now, and you can see it very well. It is a great bronze figure, the Genius of Liberty I suppose. It looks wonderful toward sundown. I love to go and look at it. The sun when it is nearly down shines on the headpiece and it dazzles and glistens like a big star: it looks quite
>
> curious …

The choice of Whitman, the great American Everyman, is significant: his presence signals an interest in a poetry of national community. But the break mid-sentence, together with the lineation, put a great deal of stress on that final word, "curious." What is Oppen's take on the idea of community? Is he skeptical? Intrigued? He certainly can't bring himself to yawp with a full-throated Whitmanesque enthusiasm. The questions are left hanging there in front of us.

Crowds and Countercultures

The countercultural movements of the sixties and seventies put different spins on the theme of solitude and multitude. Gary Snyder, for example, clearly feels the pull of the crowd in one of his most famous poems, "I Went Into the Maverick Bar." The poem begins like this:

> I went into the Maverick Bar
> In Farmington, New Mexico.
> And drank double shots of bourbon
>   backed with beer.
> My long hair was tucked up under a cap
> I'd left the earring in the car.
>
> Two cowboys did horseplay
>   by the pool tables,
> A waitress asked us
>   where are you from?

> a country-and-western band began to play
> "We don't smoke Marijuana in Muskokie"
> And with the next song,
>   a couple began to dance.
>
> They held each other like in High School dances
>   in the fifties;
> I recalled when I worked in the woods
>   and the bars of Madras, Oregon.
> That short-haired joy and roughness—
>   America—your stupidity.
> I could almost love you again.

Certainly Snyder's speaker (let's call him "Snyder," since he pretty much is Gary Snyder) feels alienated. He is, after all, disguised in the enemy camp: long hair tucked away, earring hidden, while the anthem of the hippie-bashing multitudes plays. But he feels the allure of the warm embrace: dances, horseplay, all that unselfconscious human community. I love the ambivalence at the end of the third stanza. In fact, I've always thought the poem would be better if it ended there. But instead we have another stanza, one truer, perhaps, to what Snyder really felt. Or perhaps only truer to what he thought he ought to feel:

> We left—onto the freeway shoulders—
>   under the tough old stars—
> In the shadow of bluffs
>   I came back to myself,
> To the real work, to
>   "What is to be done."

"What is to be done," of course, is the title of a famous revolutionary tract by Lenin. If there's solidarity in this last stanza, it's not to any actually experienced crowd, like the one in the Maverick Bar. Rather, it's to an abstract idea of a class-based community. Maybe it's this shift from the warmth of a real crowd to the coldness of allegiance to an abstract multitude that irks me. And believe me, I want to be on Snyder's side.

If the culture/counterculture animosity could vex Snyder's relation to crowds, it caused another kind of poet to seek to draw a crowd together. Consider the Black Nationalist aesthetic of Leroi Jones/Amiri Baraka's poem "S.O.S." Here, in a poem clearly written for oral delivery to a racially specific audience, we begin with a strong sense of the phatic function of language, with the poet seeking, apparently desperately, to connect to his community:

> Calling black people
> Calling all black people, man woman child
> Wherever you are, calling you, urgent, come in
> Black People, come in, wherever you are, urgent, calling
> You, calling all black people

The voice is like that of a lost radio operator seeking to connect to home base. But the radio-operator's voice changes, in the final lines, to something else: rather than a voice in the wilderness, trying to find contact, we suddenly get something like a host's voice, or a carnival barker's, welcoming people into whatever desirable location he inhabits: "Calling all black people, come in, black people, come / on in."

From "come in" to "come on in" is a big step: the outsider becomes the insider, and the audience, at first sought desperately, is now welcomed warmly. The move is from solitude to the hope of multitude. One senses that Jones/Baraka wants to become one of Baudelaire's "founders of colonies, shepherds of peoples," gathering "a vast family created by their genius."

Otherhood, Understood

One of my favorite contemporary poems to take up the theme of multitude and solitude is Atsuro Riley's poem "Diorama." Riley, a half-Japanese southerner, gives us a powerful, non-judgmental sense of a community gathering as a crowd at a small town summer fair. I was fortunate enough to hear Riley read the poem at the Poetry Foundation, and the man who'd introduced Riley, himself a southerner from Memphis, couldn't contain himself after the reading, and burst out saying "when I heard your poem, all I could think was those are the sounds, those are the words, I grew up with!" I get it. Riley does a great job of giving what I suppose we could call the audio landscape of a southern crowd of his youth. But then, right there in the middle of the poem, we get a moment where Riley's main character, a half-Japanese boy, overhears a conversation in which he's being talked about as an exotic alien:

> The Blue Hole Summer Fair, set up and spread out like a butterfly pinned down on paper. Twin bright-lit wings, identically shaped (and fenced) and sized.
>
> This side holds the waffled-tin (and oven-hot) huts of the Home Arts Booths and Contests, the hay-sweet display-cages for the 4-H livestock, the streamer-hung display-stages where girl-beauties twirl and try for queen. There's rosette-luster (and -lusting), and the marching band wearing a hole in Sousa. And (pursed) gaggles and clutches of feather-white neighbor-women, eyeballing us like we're pig's feet in a jar.
> *I wonder does her boy talk Chinese?*
> *You ever seen that kind of black-headed?*
> *Blue shine all in it like a crow.*
>
> This other wing (the one I'm back-sneaking, side-slipping, turnstiling into) dips and slopes down to low-lying marsh-mire: whiffs of pluff-mud stink and live gnat-pack poison, carnie-cots and -trailers camped on ooze. They've got (rickety) rides, and tent-shows with stains, and rackety bare-bulbed stalls of Hoop-La Game (*RING-A-COKE!*) and Rebel Yell and Shoot the Gook Down. Stand here, on this smutch-spot: don't these mirrors show you strange?

Crowds are gathering. Yonder there and down, the yolk-glow of a tent is drawing men on (and in) the way a car-crash does, or a cockfight sure enough, or neon. The ticket-boy's getting mobbed at the fly of the door.

No sign in sight, except for the X of the Dixie-flag ironed across his t-shirt.

I am bone-broke but falling into line.

The men upwind of me are leaking chaw-spit and pennies.

That, plus the eye-hunger spreading like a rumor through the swarm.

The rib-skinny doorkeeper's hollering: *bet now, bout's bout startin!*

Over his shoulder, a ropy yellow light.

Also: circles of white tobacco-smoke, and bleacher-rows of (cooncalling) men who know my daddy.

—And there he is, up in front with some tall man, iron-arming two black-chested boys toward the ring.

The remarkable thing about Riley's poem, for me, is the way the central moment in which we feel the main character's otherness remains undramatic. I don't mean to say that it lacks impact—it has plenty of that. What I mean is, it isn't a dramatic climax, it doesn't result in anything like the crowd turning on the part-Asian boy. It doesn't lead to a direct confrontation. In fact, it's the very ordinariness of it that makes it important: the people who ask "I wonder does her boy talk Chinese?" aren't mean-spirited or malevolent. But nevertheless we feel the sting of their words. Like the Jewish character in William Carlos Williams' "At the Ballgame," we "get it straight" about what it means to be "other." That Riley can approach this topic, one that clearly gives him much pain, with a kind of distanced, nuanced understanding is remarkable. It's one of the things that places him among the best poets I know of working on the old theme of solitude and multitude.

Between Facebook and Montparnasse:
Poetry's Lonely Years

If you want to understand the significance of Richard Hugo's 1977 book of poems *31 Letters and 13 Dreams*, you're going to need to check in with the Envelope Manufacturer's Association. Although the slim Norton edition in my possession features an envelope on the cover, the importance of communications technology—and the envelope is certainly a technology of communication—isn't the most immediately apparent thing about Hugo's book. Indeed, it comes across more as a book about solitude and loneliness than anything else, as I'm sure Hugo intended.

As the title indicates, the poems in the book come in two forms: letters and dreams. The letters are invariably given a title in the format "Letter to [name of recipient, usually another poet of the 1970s] from [name of town, usually someplace with a university Hugo was visiting, or a little western town where he'd gone to fish]." So: "Letter to Ammons from Maratea," for example, or "Letter to Simic from Boulder." The dream poems, too, have titles that follow a format of sorts: "In Your [descriptive word] Dream." Thus: "In Your War Dream," "In Your Hot Dream," and so forth.

One soon catches on that the letters and the dreams are really two different ways of addressing the same theme. The letters are the public, or semi-public, way of dealing with Hugo's sense of isolation as an aging, unattached man who spends a lot of time traveling around the country from one poetry reading or visiting writer gig to another. There's a lot of alienation, and a fair bit of non-specific frustration and detachment: "I'm awfully frightened / and I don't know why. I keep feeling revolutionary / but I have no cause," he writes in "Letter to Hanson from Miami"—"I feel I am going to dynamite / the swimming pool." It's a condition he attributes to being "as far from home / as I can get in the United States."

Letters sent to someone with whom he feels a connection, an old girlfriend, say, or to a fellow poet, become a way of trying to connect, to write his way out of isolation. It's also a way of converting pain and sometimes panic into anecdotage, reminiscence, and a presentation of himself as wistful, gently melancholy, a little stoic.

The dreams, by contrast, are private: not Hugo's way of trying to communicate to sympathetic people in the world, but his way of trying to communicate with himself. That is, they're where his unconscious feeds up images of his isolated condition, directing them to the waking mind for contemplation and interpretation. "You are riding a camel / in Athens. The citizens yell 'We are not Arab. This / is not sand'" we read in "Your Wild Dream," before discovering that, through the metamorphic logic of dreams, "the camel is a yacht. You cruise / a weird purple river. Girls doze on the bank. One / stands up and waves. You yell, 'Where is your town?' / You are alone." The imagery is weird, but the condition from which the dream springs is clear enough: isolation, displacement, a yearning to connect.

This kind of confessional poetry, in which the poet takes stock, as best and as directly as he can, of his inner needs and fears, and tries to tell them to others, is pretty out of fashion now. Indeed, reading Hugo's book side by side with Juliana Spahr's wonderful 2011 collection *Well Then There Now*, one really senses a change in style and attitude from the poetry prominent in the late 1970s to the well-received poetry of our own time. Spahr's work is about Hawaii, which one would think would give her ample cause to write about isolation and distance. But instead we get a picture of Hawaii as a place deeply interconnected with every other place: we see it penetrated by, landed on, and changed by information and bodies and species from all over the world. Like Spahr's equally fine *This Connection of Everyone with Lungs*, it is a book about connection and community, and her preferred pronoun is not "me" but "us."

If we want to understand this difference between Hugo's lonely confessionalism and Spahr's sense of interconnectivity and community, we'd do well to look at the Envelope Manufacturer's Association 2006 report "First Class Mail and the United States Postal Service: Future Strategies for This Time-Honored Medium." This, after all, throws into stark relief the very different communications regimes under which Hugo and Spahr have written.

The report, issued after a "summit meeting of former postal leaders and mailing industry leaders," is a bit panic-stricken. The envelope industry, it seems, is deeply worried about the fate of the personal letter, as the wrapping of such letters has been a major source of their revenue. But, they note, the share of United States Postal deliveries taken by first class mail (primarily letters and post-cards) has been in steep decline. Sometime around 2002 the volume of first class mail sank beneath that of pre-sorted mail (bills, large-scale business mailings, much junk mail) and the plunge has been precipitous since then. It's indicative, of course, of the rise of the internet, email, Facebook, iChat, Skype, and all the other means by which people keep in touch. Richard Hugo, back in the 1970s, wrote in a world where personal communication over great distances was either very slow, like the paper letter, or very expensive (a three-minute Sunday off-peak phone call in 1970 would cost over four dollars in today's money, which was down from the equivalent of almost 23 dollars in the mid-1960s; and when *31 Letters and 13 Dreams* was published, air travel was about two and a half times more expensive per mile than it is today, though the in-flight meals were better).

If we think about Hugo's moment, it wasn't just a time of relatively expensive communications: it was a time when American poets, novelists, and artists were more geographically scattered across the nation than ever before. In the early decades of the twentieth century, the tiny number of people privileged enough to be engaged in these kinds of creativity clustered in a few places—Greenwich Village, say, or the parts of Montparnasse where expats hung out together in cheap cafés. The expansion of the universities in the decades after World War Two allowed many more people to make their way as artists and writers, but it also scattered them across the continent. And this scattering took place at a time when it was much, much more difficult to stay in touch with likeminded people than it is today.

This combination of the growing academic-cultural establishment, and the still-primitive nature of communications technology, accounts for much of Hugo's pervasive sense of loneliness. He travels from gig to gig, from college town to college town, accumulating acquaintances but not close friends. He's uprooted, and yearns to be in touch with the people he's met who care about the same things he does. He can't go and meet them at a Left Bank bistro, because they, like him, have been scattered to the four winds by the great academic hurricane of the mid-to-late twentieth century.

This, I think, connects to a powerful feeling I had, mid-way through reading *31 Letters and 13 Dreams*, that this was a book my father would love. My dad (a ceramic artist of some renown in the field) comes, like Hugo, from a generation of artists scattered by academe, and linked only by slow or expensive communications. I remember how big a deal it was when other artists would come to visit us—the painter Toni Onley making a grand entrance landing his pontoon plane on the lake at our weekend place, John Cage making off with someone else's beaded Indian jacket, which he mistook for a gift for the Visiting Grandee, and so forth. And I remember the hand-written letters from artists all over the world. Sometimes the sense of isolation and alienation in them could be moving: I remember sneaking a peek at one left on the dining room table, in which the Florida-based artist wrote of "not feeling like part of America anymore, but more like one of a handful of eternal madmen." You get the idea: confessional, passionate, troubled stuff, born of a kind of isolation it is now difficult for us to imagine.

Nowadays, we live in a kind of dialectical synthesis of the low-tech world where artsy types had to cluster in a few bohemias, and the technological/academic world of mass culture and distance. We're scattered all over the world, as was Hugo's generation, but thanks to our iPhones and Facebook, we're always in touch, making minor small talk and nudging one another. There was no small talk in Hugo's letters—communication was too precious for that. And it would be very strange to find something like the passionate, lonely statement in that letter my father received in a Facebook update or a tweet. We're more like the gossiping Left Bank crowd, except, you know, without the affairs, the croissants, and the absinthe.

Robert Archambeau

So: one significance of Hugo's *31 Letters and 13 Dreams* comes to light when we think about the kind of statistics on letters given in the Envelope Manufacturers' Association report. That doesn't exhaust the significance, of course—but statistics on dreams are harder to come by.

Proud Men in Their Studies:
On Mark Scroggins

> Poetry, drawing away from the collective life of the court, can only withdraw into the privacy of the bourgeois study, austerely furnished, shared only with a few chosen friends, surroundings so different from the sleeping and waking publicity of court life that it rapidly revolutionizes poetic technique. Crashaw, Herrick, Herbert, Vaughn — all the poetry of this era seems written by shy, proud men writing alone in their studies.... Language reflects this change. It is a learned man's poetry.

That's a passage from Christopher Caudwell's 1937 book *Illusion and Reality: A Study of the Sources of Poetry*, in which the young writer—who'd have proved a second George Orwell, had he not been gunned down in the Spanish Civil War—describes the formal changes that came about when English poetry stopped being a public game played at court and became the pursuit of solitary men among their books. No longer something for public declamation, poetry became learned, private, knotted with a kind of profound cleverness that, requiring time and erudition to appreciate, wouldn't have pleased much as a glittering gentlemanly accomplishment at court.

Certainly twenty-first-century America has little enough in common with England in the seventeenth century, but when I read Mark Scroggins' *Torture Garden: Naked City Pastorelles*, Caudwell's passage on Crashaw, Herbert, and company came immediately to mind. Why, though? It's not as if anyone would confuse a poem like George Herbert's "Easter Wings" with Scroggins' "Perfume of a Critic's Burning Flesh":

> *Animus* deploys nurses exceptionally diligent
> attention finely tuned skills culture
> of detachment *unreliable deceptive* the
> law of the negative everlasting

> *Nay* structures of determination truth
> of the labyrinth *quasi-persons reeling*
> in customized systematic reeling pain.

But despite the very different texture, and the eschewal of reference and discursive meaning, Scroggins' poems have a lot in common with the English seventeenth century as described by Caudwell: they are learned, private, written for the few rather than the many. And, like the works of that greatest poet of seventeenth-century England, John Milton, they are angrily at odds with the dominant culture of their time.

To begin with, there are the matters of form and allusion. All 42 poems in *Torture Garden* are seven lines long, with each line limited to between five and seven stresses. Why? In part, I imagine, to say "this is formed—it may look like cacophony, but it is deliberately assembled, the product of a mind and a will." The mind and will in question may well drive in the direction of chaos, but this is no runaway car: the mind and will do indeed hold the wheel. In fact, when we look to the book's principle allusions, we see that this is very much a carefully formed entity, perhaps an obsessively formed one. The title steers us to the avant-garde composer and musician John Zorn who, with his band Naked City, released an album called *Torture Garden* in 1990. The album's 42 tracks, for which Scroggins' 42 poems are named, are short, some just a few seconds long, and give us an uncompromising cross-cutting of jazz, hardcore, and noise, in which the juxtaposition of unlike elements is, in some sense, the point—along with the evident dark humor, anger, and fetishistic eroticism (the cover of the album, featuring a whip-wielding Japanese dominatrix, caused much controversy). Behind Zorn, there's another reference, to the French decadent writer Octave Mirbeau's novel *Torture Garden*, which, like Zorn's album, is a pastiche of different styles, depicting terrible acts of violence as if they were works of art.

Looking back at "Perfume of a Critic's Burning Flesh," we can see a number of concerns reminiscent of Zorn and Mirbeau. Firstly, there's the speed of the thing: we scarcely see a clause gaining coherence before the language turns in another syntactic direction. Then there's the referencing of language from different sources: "animus" certainly brings to mind hatred, but it's also a word from Jungian psychology. This allows us to see the diligent nurses as both the agents of a psychological clinic, and, perhaps, as the agents of a malevolent system. The "culture of detachment" could indeed be something like medical professionalism, but is this detached professionalism "*unreliable deceptive*" in some Foucauldian way: is it merely the mask of cruel power? No sooner does this possibility establish itself than we hear of an "*everlasting / Nay*"—a phrase that resonates with the nineteenth-century sage Thomas Carlyle's notion of the "everlasting no," the smug spirit of the debunker and eternal critic. Is debunking of the kind that would see medical professionalism as the cold mask of power just some kind of adolescent criticism for criticism's sake? Or is it really something that reduces real people to "*quasi-persons*"? The poem jams these and many other interpretive possibilities together, quickly referencing many possible sources, then moving on, leaving nothing resolved and a residual sense of the world as a malevolent place where we wander in "labyrinths" of "systematic reeling pain."

There's something obsessive about Scroggins' concern with art in *Torture Garden*: the poems reference music, film, garden design, architecture, and quite frequently the tradition of the pastoral. To some degree, the idea seems to be similar to what Octave Mirbeau had in mind when, in his *Torture Garden*, he took us on a tour of aestheticized violence: Scroggins returns again and again to the notion that pastoral is a way of hiding both privilege and violence. But it's also interesting for how it reveals Scroggins' sense that poetry is, first and foremost, affiliated with other kinds of aesthetic expression. Poetry is at best secondarily a means of communicating information: it is primarily about formal effects and the construction of aesthetic experiences—a view common enough in our time, but far from prevalent in all times and places. There have been moments, some of them recent, when poetry was about speaking to a community about that community's needs and desires: think of the heyday of identity politics and the poetry associated with it. Scroggins' poetry isn't like that at all: it is for a smaller number of readers, particularly those willing to parse out the sudden turns of phrase, and able to pick up the quick, deft allusions. It's a poetry for art-gobbling, music-obsessive humanists, fingers at the ready on their keyboards to Google a particular phrase, or track down an allusion on Wikipedia.

This is not to say that *Torture Garden* takes no interest in community. In fact, many of the poems are dedicated to poets and critics of Scroggins' acquaintance: Tyrone Williams, cris cheek, Rita Felski, Gustaf Sobin, John Taggart, Forrest Gander, and the late Guy Davenport, among others. One suspects there are private jokes and references for these people embedded in the poems: in a poem dedicated to me, for example, I recognized several phrases from a scholarly paper I delivered at a conference Scroggins attended. And here we see another connection to Caudwell's seventeenth-century poets, who wrote for "a few chosen friends."

Affection in Scroggins' poems is directed at specific individuals, who get to recognize their words transformed; but anger is generalized, almost ambient throughout the book. There's anger at the powerful, there's anger at the bureaucratization of the world, there's anger at consumerism and commodification, there's even anger at the kind of knowing, self-reflexive verse that comprises so much of *Torture Garden*. It's very different from the specific, localized anger that most of us encounter in daily life: there's nothing like simple frustration at a local drainage ordinance that leaves one's backyard waterlogged after a heavy rain. The anger of *Torture Garden* is more abstract. It is the anger we have when we sit in our studies and look coldly at the world's corruption.

I know this kind of poetry speaks to me. I know, too, there are many who will turn from it in disdain, despair, or boredom. I suppose this tells us something about the position of poets, or, at any rate, of certain kinds of poets, in our society: that they are steeped in art and erudition, alienated from the large structures of power and corruption, affectionate to their friends, and that they address, for the most part, people much like themselves: people shy and proud in their studies, or in their offices not far from the English department lounge.

So a Poet Walks into a Bar:
Notes on Poetry Readings

So a poet walks into a bar to read his work to an audience. But what if it isn't a bar? What if it's a university auditorium, or a bookshop specializing in, say, works by women writers? What if it's a conference room at the AWP Convention, where the creative writing professors slap one another on the back and try to 'place' grad students and manuscripts with English departments and their journals? What if it's the 92nd Street Y, or a presidential inauguration, or a funeral? What if it's not a bar the poet walks into, but a recording studio, where he'll make a podcast or mp3 for an audience he's unlikely to meet? What if it isn't a poet who walks into a bar to read poetry to an audience, but a reader who walks into her study to read aloud to herself from a favorite poet's work?

Venue matters, when poetry is read aloud: indeed, in few situations does Walter J. Ong's assertion that "a writer's audience is always a fiction," seem less convincing than in a poetry reading, where the poets stand in the presence of the bodies of their listeners. Who speaks, where, to whom, and to what end?—answering these questions can tell us a great deal about the nature and meaning of performed poetry. One way to explore these questions is to adapt rhetorical theory—which has long been concerned with the specific relations of speaker, venue, and audience—to the study of poetry readings. There are obvious limits to such an approach. For example, it can tell us little of interest, perhaps nothing at all, about reading poetry aloud when one is alone, which may well be the most common form of spoken poetry. What is more, there are those who would argue that whatever situation a poetry reading creates, it is not in any meaningful sense a rhetorical situation. I'd disagree with this last criticism, but only because I'm willing to define what counts as a rhetorical situation marginally more broadly than does that most expansive of rhetorical theorists, Lloyd Bitzer.

Bitzer, an emeritus professor of the University of Wisconsin, is generally regarded as one of the most respected rhetorical theorists of his generation, and is best known for introducing the notion of the "rhetorical situation" in an essay of that name in the inaugural issue of *Philosophy and Rhetoric*. For Bitzer, there are several components to a rhetorical situation. Firstly, and most importantly, there must be "an exigence"—a problem to be solved—"which strongly invites utterance." Situations are rhetorical when the exigence, or problem calling out to be addressed, can be altered by the "bringing into existence a discourse of such a character that the audience, in thought and action, is so engaged that it becomes mediator of change." The exigence, which may or may not be consciously perceived by the speaker and the audience, is "an imperfection marked by urgency"; while an audience, to truly be a rhetorical audience, must consist "of those persons who are capable of being influenced by the discourse": the obdurate and the obtuse alike may be an audience, but stuck in their views, or incapable of growing through engaging with discourse, they aren't an audience susceptible to change. As Bitzer puts it, the situation is rhetorical if

> an actual or potential exigence ... can be completely or partially removed if discourse, introduced into the situation, can so constrain human decision or action as to bring about the significant modification of the exigence.

In addition, a rhetorical situation contains two types of constraints. The first are those inherent in the pre-existing situation, such as the audience's beliefs and attitudes, as well as pertinent pre-existing "documents, facts, traditions, images, interests." The second type of constraints originate with the speaker: personal character, established style, and the like. (Those with a background in rhetoric will recognize these as Aristotle's "inartistic proofs" and "artistic proofs"). So when a speaker enters a rhetorical situation, he or she enters a situation where some kind of change is wanted, a change that can conceivably be affected by discourse. The speaker faces people capable of being changed, if their beliefs and ideas, and the character and style of the speaker, come together in some perfect discursive storm.

Of course rhetoric doesn't take place under test-lab conditions of purity. Some rhetorical situations are simple, others much more complicated, even muddy. There may be multiple exigences in any situation, some incompatible, and an audience may consist of multiple constituencies, concerned with different exigences and with different constraints regarding the kind of discourse that will appeal to them.

Bitzer allows fairly broad latitude when defining what sort of situations count as rhetorical. While his examples include political debates and Socrates' "Apology," he also includes situations where the simple need for information is rhetorical, if the providing of that information will have an effect in the world: the need for reporters to give details about the assassination of President Kennedy in order to calm a panicked population, for example, counts as a rhetorical situation for Bitzer, one that seems to have struck him quite powerfully. The exigence, in this case, is a lack of information that could lead to panic; the audience is capable of receiving information and being calmed by it, if only because they are no longer bewildered. The speaker, knowing that he faces a worried population, and capable of projecting a certain *gravitas* in reporting the facts, will be successful in solving the exigence.

As broad as Bitzer's definition of a rhetorical situation is, it doesn't extend to poetry: in fact, he specifically excludes poetry from his scheme, apparently out of a belief that poetry (as Auden so famously put it) "makes nothing happen." It's my contention that Bitzer is too modest about the scope of his own theory, and that poetry readings tend to have some sort of *raison d'être*, that they tend, in one way or another, to ameliorate some kind of situation. In fact, one way to understand the significance of poetry readings is to look for what sort of exigence a reading seeks to address, what imperfection in the world it seeks to remedy through addressing an open-minded audience.

So a poet walks into a bar. Let's say it's the Green Mill in Chicago, where (according the PBS documentary *The United States of Poetry*), "a strand of new poetry began ... in 1987 when Marc Smith found a home for the poetry slam." For Smith, there was certainly an exigence behind the slams, with their Dionysian audience participation, ad hoc systems of judging poetic value, liberally-flowing booze, and general informality. The exigence was the perceived dryness and audience-unfriendliness of more formal poetry readings, and a resulting alienation of poetry from potential enthusiasts. As Smith put it, the slam was to be an "up yours" to poorly attended, more effete poetry readings. Smith wanted to change the culture of poetry by holding these readings, "because no one was listening to the poets." In the end, the exigence was the perceived removal of poetry from informal, non-academic contexts, and the resulting marginalization of poetry. Poetry may or may not make "nothing happen," but the poetry slam certainly attempted to make something happen. In addressing a perceived exigence, it created a rhetorical situation. The audience-based constraints (resistance to the idea of spending an evening sitting quietly in an uncomfortable chair listening to someone read) are addressed by physical comfort, alcohol, and a whole series of methods (foot-stomping, hissing, woofing, and finger-snapping are all encouraged, and have specific meanings) by which the audience is invited to participate in the performances as they happen, and in judging them when they're done. Certainly poets performing in these circumstances may face certain constraints of their own: in order to succeed they must not consider themselves or their work above spur-of-the-moment criticism, and they tend to need either a quick wit or the ability to emote convincingly in order to ameliorate the exigence. Poetry slams, of course, have evolved and changed, and can address many different exigences—my point here is simply to assert, *contra* Bitzer, that the poetry reading can indeed present a rhetorical situation.

The poetry readings associated with the Black Arts Movement of the late 1960s and early 1970s present what may be the clearest case of the poetry reading as a rhetorical situation in modern American literary history. The defining characteristic of the Black Arts Movement was its African-American nationalism, which in the early years manifested as a form of separatism. Such separatism was spurred on by events of 1965 on the national level—the assassination of Malcom X—as well as on the local level—the destruction of the relative racial harmony of the Lower East Side poetry scene of the sixties through racially-motivated violence at key reading venues. Although the movement quickly became national, the founding of the Black Arts Repertory Theater and School (BARTS) was of central importance, as was the move to Harlem by LeRoi Jones (Amiri Baraka). Poetry in the Black Arts Movement was linked with, even subordinated to, the large exigence of creating a radical culture for African-Americans outside the institutions and norms of the nation at large. As Kaluma ya Salaam has argued, the Black Arts Movement is

> the only American literary movement to advance social engagement as a sine qua non of its aesthetic.... The two hallmarks of Black Arts activity were the development of Black theater groups and Black poetry performances ... and both had close ties to community organizations and issues.

Community formation was a central goal of the movement—its primary exigence—and ideas of individualist art or art for its own sake were anathema. "Black art," wrote Ron Karenga "must be for the people, by the people and from the people. That is to say, it must be functional, collective and committing." "All art is collective," he continued, "there is no such thing as art for art's sake." Larry Neal, another founder of the Black Arts Movement, echoed these sentiments when he proclaimed, in 1968, "the Black Arts Movement is radically opposed to any concept of the artist that alienates him from his community. Black Art is the aesthetic and spiritual sister of the Black Power concept."

The exigence of Black Arts poetry readings was radical consciousness-raising and separatist community-creation. Audiences were potentially resistant for a number of reasons, not the least being that many in the potential audience were white liberals, and others were African-Americans committed to social and cultural integration, like the writer Ishmael Reed, who was never fully seen as a member of the movement for this reason. One controversial technique to render the crowd a "rhetorical audience" was simply to forbid white people from attending the readings. As the critic Daphne S. Reed points out,

> ... this very policy was endorsed by both the original Harlem venture and a number of other black-arts theatres established later in several major cities. The rationale was that the presence of whites would be potentially inhibitive ... and in any case whites should not be permitted to occupy seats needed for black people for whom the performance was intended and, allegedly, exclusively relevant.

Beyond such extreme (and short-lived) measures, other steps were taken to overcome audience resistance in pursuit of ameliorating the exigence. These included bringing the readings to places where the communities gathered, as well as adopting a mode of address that evoked the most respected institution of African-American life. Lorenzo Thomas describes both in a passage from his essay "Neon Griot":

> With self-appointed missionary fervor, Black Arts poets extended the venues for their performances beyond storefront theaters to neighborhood community centers, church basements, taverns, and to the streets. Not surprisingly, the dominant mode of poetry that proved effective in such settings drew upon the rhetorical conventions of the black church, which is the matrix of African-American culture.

The church-based conventions, which work with what Thomas calls "... the speaking voice that trespasses into song; and an antiphonal interaction with the congregation," invoked cultural authority and stressed the link between performer and audience. So important did the specifics of the speaking voice of the Black Arts poet become that at least two poets of the movement, Sonia Sanchez and Johari Amini, came to see the written text of the poem as a performance score, akin to sheet music, with the printed poem indicating exactly how the poet wanted it to be read.

As Bitzer pointed out, rhetorical situations can be complex things, and may involve multiple exigences, and multiple audiences, in a single occasion. I'd like to end by gesturing toward one such complex rhetorical situation: the situation of the contemporary African-American poet in the most prominent form of contemporary poetry reading: the academically-sponsored poetry event.

The exigences of university poetry readings vary considerably, of course; and I've been privy to more than one conversation in which it became clear that the sponsoring poet-academic and the visiting poet saw the main rationale for the reading in terms of personal career logrolling, a matter of "I'll help you put an item on your vita by hosting your reading if you help me in much the same way." But the more legitimate exigence of the university poetry reading, the reason generally given to the deans and chairs who hold the purse-strings, tends to be pedagogical. That is, the imperfection the reading seeks to ameliorate is some combination of a lack of student knowledge about poetry, and a lack of student sympathy for poetry, which the presence of a (charismatic, one hopes) poet will change.

When an African-American poet walks into a university reading situation, though, we tend to enter one of Bitzer's complex rhetorical situations, with multiple exigences and multiple audiences. To some degree, the exigence is the same as in most university poetry readings: there's a need for the audience to learn about poetry-as-poetry. But the complex web of American social history, including one of the main legacies of the Black Arts movement—identity politics—means that there's another exigence, having to do with the politics of representation. As anyone who has ever tapped an academic cultural diversity fund as a means of bringing an African-American poet to a campus knows, universities tend to recognize two real or perceived exigences related to cultural diversity: the need to show African-American students that their community is represented in university cultural programming, and the need to expose non-African-American students to African-American culture, as part of the mission of spreading appreciation for cultural diversity. So an African-American poet walks into a university auditorium. He or she is there for a multiple exigence: to increase knowledge of, and sympathy for, poetry, and to represent African-American culture for African-American students, and to non-African American students. It's a kind of palimpsest, with a more moderate, pluralist version of the Black Arts exigence of cultural representation overlaid with the discipline-specific logic of the modern university, in which poetry readings are held for the advancement of knowledge of poetry.

As we've seen with slam poetry and Black Arts poetry, the rhetorical situation of the poetry reading matters for how poetry is performed. Consider Harryette Mullen, whose success in both academic and identity politics-centered poetic contexts is rarely paralleled (she has won an award from the Black Arts Academy and taught in an Ivy League university). Her work sends out signals to a number of communities, referencing the classical canon, the modernist and avant-garde forebears of contemporary experimental work, and iconic elements of African-American culture: Mullen has described her work as a textual confluence of Gertrude Stein, Sappho, and the blues, in which "Sappho meets the blues at the crossroads." The work combines these influences in such a way that allows her, in performance, to emphasize any one of these elements in a single poem. This is accomplished largely through the polysemous nature of her language.

The critic Kate Pearcy has described Mullen's poems as involving a great deal of "homophonic punning and word play," and noted that "reading possibilities are therefore highly provisional": one may perform the poems with varying degrees of ambiguity or clarity. Here, for example, is the prose poem "Of a girl, in white," which I and others experienced, when we heard it performed, as a poem about eros and about word play—a poem, that is, in the traditions of Sappho and of Gertrude Stein:

> Of a girl, in white, between the lines, in the spaces where nothing is written. Her starched petticoats, giving him the slip. Loose lips, a telltale spot, where she was kissed, and told. Who would believe her, lying still between the sheets. The pillow cases, the dirty laundry laundered. Pillow talk-show on a leather couch, slips in and out of

dreams. Without permission, slips out the door. A name adores a Freudian slip.

Once, after I spoke on Mullen's work, the poet Tyrone Williams approached me to say that he'd attended a reading by Mullen in which the African-American audience, coming with their own expectations and interpretive norms (with, to use Bitzer's terms, different external constraints than I and my group brought when we heard the poem) received the poem as primarily about racial 'passing.' The fact that Mullen's work admits of such interpretations, and makes itself so readily available to different emphases in performance, gives an indication of one reason why Mullen's work has been so successful in the complex rhetorical situations where it is so often performed.

We get a clear sense of the possibilities for different emphases in performance in Mullen's work from this stanza of an untitled poem in her 1995 collection *Muse & Drudge*:

> you can sing their songs
> with words your way
> put it over to the people
> know what you are doing

Is singing "their songs" with "words your way" a matter of the contemporary, postmodern poet appropriating tradition, of Stein riffing on Sappho? Or is it a matter of the African-American poet appropriating white or Eurocentric traditions, the blues meeting Stein and Sappho at the crossroads? It's all in how the pronouns, which lack specific referents in the poem, are performed, how the poet chooses to perform them with the audience in the room.

I don't mean to suggest that I've done anything like perform a proper taxonomy of types of poetry readings here, nor do I want to claim I've covered all of the possibilities for slam poetry, Black Arts poetry, or the contemporary academic poetry reading (for poets African-American or otherwise). Rather, I've hoped to indicate that we will enrich our interpretations of the performance of poetry by understanding the rhetorical situation of those readings, and that we have much to gain by bringing the tradition of rhetorical theory to bear on poetic performance. It can't hurt to know what we're doing when we read.

III
Mystics and Gnostics

A Stranger from the Sky:
Sun Ra as Poet and Alien

Hardly anyone thinks of Sun Ra as a poet. A visionary outsider even in the realm of music, where his work is only occasionally taken as seriously as it ought to be, he has almost no standing in the field of American poetry, despite the fact that his poetry appeared in many Black Arts movement publications, and sat cheek-to-jowl with that of Langston Hughes, Amiri Baraka, and Allen Ginsberg in the late-sixties *Umbra Anthology*. Perhaps it's significant, in this context, that his poetry was brought to my attention not from within the poetry world, but from outside it: it was the Australian critical theorist McKenzie Wark who first steered me toward *This Planet is Doomed: The Science Fiction Poetry of Sun Ra*. When I mentioned the book to various poets and critics, none of them had heard of it. One, a jazz obsessive and semi-professional saxophonist, was stunned that Sun Ra's poetry had never appeared on his radar.

What are the poems of *This Planet is Doomed* like? Firstly, they have the virtues and vices of much spoken word poetry (the text of the book was assembled from transcripts of tapes discovered by archivist Michael D. Anderson). They hit hard when spoken aloud, when patterns of repetition and opportunities for emoting are best realized; on the page, though, they aren't as strong. Secondly, they're as weird and out-there as you'd expect Sun Ra's poetry to be. Indeed, the book's subtitle already indicates the nature of that weirdness: "science fiction poetry." We're used to genre fiction, but genre poetry? When you get past the initial oddness, though, the poems situate themselves quite strongly in several distinguished literary traditions: the literature of African-American alienation; the wing of Romanticism most strongly associated with the fantastic; and the literature of Gnosticism.

Sun Ra was an autodidact, and as idiosyncratic as they come, but only the kind of pedantic wretch who thinks the words "university transcript" are a synonym for "education" would consider Sun Ra's connection to these traditions coincidental. He arrived at his alienation existentially, and fabricated a personal and artistic identity unlike anybody else's, but he tailored that identity from some of the richest cloth in the great Savile Row of literature. It's less different from T. S. Eliot than fans of either artist might prefer to think.

Alienation from mainstream American culture was more-or-less a given for African-Americans at mid-century: indeed, both laws and the force behind them made the marginal status of African-Americans abundantly clear. But to be a gay African-American, and a genius to boot, marked one out for a special degree of alienation. We see it clearly enough in the writings, and largely ex-patriate life, of James Baldwin, who turned to Europe as an exotic elsewhere where his very outsider status freed him from the box into which America would put him and, what is more, put him on something approaching equal footing with the white Americans he met in Paris. In a 1959 essay for the *New York Times* called "The Discovery of What it Means to be an American," Baldwin tells us of the alienation he felt in America, and of the liberating feeling of becoming another kind of alien, an American abroad:

> I left America because I doubted my ability to survive the fury of the color problem here. (Sometimes I still do.) I wanted to prevent myself from becoming *merely* a Negro; or, even, merely a Negro writer. I wanted to find out in what way the *specialness* of my experience could be made to connect with other people instead of dividing me from them. (I was as isolated from other Negroes as I was from whites, which is what happens when a Negro begins, at bottom, to believe what white people say about him.) In my necessity to find the terms on which my experience could be related to others, Negroes and whites, writers and non-writers, I proved, to my astonishment, to be as American as any Texas G.I. And I found my experience was shared by every American writer I knew in Paris. Like me, they had been divorced from their origins, and it turned out to make very little difference that the origins of white Americans were European and mine were African—they were no more at home in Europe than I was.

There's nothing quite like this in Sun Ra's writing, unless we translate "Paris" to "outer space." Then things start to look familiar: the over-arching desire is for escape from a place that limits you, that confines you physically and, more importantly, that insidiously imposes its categories of thought onto your mind. Consider these lines from "This Planet is Doomed" in the context of Baldwin:

> it just breaks me all up, man
> it just breaks me all up—
> can't understand a damn bit of it
> like man, I gotta get away from it
> I gotta get away from it before they mess up
> my mind
> before they take my soul, man
> I just gotta get away
> and blast off in my rocket ship
>
> I come from a better place than this
> what in the hell am I here for—
> ....
> I gotta blast away
> I gotta get away, man
> I gotta blast off like a super megatron
> rocket on
> electro dynamic radiation

Outer space, as Sun Ra imagines it, is free from the soul-crushing ideology of mid-century America, so hostile to people like him. He envisions it as a kind of pure place where we can meet on equal footing: Baldwin may always have Paris for this, but Sun Ra has the galactic depths. And it's not only space that has this appeal. So powerful is Sun Ra's need for a place where the constraints of American race identity can be shed that, in the poem "The Government of Death," he even falls half in love with easeful death, where all are equals:

> all in the realm of death is
> nothing else but peace
> its inhabitants have all received
> equal rites
> because they have received equal rights
> that is, services, personal and
> complete,
> without prejudice of death

And later in the poem we read:

> all governments
> on earth
> set up by men
> are discriminating
> but the government of death is a
> pure government
> it treats all in an equal manner
> it is a startling, revealing picture
> of equality for all
> and in the realm of death
> is nothing else but
> peace

The need for an exotic and liberating elsewhere is a constant in Sun Ra's poems, and he even dreams of addressing an audience of alien beings, often a kind of cross between space creatures and entities out of the Judeo-Christian mythos. "let me write my music," he says in "Not for Earth Alone," "not for earth alone, but for the worlds / for those in being/those in seeming" who are also somehow "angels / and demons and devils." This yearning for elsewhere is the stuff of Romanticism, especially of continental Romanticism, and its escapism is serious stuff. By turning its back on the ordinary world, it enacts a profound criticism of that world, a near-total rejection of it as unredeemed, maybe unredeemable by anything less than an imaginative apocalypse. Readers of William Blake's prophetic works have already dialed into these frequencies, as have connoisseurs of Baudelaire. The great maverick Marxist thinker Henri Lefebvre called this kind of fantasist Romanticism the "critique of everyday life," and found in it a radicalism both profound and, ultimately, limited:

> Under the banner of the marvelous, nineteenth-century literature mounted a sustained attack on everyday life which has continued unabated up to the present day. The aim is to demote it, to discredit it. Although the duality between the marvelous and the everyday is just as painful as the duality between action and dream, the real and the ideal—and although it is an underlying reason for the failures and defeats which so many works deplore—nineteenth-century man seemed to ignore this, and continued obstinately to belittle real life, the world 'as it is.'

If Sun Ra is a part of this tradition, he is also part of an even older tradition of alienation, the line of Gnostic writing extending back two millennia. Indeed, his elaborately developed Afro-Futurist mythology is, as a way of addressing larger truths, very in accord with Gnostic thinking, which favored myth and image over discursive abstraction ("Truth did not come into the world naked," reads the Gnostic Gospel of Philip, "but in types and images. Truth is received only that way"). Sun Ra is at his most Gnostic when, like thinkers in that tradition, he sees the material world around us as fallen, broken, and not our true home (Stephan Hoeller, a contemporary Gnostic thinker, defines the material world as evil inasmuch as it diverts our attention from the imaginative journey back to our divine origins beyond the material realm—he, like many Gnostics, sees it as a barrier to the soul's journey home). When we read a refrain like "I pull the veil aside" in Sun Ra's poem "Dreams Rush to Meet Me," we're rubbing up against his Gnosticism, as we are when we read his declaration of his true home in "A Stranger from the Sky":

> I am a stranger from the sky
> far away, farther than the eye can see
> is my paradise
> a mystical world from outer space

Some of the poems of *This Planet is Doomed* are chant-like, rhythmically repetitive, and hard to extract, but even a crudely-carved out passage like this, taken almost at random from "State of the Cosmos," gives a sense of the Gnostic's yearning for breaking past the barriers of the material world into a space better and closer to the divine (it also gives a sense that, at times, Sun Ra was perfectly happy to dwell in abstractions). Watch how the "reasonable reality of the state of the world" contrasts with something truer, the "reasonable reality of the state of the cosmos":

> … the synchronization of the shadows to
> the authorized reality
> is a key to the reasonable reality of the
> state of the world
> disconnected of the shadows from the
> so-called authorized reality
> and the application of the new
> potential through resynchronization of
> the shadow
> to the unauthorized mind images of the
> cosmic idea
> is a transformation of the shadow into
> the living cosmic multi-self
> this is the key to the reasonable reality
> of the state of the cosmos
> synchronization of the shadows to the
> authorized reality is the key to the
> reasonable state of the world
> the disconnection of the shadows from
> the so-called authorized reality and the

> application of the new potential through
> resynchronization of the shadows to the
> unauthorized mind image of the cosmic
> ideas of transformation of the shadow
> into the living cosmic multi-self
> this is the key to the reasonable reality
> of the state of the cosmos

The reason of this world is not the reason of the cosmos, and it is to the cosmos that we truly belong.

Sun Ra is singular, certainly. But he doesn't come from space, even if he dreams of it as his destination. He comes out of a long tradition, several long traditions, and all of these traditions arose as balm for the dispossessed, as ways of imagining an outside to the narrow box of nightmares into which we wake. May the cosmos send us more like him.

The Open Word:

An Essay and a Letter for Peter O'Leary

1. Luminous Apocalypse

Around the time Peter O'Leary's *Luminous Epinoia* was published in 2010, another piece of his writing appeared in the pages of the *Chicago Review*: an essay called "Apocalypticism: A Way Forward for Poetry." Part memoir, part polemic, part literary appreciation, the essay argued that apocalypse—in the sophisticated sense of a sacred expression that can "unbind love from material desire, freeing it to embrace the unknown and the unspeakable"—has been erased from American poetry. In O'Leary's view, neither the old school of the workshop lyric nor the tradition of Language writing supports vatic or visionary poetry. "Why write an essay about apocalypticism?" asks O'Leary, "Why insist that it represents the way forward in American poetry?" There are surely many ways forward in American poetry, but O'Leary's own recent work constitutes as strong an argument as one could hope to find for apocalypticism as one of those ways.

O'Leary, Norman Finkelstein, and a number of other poets—one thinks of Pam Rehm, Michael Heller, Harriet Zinnes, and especially of Joseph Donahue and Nathaniel Mackey—represent a kind of Gnostic or apocalyptic movement in poetry, connected to visionary experience and ecumenical religious exploration. Theirs is a deeply rooted tradition, extending back through Duncan to Yeats and Blake, and to all manner of sacred texts. In our formally diverse but overwhelmingly secular poetic moment their work represents a true counter-culture, whose achievement has yet to be fully appreciated.

For all of Peter O'Leary's connection to a long tradition of visionary poetry, though, there's little chance anyone would mistake a passage from *Luminous Epinoia* for lines by Blake or Yeats. In *Jerusalem* Blake railed against Newtonian science, and Yeats turned to his theosophical explorations in reaction to the dominant scientific and materialistic worldview of his times—but O'Leary doesn't just accept science, he celebrates it, bringing the language of the physical sciences to bear on mystical ideas generally seen as inimical to empirical modes of thought. In this he is unique among contemporary American apocalyptic poets, and his unique position comes from the seriousness with which O'Leary, who holds a doctorate from the Divinity School at the University of Chicago, takes his background in Catholic theology.

Luminous Epinoia is a book of many things: surreal fables, sacred architecture, sermons on the meaning of love in a time of war, and the occasional jab at the policies of the Bush administration. But most of all, *Luminous Epinoia* is a book concerned with incarnation. The title of the book comes from the *Apocryphon of John*, a second-century Gnostic gospel. There, the "luminous Epinoia" is a heterodox version of Eve, who appears as a kind of coming-forth of Adam's latent spirit, both an extension of Adam and a helper who will restore to him the creative vision that can reconnect him to the full meaning of religious experience. But what's particularly striking about the book is the influence of the great Catholic theologian and paleontologist Teilhard de Chardin, who reconciled his scientific and religious beliefs through imagining the physical universe as imperfectly embodying aspects of the divine, and looked at biological evolution as a teleological process bringing us ever closer to a union with God.

Some of the most powerful passages in *Luminous Epinoia* come when the poems draw connections between the physical world, as conceived by science, and the divine. The poem "As Twilight into Noonday Knowledge Gyres," for example, splices together the language of contemporary astronomy and cosmology with the catalog of types of angels in Dante's *Paradiso*, giving us strange, haunting passages like this:

> Analogies:
> furthest and closest the Seraphim
> like dark matter, of incalculable unknown density,
>   not giving off any light, but not absorptive either. As far

> as our equations allow us to see, we still have no image
> for the highest order of angels, clothed in collapsing nanoseconds.

This isn't just a formal move on O'Leary's part, a cutting up and piecing together of radically different texts to demonstrate a procedure. We're not operating at the level of Oulipo, or of the Burroughsian cut-up. This is, rather, an attempt to get at the meaning of the world as a kind of manifestation of divine love. O'Leary reflects on the nature of this attempt in another poem, "To Suffer and Pass Through," which takes not astronomy but biology as its starting point:

> Evolution's
>
> apex remains grasses and flowers
> chlorophyll converts to life from light. Conduction of this force
>   is a message
> broadcast from the body of God, a biochemical sun
> transpiercing miraculously, glided on modulating
> radiowaves. Less a metaphor than a stopgap, this notion
> permits us crypto-angelic conceptions of how God's love
> radiates.

There's a humility to that last sentence: an admission that the visionary poet offers not prophetic truths so much as expedients that nevertheless allow us perspectives from which the world appears in holy aspect.

What doesn't come across as humble, in *Luminous Epinoia*, is the diction. It is relentlessly high-end, festooned with theological terms and arcane language from the sciences. While the English language of common usage may be described as an Anglo-Saxon lexicon studded with Latinate terms, whole stretches of *Luminous Epinoia* feel as if they come from a Latinate lexicon studded with Greek terms. This can be off-putting, but the sometimes-arduous effort the complex diction requires of the reader pays off. In the poem "Commentary on the Gospel According to Mark 9:1–6" O'Leary offers an explanation of his choice of diction: "Transfiguration's knife blade," he tells us, can take the form of an "effort to renew light in language, in a somehow holier tongue."

Since so much in *Luminous Epinoia* concerns incarnation, it would be wrong not to talk about the physical incarnation of O'Leary's text in book form, which is striking. The designer, Jeff Clark, has given us a book that looks nothing like the typical poetry book of our time. It is a large-format, shiny, silver, jacketless hardcover embossed with repeating patterns of white six-pointed stars, intricately coiled snakes, and St. George crosses surrounding the letters "L. E." in Gothic script. While the description may sound for all the world like a spellbook from the Harry Potter novels, the book itself is quite beautiful—like O'Leary's diction, it takes risks in order to point toward something somehow holy.

2. Be Thou Open: A Letter to Peter O'Leary

Dear Peter,

What has your vocabulary done to you? To me? To us? Or, to narrow it down a bit, to John Latta, who wrote, *à propos* your book *Depth Theology*:

> *Dysthymia*: *thymos* being Greek *mind*, and *dys-* ascending out of Sanskrit *dus-* meaning *bad*, *difficult*, &c. O'Leary's an inveterate neologist: in notes to *Depth Theology* he points to various "coinages from taxonomic roots: an apiologist (a word Emerson once used) is one who studies bees; a parulidologist is one who studies warblers."

Your vocabulary also staggered Broc Rossell, who said in the *Colorado Review* that the lexical "register of *Luminous Epinoia* might be the most elevated in American poetry since Hart Crane."

You make up a fair number of words, Peter, and revive many more from the realm of the *hapax legomenon*, or the deeply buried Greco-cum-Latin-cum-Sanskrit & Aramaic lexicon.

Of course there are strange words and there are strange words. I once wrote something about the difference, and it went like this:

> Consider "kuboaa," a word invented by the great modern Norwegian novelist Knut Hamsun, and put into the mouth of the starving hero of his masterwork, the novel *Hunger*. For Hamsun's delirious hero, the word was a pure sound, something outside, even above, the realm of signifying language. Always aware of the absurd, and with a longing after purity that led him into some dark corners of the psyche, Hamsun meant for his "kuboaa" to be a word free from reference. To encounter it was to encounter something alien, something of untainted otherness. You could say "kuboaa" was to be the verbal equivalent of one of Kazimir Malevich's paintings of a red square on a white background: everything familiar was to be left behind in the encounter with the unassimilated and elemental. Kuboaa was the word of the modern primitive, the word of regrounding, of beginning again, outside existing language and away from the freight of civilization. John Peck's "argura," is another made-up word, and the title of his fourth volume of poetry. But it is a creature altogether different from kuboaa. As Peck writes in the notes to his *Collected Shorter Poems*, argura "corresponds to no single Latin word, but rather to elements that derive from roots shared among several terms." This is not the neologism as word-free-of-reference; this is the polysemous neologism, the word that bears the trace of several meanings, and the weight of several etymologies, but that remains, finally, elusive. *Argentum* (silver, or money), *argumentum* (argument or evidence), and *arguro* (to make clear, but also to censure or reprove)—are all words with relevance to Peck's poetry, and lurking in argura's syllables. The point of a word like "argura" is not to lift the reader up above the trails of signification, but to send the reader down those trails in pursuit of historical and linguistic references. If kuboaa is the word of the modern primitive, argura is the word of the modern classical, sending the reader to the word-hoard of Latin antiquity.

I take the difference between a word like kuboaa and a word like argura as a cue on how to read your books, Peter—and I need cues for your books. They're among the most challenging—and most rewarding—books of poetry by an American poet of your generation (you can use that in a blurb if you like). No primitive, you, Mr. O'Leary, no primitive, but a poet whose work twines together classical references, history, and the present.

If this sounds a bit like Ezra Pound, it should: you come late onto the stage of modernism, but you belong there, I think—belong, in essence, to the same wing of modernist poetry as does Ole Ez. His, after all, is the wing of "make it new"—of the reclaiming of those elements of the cultural past that lie fallow. It's certainly not Marinetti's futurist wing of "the first dawn is now," and the shaking loose from a supposedly burdensome past—still less is it the avant-garde of denotation-free word art like Zaum or Merz, or the Dada of Hugo Ball chanting the syllables of "Karawane" at the Cabaret Voltaire.

What exactly do I mean by placing you in "the same wing" of modernism as Pound? To understand, I suppose we have to comment on the nature of the "it" in your version of "make it new." My favorite description of the modernist, and neo-modernist, project of making it new via 'argura' style vocabulary and the revival of disused words comes from a comment Vincent Sherry made about the poetry of John Matthias: "On the one hand, the pedagogue offers from his word-hoard and reference trove the splendid alterity of unfamiliar speech; on the other, this is our familial tongue, our own language in its deeper memory and reference."

What Sherry says is right, I think, but in your case I would qualify it a bit, marking out your particular space in the modernist wing of things. In your work you send us not just to the past as an end in itself, as would a good liberal humanist professor of literature, a believer in the power of cultural literacy. I mean, you're a believer, alright, but you and I both know it's not some watery liberal humanism in which you believe. What your arcane vocabulary sends us to isn't the past in general, but, most frequently and insistently, a particular set of spiritual traditions: the more heterodox branches of Catholicism, and the Gnostic tradition, in both its ancient and its perennial manifestations. And in doing so, you're not just out to remind us of history, but to redeem time.

Here's what I mean. Your most consistent poetic project, running from *Watchfulness*, through *Depth Theology* and the more recent *Luminous Epinoia*, has been redemptive, and arcane vocabulary and neologistic invention have always had a role in this project.

Of course "redemption" is a loaded word, and when I talk about the redemptive project of your poetry, I'm talking about the Gnostic sense of the word. As Sean Martin writes, "redemption" for the Gnostic, "is not redemption from original sin, which does not exist in Gnosticism, but is redemption from ignorance." Ignorance, specifically, of the divine nature, and its presence within us. This can mean a deliverance from the utterly fallen material world, but only for the more ascetic of Gnostics, and I don't think you're one of them. While some Gnostics emphasize the evil nature of material reality, others emphasize how our world, which is at a far edge of the Pleroma, many removes from the divine core of being, is nevertheless an emanation of the divine: an unglamorous exurb, to be sure, but still a part of the greater metropolitan area of divinity, if we could only see it as such. You seem more like that sort of Gnostic to me, like the scribes of the Nag Hammadi texts, who lovingly copied that passage from St. Paul's epistle to the Ephesians in which he says "our struggle is not against flesh and blood ... but against the world rulers of this darkness and the spirits of evil"—that is, against the forces that keep us from seeing the redemptive light, (in Gnostic terms, the divine spark within us and, in some iterations, in our world).

We see this already in the first poetic sequences of *Watchfulness*, "Ikons" and its subordinate parts, "Ikons," "The House of My Ikon," and "Midas." Here, you give us first the gold of Eastern Mediterranean Christian icons, which through an alchemy of perception convert wooden blocks, egg yolk, and gold dust into the instruments of spiritual transcendence. You then give us the King Midas of Greek legend, whose transformative powers are altogether less impressive, not converting matter into a pathway to spirit, but merely into other matter, ending with the materiality of gold that is only the beginning of the icon as instrument of spiritual transformation. The final image of Midas passing a golden grail ("grail"—there's a loaded word!) from hand to hand as he "changes it unavailed / from gold to gold" is a wonderful underlining of the futility of the merely material world, by the way, and a good exhibit in any case to be made for you as a Gnostic who would free us from subservience to the rulers who would keep us locked in the darkness of the merely historical and material.

Neologism and linguistic transformation come into play later in the book, in the three "Jerusalem" sections. Here, we're amid a lexicon of technical Greek and Latin, and verbs unknown to the OED. And we get some important hints about your concern with the transformation of vocabulary when you reference the word "shibboleth" and the phrase "brightness fall from the air"—the first reminds us of the inability of the Ephraimites to pronounce the "sh" sound, and their consequent slaughter by the Gileades when they inadvertently said "sibboleth"; the second refers to one of the greatest typos in the history of English poetry, when Thomas Nashe's description of the effects of the plague, "brightness falls from the hair," was accidentally reset into a much more memorable line. Both remind us of the power of linguistic transformation, whether political or literary—and in the "Ephphatha" section, we see the spiritual power of linguistic transformation.

"Ephphatha," as the contextualizing passage from the Gospel of Mark you were kind enough to quote as an epigraph makes plain, is the Aramaic word Christ used to mean "opening" or "be open," or "be thou open"— though in your quote it appears as "Ephpheta," a variant translated spelling. And this is a hint of what is to follow, when we delve into the possible etymologies of the word: a Greek transliteration from Aramaic, a Greek transliteration of Hebrew, a Samaritan's attempt to speak a Hebrew word, and so forth. We read, too, about St. Jerome's idiosyncratic apprehension of the word, morphing "eppheta" into "adapirire"—the inadvertent making of new words from old playing into the opening and closing of spiritual possibilities.

And here we come close to an understanding of the role of linguistic revival, argura-style neologism, and raids on the Mediterranean word hoard in your Gnostic poetics. Let me get at that role by describing a temptation I feel, and resist, when reading your work.

I'm tempted to say you believe in the imagination as a divine force. When you titled your book *Luminous Epinoia*, you were making an obscure reference to the *Apocryphon of John*, in which the 'Luminous Epinoia' is a term for an old Gnostic trope, the "creative or inventive consciousness sent to Adam by God in the form of Eve," (Eve, in many Gnostic texts, is the seeker of knowledge, and her plucking of the fruit from the tree a redemptive act, rather than a sin). Me, I'm immersed so thoroughly in Romanticism that I can't help seeing the idea of the luminous epinoia as similar to Coleridge's notion in the *Biographia Litteraria*, when he defines the imagination as "a repetition in the finite mind of the eternal act of creation in the infinite I AM" and the conscious poetic act as "an echo of the former." But there's something different. Coleridge speaks of creativity as an echo of the divine. You do, too, I think—but you do so in a vocabulary that specifically references the Gnostic spiritual tradition. And this leads me to resist the temptation to say you simply see the imagination as divine. Unlike Coleridge, you approach the issue through an arcane vocabulary that refers back to specific spiritual traditions. And because of this, it's better to say that you don't see the imagination as divine, so much as you see something else as divine—that something being a perennial tradition of imaginative acts. It's not as if your work is telling us "invent, and be like God!"—it's more like your work is pointing us to a long, wayward tradition, and saying, *à propos* that tradition, "*be thou open.*"

A Scribe and His Ghosts:
The Poetry of Norman Finkelstein

1. A Scribe Turned into a Scribe

Michael Palmer has said that to read Norman Finkelstein's 2009 book *Scribe* "is to pass through a series of gates into the paradoxical heart of the poem," where "the communal and the solitary" come together in the music of the poetry. He's on to something, I think: what strikes one most strongly in *Scribe* are the repeated invocations of communal experience, and the ways the influence on collectivity works its way into the forms, as well as the subjects, of the poetry.

We don't get past the first word of the first poem before we feel that we're entering a meditation on collective experience: "Like Dates and Almonds, Purple Cloth and Pearls," the poem that opens the first of *Scribe*'s three parts, begins with the collective, plural pronoun:

> We entered by the middle gate
> because the first gate frightened us
> with the ox and the pit, the destruction and the fire.
> We were old men and we were children
> old men disguised as children
> long ago and yesterday and the day after tomorrow.

By the time we're through to the end of the stanza, we're not just on a physical journey together—we've entered into a kind of community over time, bound to the distant past and the future. As we read on, it becomes clear that we are bound in this community less by the experience of a shared journey than by the experience of common texts or stories:

> We dreamed of it and spoke of it
> dreamed that we spoke of it
> spoke of it and wrote of it

> upon parchments of deerskin.
> With the meat we fed the orphans
> and on the skins wrote the five books
> and took the books to the city
> where there were no teachers
> and taught five children the five books
> and six children the six orders
> and told them: We shall return
> but in the meantime let each of you
> teach this book and all his order to the others.

What we're seeing here is nothing less than the evolution of the Torah—the five books of Moses—and the Mishnah, or Shisha Sedarim, the six orders into which the oral version of the Torah was first edited and compiled. This compiling, of course, opened up the long, ongoing tradition of commentary, redaction, and interpretation that binds the Jewish people together, through dispersal over space and time, as a people of the book.

Significantly, the poem goes on to tell us that the process of passing on these texts involves "nothing like nostalgia." There's no desire to keep a pure ur-text here, no desire to return to a lost authoritative story. Rather, Finkelstein tells us the process of passing on the textual tradition is "like a word twisted into a ring / and like a ring lost in a deep pool / and like a ring found in the belly of a fish / so it might return to the sea." What's valued are the transformations, metamorphoses, and miraculous recontextualizations of a tradition as it travels through time. The proliferation of interpretations and the evolution of reconfigured texts aren't sources of conflict, in this view: they are signs of a living tradition, and a rich, collective conversation.

Scribe's title poem enacts the kind of reconfiguration of source-texts we see praised in "Like Dates and Almonds, Purple Cloth and Pearls." The poem is addressed to us (that is, to the second person, to a "you" with whom readers are invited to identify) by an unknown speaker, and describes "our" experiences in a world that is best described as a free-style reinterpretation of Old Testament symbols, events, and settings. Here, we experience ourselves as drifting through a morphed-yet-still recognizable world, a world made from the free reinterpretation of traditional text. When we arrive at the end of the poem, we are told "you have heeded the word of the outside god / and you have heeded the word of no god at all, / like a prophet turned archaeologist, / a scribe turned into a scribe." In these lines Finkelstein draws our attention to our distance from the people who first experienced the events recounted in the Old Testament: we cannot enter into the consciousness of pre-modern prophets any more than they could enter into the scientific consciousness of an archaeologist, even though both types of person are concerned with the same tradition. But he also draws our attention to our continuity with the past, to the modern persistence of the role of scribe as preserver, commentator, and re-arranger of traditional text. In the end, we share an identity with the past, even as we are distanced from it.

The second of the book's sections is devoted to collaged text and epistolary poetry, both forms of collective creativity. Finkelstein doesn't simply celebrate collective creativity, though. In "At the Threshold," for example, Finkelstein addresses the difficult question of imaginative sympathy for a person who would not return that sympathy. The threshold imagery that runs through the poem is clearly drawn from Heidegger's thinking, particularly his writing on the poet Georg Trakl. One can certainly understand the appeal of Heidegger to a poet like Finkelstein, with his concerns about language revealing and concealing different elements of the truth over time. But the question of Heidegger's Nazism cannot be shunted aside, especially not for a poet so deeply rooted in the Jewish tradition. Finkelstein doesn't deny himself the experience of thinking-through, and thinking-with, Heidegger, but he recognizes (in yet another invocation of the collective "we") that to do so requires a special suspension of historical realities, in which people must act:

> As if we
> Too had drunk
> At the star-well

>   As if we
>   Were with him on
>   The way to language
>
>   Yellow stars
>   In a black forest

I don't know what's more resonant here, the line "The way to language," which brings to mind the title of Heidegger's *Unterwegs zur Sprache*, or the image of the "Yellow Stars / In a black forest," a haunting double-vision of the symbol the Nazis forced Jews to wear, and of the Black Forest near Heidegger's hut at Todnauberg.

The third and longest part of *Scribe* consists of poems that quote from, and riff on, passages from architect Christopher Alexander's famous book on traditional design, *A Pattern Language*. Here, again, we see an emphasis on collectivity. As Finkelstein says in an endnote to the book, he was first drawn to *A Pattern Language* because of that book's "idea of community," of architecture as an art of the social world. Many of the poems discuss the idea of community in urban and domestic spaces, but it is at the level of form that ideas of community and collective creativity come into full flower: the poems read less as Finkelstein's private thoughts than as a series of annotations and elaborations on substantial quotations from Alexander's writing. The feeling one gets is akin to that of reading scribal commentaries on a traditional text: there is a kind of collaboration at work, as a source text is elaborated and grows in meaning.

There are many versions of the poet-as-professor in the highly academicized world of contemporary American poetry: the poet-professor as hidebound formalist, the poet-professor as follower of intellectual fads and trends, and the poet-professor as obscurantist, to name just a few. In Norman Finkelstein, we're lucky to have one of the oldest kinds of academic: Finkelstein is a scribe.

2. Inside the Ghost Factory

Norman Finkelstein looks back to a legacy of Gnostic American poets: his 2010 book of literary criticism, *On Mount Vision: Forms of the Sacred in Contemporary American Poetry* is the best and most current outline we have of a Gnostic tradition in American poetry extending from Robert Duncan and Jack Spicer through Ronald Johnson, Armand Schwerner, Susan Howe, Michael Palmer, and Nathaniel Mackey. One feels the presence of Duncan in Finkelstein's poetic career, especially when he turns to that most characteristically Duncanesque form, the serial poem, as he does in the three-volume series *Track*. One feels, too, a special affinity for both Spicer and Schwerner, both of whom knew how to combine powerful spiritual impulses with comic gestures. The connection with Schwerner runs particularly deep, in that both Schwerner and Finkelstein have a keen sense of the mediation of spiritual knowledge by oral and literary traditions prone to fragmentation, distortion, decontextualization, and creative revision, but Finkelstein isn't merely an imitator of Schwerner. Where Schwerner's primary concern was with the fragmentary way the past comes down to us, and with the often comical attempt to restore the unrestorable, Finkelstein supplements these concerns with an interest in the way an unseen world presses into our own experience. Revelation, for Finkelstein, is not just embodied in fragmentary texts from the past: it is immanent, just beneath the surfaces of things.

The opening poem of Finkelstein's 2010 book of poems, *Inside the Ghost Factory*, "Instructions for the King," gives a good sense of Finkelstein's concern with the decontextualization and mediation of tradition:

> You may not cut your hair, but it shall be cut for you by a free man with a bronze knife.
>
> This is a goat, this is a dog, this is an ape: you must not look upon them, and you must forget the names for such creatures.

> You must cover your head when you go outside, for the sun is unworthy, and may not look upon you.
>
> You may not sleep during rainstorms, and if your wife hears thunder, then she is unclean until the new moon.
>
> ....
>
> None of this may be written down, for it may be forgotten, and it is not to be forgotten.

We can guess at the reasoning behind some of these ancient-sounding prohibitions. Wouldn't such frequent exposure to a free man's bronze knife help keep a king from acting too capriciously with his subjects? Could the insistence on head covering prevent the king from appearing too casual in public, and therefore help shroud him in a sense of power-enhancing mystery? Other prohibitions, though, remain obscure, their original functions lost in time, their preservation having become a matter of tradition for its own sake. The poem's final prohibition—the prohibition against the writing down of the prohibitions—has clearly been violated, as the very fact of the book in our hands makes plain. But is this preservation or betrayal? Finkelstein leaves the matter there, letting us ponder the meaning of the translation of tradition from oral culture to the culture of the book.

For all of his interest in the mediation of tradition, Finkelstein isn't primarily a poet concerned with the connection of our world and its past. He is more absorbed by the connection of our world to a mysterious otherworld lying just beyond the realm of quotidian experience. Often the connection seems to be a matter of correspondences, in the old Swedenborgian sense of the word as indicating analogies between specific things in the physical and spiritual realms. In "Tag, You're It"—a poem dedicated to Peter O'Leary—Finkelstein writes "The things above / are as the things below," an idea he elaborates upon in many other pieces in *Inside the Ghost Factory*, most notably in the title poem. Here, Finkelstein describes our relation to the ghostly inhabitants of the otherworld:

> It has been said
> that the living press down upon them, though
> they press down upon us too, until we are
>
> indistinguishable.

There's an intimacy to the quotidian and the spiritual, here, and a way in which they correspond to one another. It's fitting, then, that the poem ends with the repeated assertion "They are hiring allegorists again." It was through allegory, after all, that Dante sought the connection between the sacred and the profane.

"That's a Real Angel You're Talking To":
Robert Duncan and Mythological Consciousness

"You know, that's a real angel you're talking to." It was a dozen or so years into the current century, at a reception in Chicago's Green Lantern Gallery, that I overheard that comment. I was sipping cheap wine and talking to an old friend in the crowd that had gathered at an after-party held in the wake of the Chicago Poetry Project's symposium on Robert Duncan, and someone behind me was recalling the remark as something Duncan had said to Nathaniel Mackey after reading some of the letters to the "Angel of Dust" collected in Mackey's *From a Broken Bottle Traces of Perfume Still Emanate*. Given the provenance, the remark may be apocryphal, but it's certainly plausible, since one of the things about which Duncan was most insistent was the reality of myth, and of the figures found in myth. Indeed, the thing about Duncan that's most challenging to (and most often discounted by) contemporary audiences is just this: that he had, or at least tried very hard to have, a truly mythological consciousness—something utterly alien to most people in our time, even those who see myth sympathetically.

What it means to have a mythological consciousness is perhaps best understood with reference to Ernst Cassirer's *Philosophy of Symbolic Forms, Volume Two: Mythological Thought*. Cassirer, who goes largely unappreciated in literary circles nowadays, has a lot to offer us: after all, he was to neo-Kantian thought what Adorno was to Marxism, in that he wedded the rigors of his particular discipline to a belief that all of the humanities had something important to contribute to understanding, and took a strong interest in cultural forms. In his work on mythological thinking he is at pains to distinguish between forms of thought that merely value mythology, and a true mythological form of consciousness, something he finds primarily in pre-modern contexts (though, as his chilling study of Nazi ideology, *The Myth of the State*, makes plain, it can enter the modern world, sometimes in dangerous ways).

By and large, says Cassier, even those of us who value myths as a source of knowledge engage in some fancy footwork to make those myths compatible with our own, non-mythological worldviews. "We are accustomed to view these contents as 'symbolic,' to seek behind them another, hidden sense to which they mediately refer," he writes.

> Thus, myth becomes mystery: its true significance and depth lie not in what its configurations reveal but in what they conceal.... From this result the various types and trends of myth interpretation—the attempts to disclose the meaning, whether metaphysical or ethical, that is concealed in myths.

Those who do not truly believe in mythology as fundamentally real find the value of myth in the way myths can be translated into some other kind of knowledge. Such attempts can be quite elaborate: "Medieval philosophers," writes Cassirer, "distinguished three levels of interpretation, a *sensus allegoricus*, a *sensus anagogicus*, and a *sensus mysticus*." Even those with a great deal of sympathy for myth and a strong dose of skepticism for modern rationality tend to need some kind of allegorical or symbolic interpretive method to make sense of mythology. Even the Romantics, says Cassirer, "though they strove ... to understand the basic phenomena of mythology in themselves and not through their relationship to something else, did not fundamentally overcome 'allegorisis.'"

If one truly embodies a mythological consciousness—if one thinks not about mythology, but within it—things look different. Apollo the god, and the ideas represented by the figure of Apollo are distinct to most of us (who may be sympathetic to those ideas, but who don't expect to wake and see Apollo outside the window), but, as Cassirer points out, "only observers who no longer live in it but reflect on it read such distinctions into myth." For those whose consciousness is truly formed by mythology, the mythical figure doesn't stand for a thing: "it is the thing ... it has the same actuality"—ideas are "transposed into a material substance or being." One way to grasp this is to think of what Cassirer calls the "mythical action," when a "true substantiation is effected" and "the subject of the action is transformed into a god or demon." That is: if you go to a Catholic mass and experience the transformation of the Eucharistic wafer as a metaphor or a symbol, you may be sympathetic to the meaning of the event, but you do not experience it with a truly mythological consciousness. Only if, in your true and deepest and most fundamental understanding, you actually experience the transformation of the wafer as a real, actual, literal transformation of the object into the body of Christ, into something divine, do you really experience the event with mythological consciousness. That kind of thinking represents a challenge for most of us: but if we want to understand Robert Duncan's poetry, it's important to take up that challenge. He wants very much to experience the world with just such a consciousness.

Consider Duncan's comments on Milton's *Areopagitica* in *The Truth and Life of Myth*. Attempting to explain his own relation to mythology, Duncan quotes this passage:

> Truth indeed came once into the world with her divine Master, and was a perfect shape most glorious to look on: but when he ascended, and his Apostles after him were laid asleep, then straight arose a wicked race of deceivers, who, as that story goes of the Egyptian Typhon with his conspirators, how they dealt with the good Osiris, took the virgin Truth, hewed her lovely form into a thousand pieces, and scattered them to the four winds. From that time ever since, the sad friends of Truth, such as durst appear, imitating the careful search that Isis made for the mangled body of Osiris, went up and down gathering up limb by limb, still as they could find them. We have not yet found them all, Lords and Commons, nor ever shall do, till her Master's second coming; he shall bring together every joint and member, and shall mould them into an immortal feature of loveliness and perfection.... The light which we have gained was given us, not to be ever staring on, but by it to discover onward things more remote from our knowledge.

Most of us would read "Truth," with a capital "T," as an allegorical figure, and indeed as a figure of speech. But, says Duncan, "the mythological mind—and mine… is mythological—hears this not as fable or parable but as the actual drama or meaning of history, the plot and intention of Reality." For Duncan, "Truth was a Power, and, in this, a Person in history." To be absolutely clear: Truth, for Duncan, is not a personification—she is a person. There's a literalism here that is alien to the modern mind, and native to truly mythological consciousness.

It's not easy, though, for Duncan to maintain this mythological consciousness in a modern world that looks askance at such consciousness. Indeed, Duncan makes an admission of doubt, saying that poets who attempt mythological consciousness "must ever be troubled by the play of their genius, of true things in fictions and of fictions in true things." What is more, we find Duncan making what can seem like very willful readings, or misreadings, of other poets, in defense of mythological consciousness. We see this, for example, when Duncan discussed Dante's famous encounter with "the angel Amor" in the *Vita Nuova* (given here in D. G. Rossetti's translation, the version Duncan favored): "I felt a spirit of Love begin to stir / Within my heart, long time unfelt till then; / And saw Love coming towards me, fair and fain … / Saying 'Be now indeed my worshipper!'" Dante "is speaking literally here, not figuratively," says Duncan, he "is not illustrating some thought of his but telling us of an actual presentation in the crux of the reality of the poem." Dante's poetry, says Duncan, "insists upon the primal reality of the angel Amor" as actually real—as far as Duncan is concerned, that's a real angel Dante's talking to.

Those familiar with the medieval modes of interpretation might object that the spirit of love is no real angel, here, no record of a literal seraphic vision, but a figure of speech that fits neatly into the allegorical and anagogical modes of literary composition and interpretation with which Dante was familiar, and around which his *Divine Comedy* is structured. They may even cite no less an authority than Dante himself, who describes the angel as figurative. But Duncan will not have it. Even though Duncan admits that "Dante pleads poetic license, that this is no more than a figure of speech," he chooses not to accept this part of Dante as sincere. Rather, Duncan decides that Dante's description of the angel as figurative is merely a self-protecting lie. "Joan [of Arc] will be tried by ecclesiastic court and burned at the stake for talking with such demonic powers as Dante's angels in the *Vita Nuova* are," says Duncan, and "Ficino and Pico della Mirandola will come to trial for their practices of a theurgic magic to call up such personifications." In light of this climate of fear, Duncan decides that we must see Dante's denial of literalism in a new light, as a "pleading of insincerity [about] just what in the poem has to be sincere."

The willfulness of this reading is hard to ignore. Not only does Duncan ignore Dante's extensive use of allegorical and anagogical figures throughout his work, but he cites as evidence of a climate of fear and intimidation events that won't occur for 130 or even 150 years (the *Vita Nuova* was written in 1295; Joan of Arc went to trial in 1431; Ficino and Pico della Mirandola had their run-ins with Papal authority in the 1480s, and merely endured exile, a punishment we know from history that Dante was quite willing to undergo for his beliefs). But my point isn't to say that Duncan was right or wrong: my point is to say that his desire for a mythological consciousness put him on the defensive, and could even lead him to make claims that were more emotionally satisfying and philosophically authorizing than they were defensible. We might not learn much about Dante from Duncan's comments, but we learn something about Duncan: that he badly needed allies in his battle to maintain mythological consciousness in a milieu resistant to such consciousness, and may even have invented some of those allies out of his need.

Kenneth Rexroth's Other Worlds

The critic Michael Theune stood before the crowd that had gathered to hear him speak and slowly shook his head. Someone in the audience had opined, during the question-and-answer period, that a poem of which Theune had spoken "flowed well." "No, no," Theune intoned, "poetry doesn't *flow*, poetry *turns*." He had a point, although perhaps not a universally valid one. The turn, or the volta, is among the simplest and most fundamental of poetic techniques, and it's a simple turn, in Kenneth Rexroth's poem "On What Planet," that gives the poem all of its power—and allows it to open our consciousness to a world beyond our quotidian perception.

Much of the power of Rexroth's volta comes from how it causes us to rethink the experiences we've had reading the early stanzas of the poem. The first stanza, taken by itself, is a decent enough bit of landscape writing:

> Uniformly over the whole countryside
> The warm air flows imperceptibly seaward;
> The autumn haze drifts in deep bands
> Over the pale water;
> White egrets stand in the blue marshes;
> Tamalpais, Diablo, St. Helena
> Float in the air.
> Climbing on the cliffs of Hunter's Hill
> We look out over fifty miles of sinuous
> Interpenetration of mountains and sea.

The sense of forces moving dynamically through the landscape, the proper names of specific places, the land and water are equally important. But so what? Well, there's this:

> Leading up a twisted chimney,
> Just as my eyes rise to the level
> Of a small cave, two white owls

> Fly out, silent, close to my face.
> They hover, confused in the sunlight,
> And disappear into the recesses of the cliff.

It takes a bit of a different tack from the opening stanza, since we find we are not just looking at the landscape from on high, at a kind of Apollonian distance, as observers above the action. We're a part of the scene, and disturb it. And what's more alarming, we suddenly see the landscape—or, at any rate, its inhabitants—looking back at us. Those owls of Rexroth's are perfect for this, since they're all eyes. When I read these lines, I remember a particularly terrifying moment in my Canadian youth, when I stood on a granite outcropping high above an isolated lake, and what I'd taken to be a large white stone on the cliff's edge suddenly swiveled its head around and fixed me in its horrible, huge glare: it was a snowy owl, and I, the observer, suddenly became the observed.

The more one thinks about Rexroth's poem, the more clear it is how much Robert Hass owes to it: there's a moment in part four of Hass' "On the Coast Near Sausalito" when the speaker looks right into the living eye of the fish he's caught, and feels himself caught in that uncanny gaze—so alien, but still something we recognize, and that recognizes us—that is a moment straight out of "On What Planet."

But even with this development, the poem has yet to take its major turn. Look what happens in the concluding stanza of the poem:

> All day I have been watching a new climber,
> A young girl with ash blonde hair
> And gentle confident eyes.
> She climbs slowly, precisely,
> With unwasted grace.
> While I am coiling the ropes,
> Watching the spectacular sunset,
> She turns to me and says, quietly,
> "It must be very beautiful, the sunset,
> On Saturn, with the rings and all the moons."

The girl is a kind of further development of the owl image: just as we'd added more characters to the poem with the owls, we add another here; and just as the owls introduced the concept of a gaze other than the speaker's to the poem, the girl is given to us as a seeing entity, with her "gentle confident eyes" foregrounded. And the real turn comes when we get to see what she sees: she takes in the landscape to which we've been introduced, and combines it with her own sense of wonder, to ask about even more exotic and spectacular sunsets.

There's so much going on here I hardly know where to start. For one thing, the introduction of a younger, more naïve viewer of the landscape places the poem in the Romantic tradition, specifically in the tradition of Wordsworth's great "Tintern Abbey," where the speaker turns to his younger sister and thinks about the difference between how she perceives the landscape and how he sees it. We get some great themes, too. There's the importance of each person's particular subjective experience—how we share an objective world, but nevertheless have our own private interiority. There's also the difference between adult perception and childhood perception. Both Wordsworth and Rexroth give the edge to childhood perception, but for different reasons. For Wordsworth, the child's perception is less mediated by thought and memory than the adult's. For Rexroth, the child sort of juices up or amplifies the existing scene, allowing wonder at the present beauty to lead to even greater wonder at imagined beauties. (I think it's significant that Rexroth has the adult engaged in some mundane, utilitarian tasks while this happens—it heightens the contrast between down-to-earth or practical adult and wonder-oriented child).

To put Rexroth's poem in the Wordsworthian context is not to exhaust the significances. The girl's observation about Saturn defamiliarizes the whole scene. We've been thinking about the landscape of the early stanzas as impressive, but when we're asked to compare it to a sunset on Saturn, everything becomes less familiar. We think of the exoticness of other worlds, and then we think of our own world not as something complete in itself, but as one of many worlds—not as nature, but as one little particular articulation of galaxy upon galaxy of nature's variants. Our world doesn't just seem grand—it becomes strange, as weird and particular a combination of elements as are found on Saturn, or anywhere else. The large richness of infinite planetary beauties opens before us, and this makes our own scene not just spectacular and big, as it had seemed, but particular and small too: it's a big place of grand forces and jutting sea cliffs, but it's also, at the same time, our own dear little home in the vastness of space. The effect is to render the scene uncanny, familiar and strange at the same time.

The great moment, though, that comes with the poem's turn toward the girl and her observation, is the movement from one kind of sublimity to another, more complicated kind. The landscape in the opening stanzas of the poems is sublime in the way Edmund Burke wrote of sublimity in his famous *Philosophical Enquiry into Our Ideas of the Sublime and Beautiful*. Here, Burke speaks of the qualities of sublime objects—their vastness, ruggedness, jaggedness of line, and so forth—that mark them out from the merely beautiful. Those cliffs in the first two stanzas, and their interpenetration with the sea, are sublime stuff by Burkean criteria. But the girl takes us somewhere else, and, indeed, somewhere more profound. When she sees the grand, sublime landscape, she thinks of something even vaster. We were dwarfed by the landscape before, but now we're really dwarfed by the idea of the solar system, and behind that by the idea of the infinite plenitude of worlds, each with its own sun, its own grand vistas, its own sunsets—a deep sublimity of vastness upon vastness. But (and this is the crucial thing) we're not overwhelmed by this. In some strange sense, we've mastered it more than it has mastered us, because we—or, to be specific, the girl, and through her, the rest of us—have contained these vast multitudes in our minds. It's not just that there are an infinitude of planetary landscapes and exotic sunsets, it's that we have imagined them, and their possibility. This is one of the kinds of sublimity Kant talks about in his *Critique of Judgment*, where the sublime isn't just constituted by vastness, but by our ability to comprehend that vastness. This kind of sublime experience doesn't just tower over us: it affirms the power of our minds to take in such infinite vistas. It's a kind of affirmation not only of the outer world, but of the power of our imaginations to encompass it. The sublime experience ennobles us, as well as the world (or, in the case of this poem, the worlds).

It's particularly important that it is a child who calls us back to the power of our own imaginations. This makes such power innate, rather than learned. In fact, it makes such power latent, waiting to be rediscovered in us through our encounter with the world as seen by the child, or by the poet. This belief in the innate, but easily forgotten, power of the imagination is what marks Rexroth, for me, as a Romantic, and an imaginative mystic in the manner of Blake. And his faith in the power of something as simple as the volta to bring us to other worlds shows that he is as much a poet as a mystic: who else could believe something so unlikely, and so true?

A Strange and Quiet Fullness:

The Uncanny Charles Simic

Shop windows empty except for a dusty mannequin or a boy's suit long out of style; a seedy magician doing his threadbare act in an unpopular theater; a fat fly in a matchbox clutched by a lunatic. Charles Simic has been the primary purveyor of images such as these in American poetry for close to half a century, importing them from a mysterious region rumored to lie between the former Yugoslavia and the monstrous mountain passes of his private dream kingdom. A specialist in the uncanny, in objects removed from explanatory contexts, in stories gestured at but left untold, Simic describes his orientation as cosmic rather than historical or natural. He distrusts the tribalism inherent in history, with its chains of "begats" and its stockpiles of grievances, and he sees a direct link between the Romantic idealization of nature and a dangerously naive utopianism. He would rather reach beyond history and nature to deep enigmas of the cosmos itself—"the brain-chilling infinities and silences of modern astronomy and Pascalian thought." He finds unsettling enigmas not just in the vastness of space, but in the scenes and objects nearest to hand. When Simic looks at it, even a dog heading up the walk with the newspaper in his mouth becomes eerie and touches on an aspect of infinity.

Yet Simic's turn from history to the cosmic is itself a product of history, of the collision of his life with some of the most brutal events of the past century. A child of war-ravaged Belgrade, Simic tells us, "I've seen tanks, piles of corpses, and people strung from lampposts with my own eyes." Although they could not have known it, Hitler and Stalin were, according to Simic, "hatching an elaborate plot to make me an American poet." There is truth to this, and not just truth about Simic as an immigrant to the United States. His commitment to lyric poetry has everything to do with skepticism about the certainties of ideologies, whether of the right or the left, and his orientation toward the cosmic and the uncanny comes, too, from his traumatic childhood, from a series of events that seemed to deny any rational explanation.

Trauma figures prominently in the early memories recounted in Simic's essays. "I remember lying in a ditch and staring at some pebbles while German bombers were flying over our heads. That was long ago," he writes. "I don't remember the face of my mother nor the faces of the people who were there with us, but I still see those perfectly ordinary pebbles." The palpable fact of the pebbles was somehow uncanny, immediate but strange, within but somehow outside the human context of war. "It is not 'how' things are in the world that is mystical, but that it exists," Simic writes, quoting Wittgenstein. "I felt precisely that. Time had stopped. I was watching myself watching the pebbles and trembling with fear. Then time moved on." Moments such as these give form to Simic's imaginative reflexes and make the ordinary appear strange.

Another early memory involves a visit, just after the war, to a museum with an exhibition about wartime atrocities. The casualness surrounding unspeakable murderousness was all too evident: photos showed people chatting at public hangings, or soldiers smiling for the camera while they slit the throats of prisoners. When Simic's school group stepped outside for lunch, one of the boys had nothing but a piece of bread and scallions, which the other students found hilarious. Someone snatched the bread and threw it into the branches of a tree. Everyone, including the teacher, laughed as the boy, humiliated and hungry, tried and failed to get it down. It is a *Lord of the Flies* moment in which we catch a glimpse of the darkness just below the surface of quotidian life, sensing the failure of well-meaning efforts, such as, the exhibition, to dispel it.

Efforts to improve or perfect humanity terrify Simic, and understandably: he saw the Nazis, with their ideology of racial purification, triumph over Europe, and he grew up in a province of Stalin's empire, with its talk of a worker's utopia and the reality of its gulag. Simic is a great reader of philosophy, but like many modern philosophers he is radically opposed to the rigidities of systemic thought, whether metaphysical, political, social, or religious. "What if one doesn't buy any of these theories—as I do not?" he asks. In that case, "one just writes poems as someone who sees and feels deeply, but who even after a lifetime does not understand the world." Lyric poetry, for Simic, is about the specific case, and it stands as "the defense of the individual against all generalizations."

Commitment to the individual served Simic well in the 1990s, when his native Yugoslavia tore itself to pieces in internecine warfare. This was clearly a difficult period for Simic, who saw in the bombing of Belgrade a reprise of his youth and who found himself actively courted by the Serbian community to serve as a spokesman in America. Refusing this role, he wrote against the rise of Serbian nationalism in Serbian and German newspapers. For his efforts, he was accused of being both a traitor and a spy. "Here is something we can all count on," he wrote in 1993, the year the Bosnian Serbs scuttled an international peace plan, "sooner or later our tribe always comes to ask us to agree to murder." Nationalist ideology was no better than what he'd seen in the '40s and '50s, and Simic would have none of it.

At times this anti-ideological stance is entirely laudable, but in Simic's essays we sometimes see it harden into a kind of orthodoxy of its own. He treats the literary theory that became fashionable in universities in the '80s and '90s as if it were, by virtue of its abstraction and political commitments, no different from Stalinism, and his sense of the unregenerate nature of humanity leads him to see all efforts at making the world a better place as autobahns to totalitarian dystopia. "The dream of a social reformer," he asserts, "is to be the brains of an enlightened, soul-reforming penitentiary." Simic is not alone among Cold War–era anti-Communists in taking a hard line against social reform, but sometimes his arguments ring as hollow as those of any ideologue. In the essay "Reading about Utopia in New York City," he blasts all ideas of social reform while looking out from his Park Avenue balcony at young people enjoying themselves on a summer day. "If New York City is not already heaven, then I don't know what is," he writes. One wonders how heavenly New York would have appeared if he'd continued north on Park Avenue, hung a right on 131st Street, and taken the Madison Avenue Bridge to the South Bronx—a significantly tougher sell as the best of all possible worlds.

Simic's aversion to predetermined meanings and orthodoxies informs his poetics as well as his politics. His is a poetics of discovery rather than expression of existing ideas or observations. We might start out, in writing a poem, with a sense that "we are recreating an experience, that we are making an attempt at mimesis," he writes, "but then the language takes over.... When it first happened I was horrified. It took me years to admit that the poem is smarter than I am." He courts, rather than spurns, those moments when the poem takes an unforeseen turn, as in a series of poems he wrote in the '70s with James Tate:

> Tate and I collaborated on some poems in the following manner: We'd take a word or a phrase and then we'd turn ourselves into a 'pinball machine of associations,' as Paul Auster would say. For example, the word 'match' and the word 'jail' would become 'matchstick jail.' At some point we'd stop and see what we had.... We'd revise, free-associate again, and watch an unknown poem begin to take shape.

Simic invites chance into his poems, but does not give it carte blanche. He is more like André Breton who, caught revising his automatic writing, shrugged and claimed, "It wasn't automatic enough." Simic submits to chance "only to cheat on it." The resulting poetry is a close cousin to the works of the visual artists to whom Simic is drawn: Giorgio de Chirico, Eva Hesse, Joseph Cornell, and Odilon Redon. His work, like theirs, is pregnant with meanings always about to be born, with significances hovering on the verge of expression.

Like Cornell or de Chirico, Simic often works by juxtaposing powerful but seemingly unrelated objects, chosen not so that the relation can be explained—as John Donne would explain, say, the surprising similarity of parted lovers and a compass drawing a circle—but to place them in a suggestive relationship. The technique goes back at least as far as the proto-Surrealist poetry of Pierre Reverdy, who claimed, in 1918, that a powerful image is born from "a juxtaposition of two more or less distant realities"—the more distant the relationship between those realities, the stronger the image. In de Chirico we may see, for example, a composition in which a classical bust and a rubber glove sit side by side. The first is an object of artistic beauty, a memorial to an individual, a survivor from ancient history; the second is utilitarian, modern, industrial. Side by side they register a common status as traces of human presence, and we sense something important in their relation without being able to define it.

Similarly, Simic will pull two realities together, teasing us toward a sense of significance. In the poem "Eternities," for example, we first behold:

> A child lifted in his mother's arms to see a parade
> And that old man throwing bread crumbs
> To the pigeons crowding around him in the park,
> Could they be the very same person?
> And then, in the second and final stanza, we are told:
> The blind woman who knows the answer recalls
> Seeing a ship as big as a city block
> All lit up in the night sail past their kitchen window
> On its way to the dark and stormy Atlantic.

The first image gives us a sense of the cycle of life from youth to age, the second an eerie image of immense mechanical power setting out into an ocean that renders such power insignificant. We hover on the brink of a revelation, a statement of some kind about our status in the vastness of time and space—and remain hovering.

"If you worship in the Church of Art with a Message," Simic writes in an essay about a Surrealist art exhibition, "stay away." The sentence would make good jacket copy for just about any collection of Simic's poetry, including *The Lunatic*, a book full of images of people waiting for messages that will not come: a man sitting by a dead telephone telling himself it may yet ring; a blind man holding a fortune cookie at a Chinese restaurant, hoping the waiter (who has gone home for the evening) will read it to him. The poems gathered here do not so much make sense as express a sensibility—dark, deadpan, insomniac, haunted. Even the consolations of the pastoral rapidly peel away, revealing something eerie, as in the opening stanzas of "As You Come Over the Hill":

> You'll see cows grazing in a field
> And perhaps a chicken or a turtle
> Crossing the road in their sweet time,
> And a small lake where a boy once
> Threw a girl who couldn't swim,
> And many large maple and oak trees
> Offering ample shade to lie in,
> Their branches to hang yourself from,
> Should you so desire

"Over the Hill" may be a play on words, given how frequently the idea of aging finds its way into this book. Sometimes we see sex standing in the shadow of death—a girl in a red flamenco dress walking past a funeral parlor, a prisoner who finds happiness in the arms of the executioner's daughter—we get a sense of our powers and vital energies dwarfed by the vastness of time, like that "ship as big as a city block / All lit up in the night" as it sails past the kitchen window "on its way to the dark and stormy Atlantic."

The idea of mortality doesn't drive Simic any closer to religious or philosophical certainties, though. Instead it heightens his sense of mystery, and of how we remain strangers even to ourselves. "Have you introduced yourself to yourself?" he asks in "Late-Night Inquiry." "Have you found a seat in your room / For every one of your wayward selves?" And can you do so "before they take their bow and the curtain drops / As the match burns down to your fingertips?"

War, deprivation, atrocity, hunger, and dictatorship hurt Simic out of certainty and into poetry. His poetry avoids easy consolations: there are no gestures at transcendence or divine union, no visions of ideal love, no celebrations of community. But in the austerity of his poems, in their odd juxtapositions of images, there is a strange and quiet fullness. We get a sense of what this means to Simic when, in the essay "The Power of Ambiguity," he writes that he prefers empty rooms, "spaces where a single chair or an empty birdcage can do wonders for the imagination" because "in such rooms one has the feeling that time has stopped, that one's solitude and that of the remaining object are two actors in a metaphysical theater." We may count ourselves lucky to have tickets to the show.

John Crowe Ransom's Quarrel With God

We make out of the quarrel with others, rhetoric, but out of the quarrel with ourselves, poetry.
—W.B. Yeats

Once, in the waning days of the nineteenth century, a southern preacher's son quarreled with his father about the place of human happiness in God's plan. He pointed defiantly to the world's disorder as proof that God cared little for our desires, but he was too much his father's son not to doubt his own position, not to wonder if benevolent Providence could be real. He carried his doubts with him when, years later, he sat down to write. That preacher's son was John Crowe Ransom, and the quarrel with the father became a quarrel with himself, from which sprang his poetry. Later, his doubts resolved, he took up quarrels with the world and modernity. From this sprang prose and, eventually, disciples both political and literary. The poetry of the old inner quarrel was never quite abandoned, though the font of inspiration ran close to dry. Instead, the poems were rewritten, ironed smooth, the self-division suppressed, chastened, or ironized. What remained was assured, refined, supple—but somehow confined. One thinks of Rilke's panther in its cage.

During Ransom's lifetime, many thought that what he'd wrought in poetry was great, and numbered him among the storied names. Robert Lowell, speaking of the generation of American poets born in the 1870s and '80s, listed Frost, Williams, Pound, Moore, Eliot, and Ransom as the masters, sure of lasting fame, adding only "who outranks whom will be disputed." Randall Jarrell said Ransom's poems would "outlive Mother Goose." And at the height of his own fame Robert Frost told a fawning audience at Kenyon to redirect their enthusiasm, because the greatest living poet was their own Professor Ransom.

From certain perspectives, Ransom's legacy may count for more than that of more enduringly famous poets. His students went on to serve in numerous English departments, and through them he changed our expectations for what a poem is, and what it means. But to rank Ransom's poetry with that of the august company listed by Lowell would today be the act of an eccentric, or the willful assertion of one who knew and loved the man, an act redolent more of *pietas* than critical acuity. It is at times like these, when the sun of a once-great literary reputation has set, that we should be grateful for an opportunity to re-assess the work, to see it again, as if for the first time. When we look with fresh eyes at the poetry of John Crowe Ransom, what we see is a journey through dark doubt to something like stoic certainty. What is more, we see the often-baleful effects of revisions that subjected complex poems to the hard-won philosophy of the mature man.

Ransom, wrote Robert Lowell, "liked to be a poet, but not to be seen as one; he preferred the manner of a provincial minister." This should come as no surprise: both Ransom's father and grandfather were ministers of the Methodist church, and like them he lived the greater part of his life in the provinces. His origin as the scion of the provincial clerical class formed much in Ransom's sensibility: approaching his 80th year, he would affirm he was "neither capable nor desirous of abandoning the instruction I received in my father's parsonage." But that instruction was never simply dogmatic. His father's substantial library included works of great Victorian doubters like Arnold and Hardy, and the religious controversies of the day were openly discussed with visiting clergyman in the Ransom home. It was after a sermon by one such visiting minister that the young Ransom had his first great argument with his father about God and the meaning of suffering. Belief in God was in Ransom's background, one might say in his blood—but who was this God who could countenance evil, and what could he mean to us?

Poems About God, Ransom's first book, worried over these questions. Like all of Ransom's verse, the poems here tend toward the anecdotal; and like all of Ransom's verse, they are haunted by the nearness of death. What is unique to *Poems About God* in the Ransom *oeuvre* is the inconsistency of viewpoint among the various poems. The poems constitute something like an anatomy of possible human attitudes toward the divine. In "Sunset," for example, we hear the voice of a man who loves, but cannot understand, a woman who looks past the things of this world toward a distant and transcendent God. The narrative frame of the poem hints that we should draw parallels between the man and the cows in the nearby farmyard, or the little dog that accompanies him—he is the animal self, satisfied with fat fields and the beauty of the shifting light. She, though, is wed to something distant, beyond his comprehension, and he attends her with all the affection, and as little comprehension, as his dog attends him.

If God is an otherworldly mystery in "Sunset," he is quite the opposite in "Noonday Grace." The scene begins with the speaker's father saying grace over an ample and rustic meal. The prayer reminds the speaker of sermons, which leave him cold:

> Sunday the preacher droned a lot
> About a certain whether or not:
>
> Is God a universal friend,
> And if men pray can he attend
> To each man's individual end?
>
> They pray for individual things,
> Give thanks for little happenings,
> But isn't his sweep of mighty wings
> Meant more for the businesses of kings
> Than pulling small men's petty strings?

The sermon speaks to Ransom's own persistent question about the place of our happiness in God's creation, but says little to the speaker of the poem, who finds it abstract, and too grand for such as him. He isn't indifferent to God, though: instead, he finds the divine in the things of this world, especially in the abundant meal his mother prepared for the family. Bread becomes the body of the Lord in a humble, quotidian act of transubstantiation—the poem argues for

God's immanence, and invites us to partake of him through the fruits of this world.

The poems of Ransom's first volume stake out their different positions on the question of God without the inner balance and subtle irony found in his mature work. But one poem, "Grace," is a rarity in *Poems About God*, and looks forward to the path Ransom will take in later poems: it holds radically different notions of God together in a subtle equilibrium. It doesn't start out that way, though: a reader making a forecast based on the opening stanza alone would likely declare that this will be a poem about God's unmitigated malevolence:

> Who is it beams the merriest
> At killing a man, the laughing one?
> You are the one I nominate,
> God of the rivers of Babylon.

Soon, though, the dark view of the speaker, a farmer who seeks satisfaction only in the worldly appetites, is set in counterpoint to the beliefs of his hired man, who sings hymns of praise as he works the land. Then, on a blazing hot day, the hired man dies of heat stroke, and the world seems to make a mockery of his faith. The body lies in the field,

> And God shone on in a merry mood,
> For it was a foolish kind of sprawl,
> And I found a hunk of heaving meat
> That wouldn't answer me at all
> And a fresh breeze made the young corn dance
> To a bright green, glorious carnival

The very beauty of the world at a time of grief betrays God's indifference to our dying flesh.

What possible value can faith hold in this situation? Faced with death, can we see God as purely good? The speaker can't, and declares that God "shall not have my love alone, / With loathing too his name is named." But there is a turn at the poem's end. Here, the whole of nature praises God—the whole world, that is, except the speaker and his corollary, a crow whose caw represents a dissonance in the general outpouring of beauteous song. The juxtaposition of the crow and the celebrating world gives us a variation on the ending of Hardy's "The Darkling Thrush," where a desolate Hardy listens to a thrush's outpouring of joy and feels it must represent "Some blessed Hope, of which he knew / And I was unaware." Ransom's poem, like Hardy's (surely its model), doesn't deny the possibility of hope and grace—but cannot in good conscience embrace them either.

Such tentative faith as Ransom retained was sorely tested during his army service in the First World War, including four months at the front. Like his contemporary J. R. R. Tolkien, Ransom doesn't address the ghastliness of the war directly, but transposes it onto an imagined medieval world. In "Necrological," from the 1924 volume *Chills and Fever,* Ransom depicts a friar who visits a battlefield after the victorious army has moved on. There he finds the bodies of the slain:

> Close by the sable stream that purged the plain
> Lay the white stallion and his rider thrown,
> The great beast had spilled there his little brain,
> And the little groin of the knight was spilled by a stone.

The spectacle of carnage bewilders the monk, who

> … sat upon a hill and hung his head,
> Riddling, riddling, and lost in vast surmise,
> And so still he likened himself unto those dead
> Whom the kites of Heaven solicited with sweet cries.

Are these kites of Heaven simply scavengers, feeding on mere meat? Or is there something more, some yet-ungrasped redemption? We end in much the same place we find ourselves in with the closing lines of "Grace," but the intensity is greater, the pain more palpable.

Elegy is the great mode of Ransom's imagination, because it provides the occasion for him to express both despair and the yearning for grace at their most poignant—and it is in his balancing of the two that he earns the title bestowed on him by Miller Williams, that of "supreme equilibrist." "Dead Boy," from Ransom's final book of new poems, *Two Gentlemen in Bonds*, stands as the most refined of his elegies, and represents the height of his achievement in juxtaposing cold, cosmic indifference with human emotional needs. The poem begins with an assessment of the situation so detached and rational as to appear almost inhuman:

> The little cousin is dead, by foul subtraction,
> A green bough from Virginia's aged tree,
> And neither the county kin like the transaction,
> Nor some of the world of outer dark, like me.
>
> He was not a beautiful boy, nor good, nor clever,
> A black cloud full of storms too hot for keeping,
> A sword beneath his mother's heart,—yet never
> Woman bewept her babe as this is weeping.
>
> A pig with a pasty face, I had always said,
> Squealing for cookies ...

"Subtraction," "transaction"—these are words of a mathematician or accountant, not one who grieves. But they are the least offensive of the speaker's terms: the description of the boy is so far from keeping with decorum as to border on heartlessness. But what are we to make of those who do grieve? Theirs is a world of emotion, to be sure, but not an entirely sympathetic one. They love the boy less for himself than as an extension of their illustrious family: "Their hearts," we read, "are hurt with a deep dynastic wound." The speaker's objectivity may chill us, but the mourners' sorrow is tribal and, in its way, exclusive: for the Virginian family the world splits into two categories: "county kin" and "outer dark."

The detached and rational; the intimate and tribal—both sets of values are judged, and each set of values subverts the other. If the Ransom of *Poems About God* let his poems argue with each other, the Ransom of *Two Gentlemen in Bonds* has moved beyond such arguments, and arrived at a kind of conviction. For him, there will always be a subjective, needy, yearning humanity, never so virtuous as it should be; and there will always be a cosmos that seems not to care for who we are and what we need. If there is a God who loves us and cares for our happiness, his way of loving us is something we can never understand.

By the time he wrote "Dead Boy," Ransom had settled his old quarrel with his father, and with himself—and resolved it so thoroughly that he could present the resolution as doctrine or dogma. This resolution marks the birth of Ransom as an abstract thinker, and his death as a poet.

Since his student days, Ransom had dreamed of writing a great philosophical work, but until 1930 he had failed to realize the dream. Then came the idiosyncratic theology of *God Without Thunder*. Subtitled "An Unorthodox Defense of Orthodoxy," the book maintains there is no afterlife, no divine revelation, no divinity to Christ, and that God, indifferent to our prayers, is the author of evil as well as of good. The book was "orthodox," then, in no orthodox sense of that word—and it's little wonder that an early reviewer claimed "Mr. Ransom's book, far from being a defense of orthodoxy, is a repudiation of the Christian religion."

God, writes Ransom, does not govern the universe in order to accommodate the needs of humanity—a fact we have found hard to stomach. Instead, "we wanted a God who wouldn't hurt us, who would let us understand him; who would agree to scrap all the wicked thunderbolts in his armament." This is the God (for Ransom, the false God) of the New Testament, of Christ as "the principle of social benevolence and of physical welfare." But why does Ransom take issue with the notion of God in Christ, of God as redemptive mercy and universal love? Not only does the idea grate against his hard experience, as expressed by the torn corpses on the battlefield of

"Necrological"—it tempts us into arrogance, selfishness, and errors of grave consequence. "The fear of the Lord is the beginning of wisdom," wrote Ransom to Allen Tate in 1929, but the New Testament errs by claiming "the love of the Lord is the beginning of wisdom." This is a manipulative and arrogant love, "the kind of love," says Ransom, "a scientist bears to the gentle, tractable elements in his test-tubes, which so gladly yield him their secrets, and work for him." Ransom's God is inscrutable, beyond our understanding, and certainly unconcerned with interceding on our behalf: prayer exists to reconcile us to our condition, not as a means to petition God to accommodate our needs.

The on of his quarrel with himself left Ransom free to quarrel with the world, and the social implications of his theology were clear. The belief that we can understand the mysteries of God and his world leads to the belief that we can perfect not only our souls but our polity. Belief in the inscrutable God of the Old Testament serves as our best, indeed our only, defense against a host of ideologies noxious to Ransom's disposition. It is, says Ransom, the only defense against "our vicious economic system; against empire and against socialism, or any other political foolishness." An old-style conservative such as Edmund Burke may not have embraced Ransom's theology, but he would have appreciated Ransom's choice of enemies.

Rationalizers and reformers are the villains of Ransom's social vision, and modern industrial society, with its implicit belief in technologically based human perfectibility, is the baleful result of their triumph. Ransom would work against it: during the same period he was composing *God Without Thunder* he and Tate were discussing the project that would become *I'll Take My Stand*, the manifesto of the Southern Agrarian movement. An agrarian society kept mankind in close relation to the elements, reminding us of the awesome power and incomprehensibility of God; it was, moreover, immune to the vices of social schemes doomed to create totalitarian dystopias or, at best, the fool's paradises of materialist consumption.

An aesthetics as well as a politics grew from Ransom's theology. The error of concocting a God who would let us understand him leads us to over-value reason and to value abstractions above particulars. In our infatuation with abstractions we forget what Ransom calls "the world's body"—a term so important to him that in 1938 he used it as the title for his first book of literary criticism. There he argues for an unparaphrasable poetry that combines ideas with the world of the senses in images irreducible to mere concepts. Particularity and concreteness join equilibrium and subtle irony among the desiderata of poetry, and the poem's structure, or prose argument, is not to take precedence over its texture, the particular connotations of its individual words and images.

Ransom was never a prolific writer of verse. He wrote fewer than 160 poems from his late start at the age of 28 to the publication of *Two Gentlemen in Bonds* 11 years later, and subsequently added only a half-dozen new poems to his *oeuvre*. Allen Tate claimed Ransom had simply said all he needed to say, and there's some truth to this: Ransom had answered the questions he most urgently needed to answer, and could move from inner debate to building intellectual systems. He turned with relish to literary criticism, all but abandoning the writing of poetry in the process.

In abandoning poetry, though, Ransom did not abandon his poems. Instead, he revised them compulsively. Many of Ransom's revisions to his poems were quite minor: matters of punctuation or a smoothing out of rhythm. But the more substantial changes tended to tame unruly elements, to substitute simplicity for complexity and certainty for uncertainty. At the end of the version of "Necrological" published in *Chills and Fever*, for example, we read that the friar "hung his head, / Riddling, riddling, and lost in a vast surmise." When Ransom revises the poem two decades later, we find that the friar "bowed his head, / Riddling, riddling, and in a deep surmise." Can the friar sustain his faith in the face of tragic carnage? Will he remain lost in the vastness of uncertainty? In the later version, the bowed head implies piety, and the monk "in deep surmise" is less bewildered than the monk lost in unfathomable vastness. The revisions move us from greater to lesser ambiguity.

Ransom's theories of poetry allow for, and even embrace, the poem whose elements complicate its argument, but often it is just these subtleties he edits out as he revisits the poems of his younger days. Many of his most careful readers lament the changes: Robert Lowell found the poems in their later forms "curiously and dubiously revised," and Tate decried the destruction Ransom "inflicted upon many of his finest poems." Others defend the old Ransom against the young, praising the greater simplicity and consistency of the newer versions: the novelist and critic Donald A. Stauffer, for example, lauds the revisions, writing that Ransom, in his theory, "may go too far in the separation of texture and structure. What a poem needs is not an irrelevant word but the relevant word, whether it is expected or unexpected."

The judgment of Ransom's revisions is, of course, a matter of taste, and matters of taste are best adjudicated on the basis of our own direct experience of the texts in question. For too long this was difficult to do, with Ransom's different version scattered in various journals and books. Back in 1976 ago Ransom's biographer Thomas Daniel Young spoke of the urgent need for a variorum edition of Ransom's poetry, and after a delay of thirty years do we have one—which means we are finally in a position to undertake something of which Ransom, as godfather of the New Criticism, would heartily approve: a long and careful close reading of the texts.

History, Totality, Silence

We have it on the best of authorities that the poetry of John Matthias has heretical tendencies. Here's what Robert Duncan said about Matthias in an undated letter from the early 1970s:

> Matthias is a goliard—one of those wandering souls out of a Dark Age in our own time ... carrying with him as he goes in his pack of cards certain key cards that come ever into his hand when he plays: the juggler (as he was to be portrayed later in the Tarot), the scholar whose head is filled with learning and of amorous women and the heretic remembering witch-hunts yet to come.

A goliard! Already Matthias is in trouble, the goliards being clerical students of the Middle Ages who affirmed the flesh and derided the corruption of Mother Church. And not just any goliard, but a goliard Duncan associates with the juggler of the Tarot (in esoteric decks, a figure for the magus who masters dark arts) and with the heretic seeing into a future of persecutions. We may as well call in Torquemada's inquisition and get this heretic burning. But Duncan is talking about the Matthias of the sixties and early seventies, and thinking of Matthias' political radicalism and of his early obsessions with alchemy and witchcraft. What of the later Matthias?

Consider three long poems of Matthias' that form a poetic suite: "An East Anglian Diptych," "Facts from an Apocryphal Midwest," and "A Compostella Diptych," written between 1984 and 1990, and published collectively as *A Gathering of Ways*. The general project of the poems indicates a turning-away from the Matthias described by Duncan: they are attempts of coming to terms with what Matthias called his "post-activist consternation" and alienation from American life. "An East Anglian Diptych" is Matthias' attempt to make a psychological home for himself in England, and "Facts from an Apocryphal Midwest" represents a similar home-making project in America. This is no longer the radical wanderer, but the poet in search of stability. Indeed, "A Compostella Diptych," takes as its subject the ancient pilgrim routes across France and Spain to Santiago de Compostella. It's an attempt by the post-activist Matthias to come to terms with, and possibly make himself at home in, both the history of the West and the dominant spiritual tradition of the West, Catholicism.

But to what terms does he come? If I were to try to sum them up, I'd say this: in "A Compostella Diptych," Matthias attempts to present a totalized history of the West and of Catholicism. But he fails to find a happy totality, and this drives him toward an otherworldly yearning, a yearning for a world beyond history, an eternal world of free of violence. This is essentially a Gnostic yearning for some eternal, infinite elsewhere of light, a yearning from which he only escapes at the very end of the poem.

When I speak of a "totalized history" in "A Compostella Diptych," I want to use the term "totality" in a vaguely Levinasian sense: as something finite, in which diverse elements are reduced to "the violently pacified empire of Same" or "the counted-as-one" (to use Dominic Fox's glosses for Levinas' "totality"). With regard to history, we can think of totalization as the opposite of an unending series of discrete events—the opposite, that is, of Henry Ford's version of history as "one damn thing after another"—or perhaps we can think of it as the hammering of such discrete phenomena into something whole, in which apparently disparate parts are in fact manifestations of a single force, or repetitions of a single pattern. We're on the same page about this if you're thinking of one of the most famous passages in the works of Walter Benjamin, which reads:

> A Klee painting named *Angelus Novus* shows an angel looking as though he is about to move away from something he is fixedly contemplating. His eyes are staring, his mouth is open, his wings are spread. This is how one pictures the angel of history. His face is turned toward the past. Where we perceive a chain of events, he sees one single catastrophe which keeps piling wreckage upon wreckage and hurls it in front of his feet. The angel would like to stay, awaken the dead, and make whole what has been smashed.

But a storm is blowing from Paradise; it has got caught in his wings with such violence that the angel can no longer close them. The storm irresistibly propels him into the future to which his back is turned, while the pile of debris before him grows skyward.

This is a vision of history as total, and as total disaster. And this is very much the vision of history that Matthias gives us in "A Compostella Diptych."

It doesn't seem that way at first, though. "A Compostella Diptych" begins with what seems to be a happy vision of the many pilgrims who have trodden the various routes through France and Spain to the cathedral at Santiago de Compostella. There's a barrage of proper names of people and places: some 41 different proper names in the first 45 lines of the poem. On the face of it, this doesn't seem like the writing of a man who would present history as a totality. Nothing, after all, insists on irreducible specificity more than a proper name. Indeed, proper names will be very significant at the end of the poem, when Matthias shakes himself free of a totalized version of history—but I'm getting ahead of myself. The point I want to make here doesn't have to do with proper names, but with a collective pronoun, "they." Unlike proper names, collective pronouns reduce the many to the one, and what we see happen in the opening of "A Compostella Diptych" is a reduction of the people of different European nations and centuries into a single, collective, "they"—a trans-historical subject for the people of Catholic Europe. Here we have the multitudes "counted-as-one." It doesn't seem, at first, to be anything but a joyous affair, a holy journey uniting the many. But this all changes a few pages into the poem. After Matthias gestures toward the song of the pilgrims, he adds this:

> And there was another song—song sung inwardly
> to a percussion of the jangling
> manacles and fetters hanging on the branded
>
> heretics who crawled the roads

> on hands and knees and slept with lepers under
> dark facades of abbeys
>
> the west portals of cathedrals ...

There is a dissonance in the happy totality of history: those who do not fit, those who are expelled, despised, oppressed. This is a vision of the violence of the totality, and soon the history his poem recounts becomes a history of crusade, jihad, and inquisition, while a small minority yearns for an escape into timeless peace. Indeed, history becomes totalized in a new way—as Benjamin's totality of "one single catastrophe which keeps piling wreckage upon wreckage."

Matthias creates a sense of this catastrophic historical totality through four main techniques. I call them coincidence in place; rhyming actions; musical refrain; and musical reprise.

Coincidence in place presents history as total catastrophe by giving us a series of almost archeological sections in which the same geography hosts similar events over time. For example, Matthias shows us Charlemagne's minions slaughtered during a crusade in Spain. These events coincide in space with later massacres of the Spanish Inquisition centuries later, and with still later massacres perpetuated by Napoleon in the Peninsular War. We dig into the history of particular places, and, like Benjamin's angel, see only wreckage piling upon wreckage.

By "rhyming actions" I mean historical events that Matthias presents as essentially parallel. Notable among these is the fate of the cathedral bells of Santiago. Early in the poem we see these hauled away by the conquering armies of Islamic Spain under Almansor, who hangs them upside down in his great mosque and uses them as candelabra. Much later in the poem and in history we see Alfonso VI of Castile sack the mosque and take the bells back to Santiago, installing them in the cathedral for their original use. The effect of these actions, which echo one another, is to remind the reader of conflict, and of the hubris of conquerors, as the constants of history.

There are many refrains in "A Compostella Diptych," but among the most resonant refrains is the phrase "darkness fell at noon." We hear it at many moments in the poem when political disaster falls. The refrain not only serves to unite these moments—it also connects those moments to more modern disasters. *Darkness at Noon* is, after all, the title of Arthur Koestler's novel about the evils of Stalinism.

Musical reprise is a technique quite common in opera and musical drama, but unusual in poetry: the passing of the same lyrical part from one voice to another in different contexts. A number of different passages get a reprise in "A Compostella Diptych," but the most insistent one is Charlemagne's dream of war, an 18-line passage lifted from the *Chanson de Roland*. We're first given it as a prophetic dream in the mind of Charlemagne, but we hear it again, in whole or in part, in the voices of other characters (notably Aimery Picaud, the chronicler of the pilgrim routes, and John Moore, the English general killed while fighting Napoleon's armies at Corunna), or with reference to other conflicts, including modern acts of terrorism by Basque separatists. The effect of the reprise is to make all of history into Charlemagne's nightmare of war—a nightmare from which we seem unable to wake up.

Not that some characters in Matthias' poem don't try. Accompanying the long nightmare of history recounted in "A Compostella Diptych" is another story, a story of Gnostics who long for a world beyond this broken, bruised, and evil one in which we seem perpetually imprisoned. This group includes the historical Gnostics and heretics of the times and places covered by the poem (Cathars, Albigensians, and the like). But Matthias interprets Gnosticism broadly, and includes in it the Eleusinian mysteries, the practitioners of the medieval Trobar Clus, and the Sufi mystics of Islamic Spain. He even includes Ezra Pound, wandering as a young man through the south of France, and dreaming of a light beyond the nightmare and wreckage of history.

There is much in "A Compostella Diptych" to indicate that Matthias would join with the Gnostic tradition, especially in the poem's final section. Here, Matthias presents us with a moment where we seem to leave history, and indeed this world, behind, in an intersection of the timeless with time. The occasion for the intersection is the explosion of an enormous Spanish armory, an explosion that shakes foundations and, from many miles away, creates shockwaves that ring the Santiago cathedral bells, the same ones that had been hauled away by conquering Moors and hauled back by crusaders. Now, we're told

> Men
>
> whose job it was to ring them stood
> amazed out in the square & wondered if this thunder
> and the ringing was in time for Vespers
>
> or Nones or if it was entirely out of time …

As it turns out, it's the latter: the explosion is followed by a stillness that Matthias identifies with the silence before the existence of time. We are taken to a place of stillness "As it was … in the silence that preceded silence" when "there were neither rights nor hopes nor sadnesses to speak of," where "in the high and highest places everything was still." We're outside of time, and certainly outside of the totalized, catastrophic history with which the poem has presented. Indeed, inasmuch as we are in some boundless place, we have escaped totality, and encountered the infinite.

Another kind of poet would end things here. Indeed, a properly modernist poet would end things here—gathered into the artifice of eternity (as in "Sailing to Byzantium"), or purged of worldliness by fire (as in "Little Gidding"). But Matthias doesn't. Instead of turning from the world of history, he returns to it—in fact, for the first time in the poem, he enters history by name, appearing with his wife Diana on the pilgrim trails. Here's the passage:

> Towards Pamplona, long long after all Navarre
> was Spain, and after the end
> of the Kingdom of Aragon, & after the end of the end,

> I, John, walked with my wife Diana
> down the Somport Pass following the silence
> that invited and received my song

It goes on, in prose saturated with more proper nouns—29 in 21 lines—to describe John and Diana "blest and besotted" in Spain, and in their moment of history. Escape to a timeless realm would be the Gnostic's happy ending, but the true spiritual tradition informing "A Gathering of Ways" turns out to be something rather different, the best analog for which is the philosophy of Emmanuel Levinas. For Levinas, the encounter with the unbounded or infinite is not an end in itself: rather, it returns us to experience with a sense of wonder, and an invitation to enter into dialogue with the world. And this sort of return and invitation is what we get in "A Compostella Diptych" when Matthias appears in the historical terrain of his poem, and when the silence "invite[s] and receive[s]" his song. The encounter with the infinite releases him from a sense that history is catastrophe and nothing more. Moreover, by inviting Matthias' particular song, the infinite shows it welcomes proliferation, rather than the reductions of totalization: Matthias' song is just one voice in a boundless infinity, not the total summation of all things.

It's important to note the role of proper names here, because it underlines a slight difference between Matthias and Levinas. For Levinas, the encounter with the infinite comes about through confronting a human face, in all its particularity. For Matthias, though, the encounter with the infinite is with something still and silent and beyond us. But the effect of that encounter is to return us to the world of specific people and places, the world of proper names—and to show us that this world is not reducible to some totalized history of catastrophe. Particularity trumps totalization at the end of the poem, as a litany of proper names unassimilated into a grand pattern of catastrophe leaves us blessed and besotted. In the end, it is this return that prevents Matthias from being a Gnostic. As much as he is fascinated with that tradition, he can't join it: he is too much in love with all of us who can be named.

IV
Others

An ABC of Gertrude Stein

A is for Alice, or Artist's Wife. When I began to learn about Alice B. Toklas, I knew I'd seen her kind before. I grew up as an art school brat in the 1970s, and back in those days when male egos swaggered and feminist consciousness had permeated less thoroughly through the cultural sphere, it was common enough to see, in the shadow of each male would-be genius in paint-spattered denim, a quiet figure, attending to all the banalities of life and the social obligations, a self-abnegating figure who had nevertheless made herself so essential to the artist's ability to function that he would fall apart if he left her, as he sometimes did. Alice never walked out on Gertrude, but if Ernest Hemingway is to be believed, she made it perfectly clear that she could and she would, and it made Gertrude tremble (see P, below).

B is for Bile, or Biting Remark. Gertrude Stein was tremendously jealous of the success of other writers, especially if they were of her generation, or if they had once sat at her feet at her salons, and she knew just what to say to hurt them. Sinclair Lewis only sold so many books because he "is the typical newspaperman and everything he says is newspaper," she'd remark. Or "Hemingway," (see H) she'd say, after his books began to sell, "after all you are ninety percent Rotarian."

C is for Cézanne. No one cared about Cézanne until 1906, when a posthumous exhibition of his work was held in Paris. Or almost no one, except for Stein and her brother Leo. Leo in particular saw that Cézanne had set about solving the problem of composition as no one else had; absorbing what the Impressionists had taught about color but looking for a way to re-introduce order to the visual plane. He did it by distorting the objects he represented, and using inconsistent perspective. That is: by almost inventing Cubism. Stein hung Cézannes in her salon, and wrote *Three Lives* while staring at one of them. Picasso came by and liked them too.

D is for Deterritorialization. Gilles Deleuze speaks of deterritorialization as the moving out from a defined sphere, and Stein certainly did that when she broke with mimesis as a principle of writing. But she was also deterritorialized in a more down-to-earth sense: until she arrived in Paris, she belonged nowhere. She'd lived in hotels and boarding houses and with relatives, and in a big house in Oakland isolated from everyone else, and among people with whom her affluent, cosmopolitan family had nothing in common. When her parents died she connected with no one and nothing except her books and one brother, who confesses that he and Gertrude knew nothing of each other's inner lives. But bohemian Paris was a special territory, inhabited by refugees from all sort of backgrounds, all united by some concern with art. It was a territory for the deterritorialized, and if there was a home for Stein, it was there that the there would be.

E is for Everybody. Not many people read *Everybody's Autobiography* anymore, and almost no one has ever read all of *The Making of Americans'* 1000 close-set pages, but these books are fascinating because of the ambition to talk about, well, everyone. *The Making of Americans*, which starts out as a family chronicle, shifts gears on the fly and suddenly concerns itself with creating a universal psychological typology, accounting for the inner lives of all possible kinds of humans in all possible kinds of conditions. It's the sort of thing you write if you feel alienated from the world, if you'd been cut off from it by your isolated early life and your out-of-stepness with your peers and your self-involved narcissism (see N, below). It's the sort of thing you write if you're making a willful effort to empathize with a world that has not much empathized with you.

F is for Fleurus, not Flowers. Every Modernism geek knows that Stein's salon at 27 rue de Fleurus was one of the great epicenters of modern art and literature. Except me, for many years: I thought it was 27 Rue Des Fleurs, 27 Flower Street. But no, it's Fleurus—a the particularly dull town in a dull part of Belgium. It's as if the greatest and most glamorous gatherings of Modernism took place on Hoboken Road.

G is for Genius, that is: Gertrude Stein. I refuse to believe there was ever another human as dedicated as Stein was to calling herself a genius (see N, below). But if you look at how the category of genius has come down to us through Kant and a host of neo-Kantians, you'll see that there are a number of boxes to check—originality, signature style, freedom from the rules of taste and the demands of the audience, the ability to inspire the originality of others (see H)—and Stein checks them all. Coming from her particular background—unaffiliated with any group or region or religion (see J)—she clung to the idea of herself as a genius because it was what counted in the only milieu where she ever felt as home (see D, above).

H is for Hemingway, who kind of fell in love with Stein. I mean it. You should read what he wrote about wanting to seduce her. Alice Toklas was even worried about this, and worked to drive the two apart. Her plan may have worked even if Hemingway's fame hadn't made Stein jealous (see B, above). In any event, Stein really set out to hurt Hemingway in *The Autobiography of Alice B. Toklas*, where she presents him as clumsy and fragile. Hemingway struck back in the introduction he wrote to the memoirs of Jimmie Charters, his Montparnasse bartender. There's hardly anything of substance in there about Jimmie or drinking, but plenty of proof that Gertrude got his goat.

I is for Intrigue. By Alice. See A and H.

J is for Judaism. It never meant much to Stein, or at least she never admitted to it, though she must have been conscious of how other people marked her off as other: her brother Leo reports on painful anti-Semitic remarks at school. She seems to have been naïve about what it meant to be Jewish in Europe in the thirties. Not long before the German tanks rolled into France, she talked about how vulnerable the French were, and how above vulnerability she thought herself. As it turned out, she made it through the war by keeping her head down in a small town in Vichy France, with some help from her friend

Bernard Fäy, an important man in the cultural wing of the Pétain administration. Stein, whose sympathies were never democratic, had a disconcerting degree of sympathy for Pétain and the French right wing that can't quite be explained away as a matter of survival, though some of my friends who love Stein plug their ears if anyone says so.

K is for Kahnweiler. Daniel-Henry Kahnweiler was the art dealer who sold Stein her Picassos. He more or less invented the idea of the dealer as someone who would contract to buy all of an unknown or unappreciated artist's output, then hustle to create the taste for that artist's work. Without being an artistic genius, he nevertheless manufactured more genius reputations than anyone else in all of Paris. Without him, there's no sure bet that the throngs would have assembled at Stein's place to see what was on the walls (see S, below).

L is for Lectures. Stein didn't want to do them at first, feeling insecure about leaving the salon where she had the world very much on her own terms, where she swam comfortably among the shoals of admirers. But when she was invited to speak at Oxford and Cambridge she discovered she liked it. She especially liked the way what she said divided the audience, how professors would hop up to snipe at each other during Q & A—little frogs in their own little pond.

M is for Money. When Stein's father died, his affairs were in disorder, and her oldest brother Michael sat down to unravel them. What he found when he got to the end of all the knots wasn't much, mostly some railroad stocks he took to the great rail magnate Collis Potter Huntington, along with a plan for streetcar consolidation. Huntington didn't much care for the stocks, but he liked Michael, and bought him out as a way of bringing him into the company. This set all the Stein siblings up with modest prosperity for life. If Michael had put on a bad show, or if Huntington has let a subordinate deal with the meeting, Gertrude would never have assembled all her paintings, and never settled at 27 Rue de Fleurus. She'd probably have finished med school at Johns Hopkins and spent a lifetime lancing boils in Baltimore.

N is for Narcissism. This might be the key to understanding Stein, although it's hard to scrape the barnacles of judgment off the term enough to use it as simply descriptive of Stein's psyche, rather than as some kind of condemnation. Stein rings all the bells for the old DSM-IV definition of narcissism: a grandiose sense of self-importance; fantasies of unlimited brilliance; a sense of specialness accompanied by a sense that only other, special people can understand her; a need for excessive admiration; a sense of entitlement to special or favorable treatment; a tendency to take advantage of others (read: Alice); envy of others or a sense that others envy her; and arrogant or haughty behavior. The causes for the condition are generally thought to relate to early affective deprivation—the lack of a sense of belonging and being loved (Stein's parents died when she was in her early teens, and had been distant when she was a child). The only criterion of narcissism that Stein didn't seem to exhibit was a lack of empathy. She was a good listener, and she tried hard to understand what made other people tick (see E, above). There's a longstanding myth about the link between mental illness and genius. But I'm quite sure that if Stein hadn't been hurt into the narcissism that made her so difficult to get along with (she lost friends as fast as she made them) she'd never have striven for genius, and never have arrived there (see G, and maybe D).

O is for Oakland, where there was no there.

P is for Pussy, one of Stein's favorite nicknames for Alice, and the one she used when Hemingway overheard an argument upstairs at 27 Rue de Fleurus, one that made clear just how much power over Stein the self-effacing Alice really had (see A, above). "I heard someone speaking to Miss Stein as I had never heard one person speak to another; never, anywhere, ever," Hemingway reports, "then Miss Stein's voice came pleading and begging, saying, 'Don't, pussy. Don't. Don't, please don't. I'll do anything, pussy, but please don't do it. Please don't. Please don't, pussy.'" This unflattering portrait of the Stein-Toklas relationship may have been colored by the feud that grew between Hemingway and Stein after she became jealous of his success (see B and H). If she knew how to sting him with charges of physical fragility, he knew how to counter-attack, making the narcissistic and formidable queen of a grand salon (see N and S) appear needy and vulnerable.

Q is for Queer, or *Q.E.D.* Early on Gertrude Stein wrote a novella called *Q.E.D.*, which addressed her lesbianism more frankly than she was comfortable with in a public document. She suppressed the book, which wasn't published until after her death, under the title *Things as They Are*. One thinks of E.M. Forster's inscription on a note attached to the manuscript of his homosexually-themed novel *Maurice*, which was left unpublished at his death—"publishable, but worth it?" But Stein had something that Forster never had: Cubism. She was able to put bits and pieces of obliquely rendered same-sex eroticism into *Tender Buttons*, where they peek out from behind the dazzle of different perspectives and syntactical shake-ups the way bits of a guitar or portrait peek out behind the shattered planes of Picasso's Cubist works.

R is for a Rose, which is a rose, is a rose, of course. It was on her stationery.

S is for Salon. Edmund Wilson correctly described Stein not as the hostess but as the *ruler* of a salon, where ambitious young literary men literally sat at her feet (she sat cross-legged in a renaissance chair, they did the same on the floor nearby). Artists were drawn by the unprecedented collection of modern paintings—no one else with the means to buy such things wanted to. And Stein knew how to cultivate artists: at one large dinner party, she arranged for each artist to sit across from one of his own paintings, which put them all in good moods, except Matisse, who caught on to the trick, and tut-tutted her on his way out the door.

T is for Tender Buttons. See Q, above.

U is for Unconventional. Stein's style was certainly that—in writing (it was necessary for a genius to have a signature style) and in appearance. The Canadian poet John Glassco once wondered if the dress in which he saw Stein appear was in fact a burlap sack, but it was probably just the threadbare brown corduroy she liked so much. Apollinaire reports that Stein would sometimes find herself expelled from more conventional French cafés because of her dress (her sandals were a particular concern to many proprietors), but in the more bohemian venues she was as welcome as in her own salon. As F. Berkeley Smith put it describing the bohemian cafés of Paris, the codes in such places were considerably relaxed. "Should you happen to be a cannibal chief from the South Seas, and dine in a green silk high hat and necklace of your latest captive's teeth, you would occasion a passing glance perhaps, but you would not be a sensation." Add this to the file on why Stein ended up in Paris (see also D, M, and O).

V is for Vichy. It was difficult living in southern France during the war, where cigarette rations were meager for men and nonexistent for women (see also J).

W is for William James, Stein's favorite professor at Radcliffe. She skipped his final exam, writing on the paper that she was not in the mood to take an exam that day. He wrote back that he understood, having many days where he felt much the same. Many people have speculated about James' experiments in the psychology of automatic writing influencing Stein, but no one ever talks about how his theories of genius may have lodged in her mind and conditioned her sense of herself (see N and G, above). Someone should look into this and get back to me about it.

X is for X-Rated, see Q and T, above.

Y is for Youth. Stein claimed she didn't have an unhappy childhood. "What is the use of having an unhappy anything?" she wrote, but without the question mark (see U, above). But her brother described things differently, and she lets slip a few comments that indicate he may have been right. Read some of the stories she wrote at Radcliffe sometime and decide for yourself (see also N).

Z is for Zürich, the birthplace of Dada in 1916, years after Stein's equally radical experiments with language. It took a war to drive Tzara and company to such extremes. All it took for Gertrude Stein was her unshakable sense of genius (see G and see N, see, always, N, N, N, without which none of these letters could appear).

The American Poet as European, or:
Egon Schiele's Ladder

John Matthias is so thoroughly a European poet he could only be American. That is, his poetry is so saturated with European geography, history, and, most importantly, personages from the history of high culture, that a reader coming to it for the first time would see at once an affiliation with Europhile American poets like Pound and Eliot. Like those poets, Matthias spent a considerable period of his life in Europe (mostly England), and like them he has read widely in the poetry of the continent. Like them, too, he takes Europe as a kind of whole, and as a single living tradition—very much an American thing to do, and not at all English, or Spanish, or Lithuanian. Every inch of Europe seems to open out into a richly storied past, and one senses that at least part of his attraction to Europe is that it offers an escape from a perceived American historical shallowness, the sort of thing Harold Rosenberg described when he said that America "builds and acts on a thin time crust—its constructions reach upward rather than down, its politics take account of the immediate future rather than the past."

One thing that the opportunity the three volumes and 900 pages of his collected poems offers is the chance to see the consistent appeal of Europe to Matthias, and to recognize a fundamental pattern in the way Europe plays into the poetry. Despite the serious religious concerns of poems like the 45-page "A Compostella Diptych" (which traces ancient pilgrim routes across France and Spain), Matthias does not seek in Europe a path back to a meaningful religious communion, as did Eliot. Nor does he use the European past as a way to cudgel Americanized modernity, with its preference for mass-produced plaster over artisanal alabaster, as did Pound. Instead, Europe, and especially Europe's past, provides a kind of Archimedean point outside of Matthias' immediate experiences from which he can re-imagine them. From his earliest poems to his most recent, we find Matthias changing his perspective on experiences—often difficult or painful ones—by placing them in the context of distant geographies, remote pasts, or foreign lives.

Even the erotic poetry of Matthias' youth works this way. Consider "What They Say," a short poem written when Matthias was twenty and published for the first time in volume one of the *Collected Shorter Poems*. Grouped with other erotic poems like "Female Nude, Young" and "Swimming at Midnight," it describes the Viennese painter Egon Schiele in his studio, posing his models and friends as "onanistic nudes," then climbing a ladder to a loft to get the odd angle he desired. "And it's the perspective that distorts," writes Matthias, "The ladder and the beds / were Egon Schiele's." while "The postures and / the gestures / were all theirs." It's a simple poem, and very much juvenilia, but in a way it contains the poetic career that would follow for another half century and more. It's not just that Matthias' erotic imagination, here, runs toward the visions of long-dead artists in faraway Europe rather than the proximate body of a lover: it's that the important thing, the thing that makes Schiele more than a pornographer, is his distancing himself from his material, his climbing of a ladder to gain exactly the right point of distance and perspective.

Much later, when Matthias was in his mid-sixties, he would title one of his longer poems "Kedging in Time," and describe his poetic technique of reflecting on the present in the context of the long ago and far away as "kedging," a word for which he helpfully provides a definition:

> [Kedge, v. intr. A. To warp a ship, or move it from one position to another by winding in a hawser attached to a small anchor dropped at some distance; also trans. To warp. B. Of a ship: To move by means of kedging.] Poets, too, may cast an anchor well before them, pulling forward when attached to something solid, only then to cast their anchor once again.

It is this ladder-climbing or kedging that we should bear in mind when we think about Matthias as Europhile, this seeking in things distant a way to move himself in relation to his material.

The technique manifests in many ways. Even when Matthias writes, in "Edward," about the illness of his uncle, he breaks away from painful family experience into an old Scottish ballad, concluding what seemed like a confessional poem with "Edward, Edward, *howe we fear our ain, / Sic counseils O / they give us of mortality.*" The passage of the ballad is apt, in that it speaks of how we feel our own kin (our "ain") when their illness reminds us of mortality. But it makes a difference that the final lines aren't spoken in colloquial American English, but quoted from centuries ago and an ocean away. The old lines take the individual experience of pain and show us that it is shared: they make us less alone. Something similar happens in the poems Matthias wrote during his period of activism against the American war in Vietnam. A series of poems addressing state violence against protestors (Matthias ranked among those who suffered physically at the hands of the police) concludes with "Nightmare After Mandelstam: Who Spoke of the Language Itself." "I see America closing in on my friends," writes Matthias, thinking of his radical friends and the rioting police of Chicago in 1968. It is a poem of terror, in which Matthias fears the "knock at the door" of the house where he cannot protect his wife and daughters, and where he is convinced "they will murder us, simply." It offers no real consolation, especially in its appeal to Mandelstam, the Russian poet who died en route to Stalin's gulag. No consolation, that is, except this: that there is a kind of historical rhyme between the events of the past and the present. Mandelstam's suffering isn't just a sign of suffering and defeat, parallel to the suffering and defeat of Matthias' moment: it offers a way to think about present experience with some distance. The presence of Mandelstam in Matthias' poem does not deny panic and terror: it just allows us to place them far away, to think of our own fears in the way we would think about those of another person's, on another continent, in another time. We can climb up our ladder and look at experience from a distance that is both historical and aesthetic.

Since indirection is our theme, it may be appropriate to gloss this process by turning to Seamus Heaney, a poet Matthias admires, as he quotes and glosses the scholar and psychiatrist Anthony Storr, who in turn quotes and glosses Jung:

In his introduction to Jung's psychology, Anthony Storr gives an account of a case that bears closely upon the situation of the poet in Northern Ireland or the poet anywhere else: Jung describes how some of his patients, faced with what appeared to be an insoluble conflict, solved it by "outgrowing" it, by developing a "new level of consciousness." He writes: "Some higher or wider interest appeared on the patient's horizon, and through this broadening of his outlook the insoluble problem lost its urgency. It was not solved logically on its own terms, but faded out when faced with a new and stronger life urge." The attainment of this new level of psychological development includes a certain degree of ... detachment from one's emotions. "One certainly does feel the affect and is shaken and tormented by it, yet at the same time one is aware of a higher consciousness looking on which prevents one from becoming identical with the affect, a consciousness which regards the affect as an object, and can say "I know that I suffer."

The insoluble conflicts in Matthias' poems are legion—familial, political, medical, Oedipal—but they are outgrown by his turning to higher and wider interests, the moments of the European past that resonate with his personal experiences. The detachment helps. As Matthias wrote in "Bucryus," an early, long, and important prose poem excluded from these volumes, "necessities become conscious, become emotion and thought. The change is the emotion on thought." Matthias cannot change his circumstances or his thoughts, but he can—through a technique we could call ladder climbing, or kedging, or simply finding the historical parallel to the present—change the emotions that attend his thoughts and circumstances.

The poems in volume two of Matthias' *Collected Shorter Poems* remain closer to native soil, but even here we sense the European presence: a poem about the schooldays of Matthias and his friends in Columbus, Ohio, is tellingly titled "Francophiles, 1958." And the technique of the indirect approach to experience with reference to European culture remains in play even where we'd least expect it: the two parts of "Hoosier Horologe," for example, come to the matter of Indiana by addressing T.E. Hulme and Geoffrey Hill, respectively. Sometimes, though, the indirection stays strictly American. "Missing Cynouai," for example, a painfully moving poem about Matthias' estranged daughter, approaches personal emotional loss through memories of Matthias' onetime teacher, John Berryman, and Berryman's poem about his own daughter. One way or another, though, Matthias is still Egon Schiele, climbing the ladder to get to the proper distance.

There is more to Matthias, of course: he has, for example, invented a minor poetic genre. We might take as our model the German term for the novel of an artist's life, the *künstlerroman*, and call this genre the *komponistgedicht*: the poem of a composer's life. Matthias writes poems based on incidents in the lives of a legion of composers, mostly modern and mostly European—Stravinsky, Janáek, Messiaen, Percy Grainger, Shostakovich, Schoenberg, Vladimir Dukelsky, Alban Berg, although he sometimes dips deeper into the past, writing on Berlioz, Haydn, and Schubert. And Samuel Barber shows up to represent the United States.

It is in Matthias' long poems that we see his most extended investigations of Europe: "Northern Summer" takes us to Scotland, "An East Anglian Diptych" to England, "A Compostella Diptych" to France and Spain, and "Cuttings" to Kew Gardens. In each case, the journey is into the past as well. It is hard to say where "Automystifstical Plaice" takes us, except perhaps right into the heart of European and American modernism, via the history of *Ballet Mécanique* and associated events. The most American of the long poems, "Facts from an Apocryphal Midwest," was written almost under duress, when circumstances conspired to keep Matthias in America when he'd rather have been abroad. The poem works, paradoxically, to make Matthias at home in America by making America exotic: it delves into the history of Matthias' region, looking to French explorers and Neolithic travelers as the context for contemporary experience. In this paradox it confirms Matthias' identity as America's leading European poet.

Poetry Ha Ha

Comedy is a funny kind of art: much loved, but rarely held in the highest esteem. Aristotle ranked it lower than tragedy, and the last unambiguously genre-specific comedy to win the Oscar for best picture was *Annie Hall*, in 1977. Comic poetry suffers a similar fate: it is under-represented in anthologies and rarely given systematic critical consideration. But do we even know what comic poetry is? Well, it's poetry, for starters, although the worms that spill out of the can when we ask what constitutes poetry are too numerous to count. As for what constitutes comedy, the theories are a bit more manageable, and fall into three main categories: incongruity theory; relief theory; and superiority theory. All of these are encompassed, implicitly or otherwise, by Henri Bergson's treatise *Laughter: An Essay on the Meaning of the Comic*, which forms the basis of Aaron Belz's theoretical speculations on comedy. If I'm not mistaken, though, Belz warps Bergson's theory in interesting ways, ways that help us understand the very serious intent—and rather dark view of the world—of the comic poetry in Belz's book *Glitter Bomb*.

Theories of comedy are no more comic in themselves than theories of sexuality are sexy. Immanuel Kant, for example, is no one's idea of a comic writer, but he is the great promulgator of the incongruity theory of humor. "In everything that is to excite a lively convulsive laugh," he writes, "there must be something absurd," something that thwarts our expectation, that for some reason just doesn't fit. Kant provides several examples, none of which undermine our sense that he'd make a lousy *Saturday Night Live* host. The least bad involves an Indian dining at the table of a British merchant in Surat, who

> … saw a bottle of ale opened and all the beer turned into froth and overflowing, testified his great astonishment with many exclamations. When the Englishman asked him, "What is there in this to astonish you so much?" he answered, "I am not at all astonished that it should flow out, but I do wonder how you ever got it in."

We (and by "we" I mean "we eighteenth-century Europeans, with our condescending attitudes to other cultures") were expecting the Indian to marvel at one thing, but he marvels at another, and our expectations are dashed. Mikhail Bakhtin makes much of a more specialized notion of incongruity, claiming that comedy is to be found in the treatment of the highly regarded in terms of, or in proximity to, the low and bodily—the transcoding of the one upon the other. Aeschylus's depiction of Odysseus, mid-heroic quest, being conked on the head by a hurled chamber pot presents a case in point, and provides evidence that the practice of comic transcoding existed long before the theory.

For Bergson, though, incongruities of all kinds are incidental to comedy. The core of laughter, he tells us, resides in the principle of something mechanical imposed upon life. We laugh at the absentminded professor putting a tea cozy on instead of his hat because we find it funny that he is on a kind of auto-pilot; we laugh at an orator who predictably thumps the lectern to emphasize each point because of the rigidity of his gesture; we laugh at a pratfall because where we'd hope for bodily gracefulness we see bodily rigidity, and so forth. When incongruity comes into play, it is simply a way of drawing our attention to the still or mechanical nature of things: all solemn ceremonies are ridiculously artificial, but we have become habituated to this, and it is only when something incongruous happens—a graduation speaker in full academic regalia farts audibly near a microphone, for example—that the laughably mechanistic nature of the situation is made evident to our jaded eyes. The situation is doubly funny, since in addition to this, we laugh at the manifestation of bodily needs that appear when a more intellectual or spiritual context is meant to prevail. Bakhtin's notion of transcoding is one way to describe the phenomenon—the farting graduation speaker has made an incongruously low noise at an occasion of high sentiment—but for Bergson, the root of the comic lies deeper, in the way the needs of the body are mechanical, and impose themselves on other aspects of life.

For Freud, the various permutations of laughter are matters of relief: we constantly expend psychic energy, but things that make us laugh relieve us from having to do so, and the excess energy manifests as laughter. Jokes that let us talk openly about sex or various vices, for example, let us stop repressing our forbidden thoughts and urges, and the energy that had gone into repression dissipates in giggles and guffaws. Bergson, too, sees a release of energy in comic situations, but again it becomes a manifestation of his central idea of the mechanical imposed upon the living. What, wonders Bergson, accounts for the affection we feel for comic characters—those laughable characters we surely wouldn't want to be? A part of us, as it turns out, *would* like to be them, because a part of us wants to give up the effort of trying to be gracious and socially acceptable and lapse into the automatism of our urges. We'd like to let ourselves go and be as gluttonous as Falstaff; we have moments when we'd like to stop repressing our anger and scream like Yosemite Sam. A part of what happens when we laugh is that we allow those automatic urges a place: we acknowledge the things we usually repress.

This is not to say that we fully embrace comic characters. Indeed, if Hobbes is correct, the central fact of comedy is our superiority to the objects of our laughter. "The passion which maketh those *Grimaces* we call LAUGHTER" wrote Hobbes in *Leviathan*, occurs either when people experience some sense of self-satisfaction, or "by the apprehension of some deformed thing in another," in either case it is a matter of "comparison, whereof they suddenly applaud themselves." Casting as cold an eye on comedy as he casts on politics, Hobbes maintains that we laugh because we feel better than the people at whom we laugh. Despite his understanding of our affectionate impulses toward comic characters, Bergson sees the truth in this Hobbesian observation: for him, laughter has a kind of cruelty to it—and it is in its very cruelty that its importance lies. In mocking rigidity of mind and morals, comedy encourages the kind of fluidity and adaptability that we need to live well together. It polices against traits that we, as a society, wish to discourage. "Laughter," says Bergson, "is, above all, a corrective" and its function is to "intimidate by humiliating." Those who fail to attain a certain fluid gracefulness—those who allow mechanical habits or automatic urges to take over—will be punished, and laughter is the scourge. At the conclusion of his essay Bergson compares laughter to the delightful froth generated by ocean waves lapping up against the shore—it delights, but is "a froth with a saline base. Like froth, it sparkles. It is gaiety itself. But the philosopher who gathers a handful to taste may find that the substance is scanty, and the after-taste bitter." (We might experience another kind of bitter after-taste when we consider how overwhelmingly male the theory of comedy has been in our tradition—but an amelioration may be underway, especially if the brilliant Sianne Ngai expands her theory of the zany from the study *Our Aesthetic Categories* into a full-scale theory of the comic).

*

Bergson's theory goes a long way to explaining a great deal of poetic comedy. Consider Kenneth Koch's "Variations on a Theme by William Carlos Williams," which riffs on Williams' famous "This Is Just to Say":

> 1
> I chopped down the house that you had been saving to
>   live in next summer.
> I am sorry, but it was morning, and I had nothing to do
> and its wooden beams were so inviting.
>
> 2
> We laughed at the hollyhocks together
> and then I sprayed them with lye.
> Forgive me. I simply do not know what I am doing.
>
> 3
> I gave away the money that you had been saving to live
>   on for the next ten years.
> The man who asked for it was shabby
> and the firm March wind on the porch was so juicy and cold.

> 4
> Last evening we went dancing and I broke your leg.
> Forgive me. I was clumsy, and
> I wanted you here in the wards, where I am the doctor!

Firstly, there's the simple fact of imitability: we are imitable only inasmuch as we are predictable, and our gestures automatic or mechanical. Here, it's less that Williams himself has mechanically gone about writing the same poem over and over, but that two of his poems (this and "The Red Wheelbarrow") have been repeated and anthologized and taught and cited so relentlessly that we come to associate them automatically with Williams, and the recognizable nature of the tropes forms a big part of the comedy. Then there's the speaker's mechanical repetition of similar actions, his refusal to grow or learn ("I simply do not know what I am doing"), which, combined with the way his urges govern him, freezes him into a comic type. For Bergson, the root of our laughter is social, even when we're as far from political satire as we are in Koch's poem. We don't need to be reading Bertolt Brecht's bitterly funny poems about capitalists or T.S. Eliot's early satires of the anemic culture of Boston Brahmins for laughter to function socially. When we laugh, we're policing against the undesirable. In Koch's poem, the implicitly undesirable things include a narrow sense of poetic canon as well as a failure to learn from our actions and the inability to stop our urges from ruling us.

Even something as dissimilar from Koch's poem as Lewis Carroll's "Jabberwocky" makes sense in light of Bergson's theory of the comic. It's easy to be delighted by lines like these, but what exactly makes us smile when we read them?

> 'Twas brillig, and the slithy toves
>   Did gyre and gimble in the wabe:
> All mimsy were the borogoves,
>   And the mome raths outgrabe.

There's a distinction, says Bergson, between comedy expressed by language, and comedy created by language. The first type has to do with actions and scenes, but the second, which is untranslatable, "does not set forth, by means of language, special cases of absentmindedness in man or in events. It lays stress on lapses of attention in language itself. In this case, it is the language itself that becomes comic," rather than anything to which the language may refer. Lewis Carroll's poem traffics in this second type of comedy, in which language seems inattentive to its own content. When a poem gives us absurd words in a well-established poetic form like Carroll's rhythmic quatrain, it isn't merely the incongruity of semiotic disorder and prosodic order that amuses: it is the automatism, the sense of language filling out its regularities (ABAB iambics, here) while forgetting to cohere into meaning. Moreover, the nonsense words remind us of the material body of language as sound, giving precedence to this over the meaning we'd expected—and we're amused just as we are when bodily needs take precedence over more elevated aspirations. We're not all that far from the farting graduation speaker.

The human body, like the body of words, is funny when it draws our attention in contexts where we'd like the moral or spiritual to come to the fore—and so, says Bergson, "we laugh every time a person gives us the impression of becoming a thing." Much of the comedy in Belz's early poetry comes from a kind of deadpan execution of this principle, as we see in "Pioneers at the Foot of the Rockies":

> "Bit of an impasse" says one—
> hardy farm gentleman, six horses
> pulling all his possessions.
>
> "Maybe we head north a while,"
> says another. And just as he says
> it, a fierce wind descends upon
>
> them, and their hats sail away
> into the twilight. "Lost our hats,"
> says one, patiently. "Believe

> you may be right about heading
> north a while," he adds, scratching
> his forehead and chewing a bit
>
> of leather, patiently. "Believe
> you're right," he says, more quietly,
> scanning the horizon to the north
>
> and just as he gets back on his horse,
> another fierce wind comes down
> upon the two gentlemen and blows
>
> away their families and wagons,
> so now it is just them sitting
> on their horses at the foot
> of the Rockies. Says the other, "I
> think we're alone now."

It goes on, leading to a comic homily about the founding of the city of Denver. But it's the fatalism of the men, their automatic acceptance of the loss of their hats, combined with the reduction of their families to mere things, bits of litter blown by the wind, that gives the poem its odd, goofy feel.

Readers of poems like "Pioneers at the Foot of the Rockies" wouldn't be surprised, if they were to delve into a research library's stacks and crack the pages of Belz's unpublished doctoral dissertation, to find that it is the body/spirit dichotomy that most fascinates Belz in Bergson's work. *Something Mechanical: Popular Comedy's Influence on Modern American Poetry, 1900–1960* is a Bergsonian study of comic poetry, its chapters pairing up modern poets with pop culture figures—e.e. cummings with the now-forgotten Henry Wheeler Shaw; T.S. Eliot with Groucho Marx; Gertrude Stein with Charlie Chaplain; and Jacques Tati with John Ashbery. Belz is drawn to the Bergson who wrote passages like this:

... a living body ought to be the perfection of suppleness, the ever alert activity of a principle always at work. But this activity would really belong to the soul rather than the body. It would be the very flame of life, kindled within us by a higher principle and perceived through the body, as if through a glass. When we see only gracefulness in a body, it is because we disregard in it the elements of weight, of resistance, in a word of matter; we forget its materiality and think only of its vitality, a vitality which we regard as derived from the very principle of intellectual and moral life.

"Rigidity, or resistance between body and soul," Belz argues, is corrected through laughter." And the purpose of Bergson's essay, Belz goes on to say, "is to propose an ever-elusive telos for laughter: to reunite body and soul." Bergson's theory of laughter, then, has "a redemptive dimension." Comedy reminds us of just how far from grace and gracefulness we have fallen by providing negative examples: we infer from them what a redeemed condition might be.

This is a strange conclusion to draw from a philosopher whose essay ends with an image of the bitter, saline base beneath the froth of laughter. Certainly there's a telos to comedy: as Bergson sees it, the social usefulness of comedy is what makes it an impure art. But the telos of comedy has to do with the somewhat cruel policing of human behavior, about which Bergson is clearly ambivalent. Belz repositions Bergson—one might even say Belz reinvents Bergson as someone with a more Christian outlook, whose laughter seeks to bring our fallen lives closer to the world of the redeemed soul. In his doctoral dissertation, then, Belz proves himself a true poet, not a critic who writes poetry: the true poet never met a theory he couldn't bend to suit the needs of his own temperament. And Belz's temperament, for all of its goofball, deadpan, witty affect, inclines toward a sense of the fallen nature of the world, and the distant hope of redemption. The blending of this affect with these inclinations is the genius of the poems collected in Belz's *Glitter Bomb*.

*

Robert Archambeau

Life, says Bergson, progresses and evolves. It does not repeat or reverse itself—but when it appears to do so, it seems rigid, mechanical, and comic. Belz applies this principle to language itself, as in these palindromes from *Glitter Bomb*:

Hopkins Palindrome

I caught this
morning morning's
minion, then gushed
glossolalia thus:
"Suh tail a loss
olg deh sug neht!
Noinims gninrom
Gninrom sihth!
Gu aci!"

Famous Palindrome

My girlfriend has a freaking weird name:
Eman Driewgnikaerfasahdneirflrigym.

We're expecting wit, here: a palindrome promises that the reversed letters of the initial phrase will cleverly create a new phrase in the manner of the famous palindrome about Napoleon, "Able was I ere I saw Elba." But instead we get flat-footed repetitions of letters, mere nonsense, and built-in justifications for nonsense as glossolalia's speaking-in-tongues, or as a "freaking weird name." Bergson would see it as a mechanical fulfilling of formal requirements without an accompanying attention to sense—a comedy much in the manner of "Jabberwocky," and like that poem it is essentially untranslatable.

The comedy of *Glitter Bomb* often involves a warping of a received phrase, one of Bergson's classic forms of the comedy in the absentmindedness of language. In fact, Belz seems to have invented a form I call the two- or three-line one-liner, a quick little squishing or mashing of something we've heard a million times (these bump up against the outer border of what some would consider poetry, but if we think of them as drawing attention to idioms as idioms, they stand squarely in the middle of what linguist Roman Jakonson considered the poetic function). Belz's poem "Ice Cream," for example, reads "I scream, you scream, we all scream / when we get stabbed in the heart" and his "Michael Jashbery" mashes up a John Ashbery title with a Michael Jackson lyric "I'm starting with the man / in the convex mirror." The goofiness here cuts against a certain darkness: the literal or emotional pain of "Ice Cream," or the hints at hopelessness in "Michael Jashbery." The Jackson lyric is, after all about self-transformation coming from the insights of self-examination. But what insights, what transformations, can we hope for if our reflection is only the distorted one we find in Ashbery's *Self-Portrait in a Convex Mirror*? The darkness underlying this side of Belz's writing is clear enough in a similar poem, "Team,",: "There's no I in team, / but there's one in bitterness / and one in failure."

The mashing up of familiar bits of language we see in "Michael Jashbery" gets a fuller treatment in "Thomas Hardy the Tank Engine," which also begins to hint at the redemptive urge in in Belz's poetry, its sense of how we can survive bleakness by turning toward the not-quite-serious. To the best of my knowledge, Hardy attempted comedy only once in his poetry, in the utterly ghastly "The Ruined Maid," which rivals Wordsworth's flat-footed failure "The Idiot Boy" as the most powerful evidence that sincere poets of English rural life should keep the comic urge at bay with a pitchfork. Otherwise, Hardy's poetry stuck to the kind of bleak hopelessness that has crushed the spirit of many a reader of *Tess of the D'Urbervilles* or *Jude the Obscure*. And it is to this kind of poetry that Belz appears to pledge himself in the opening stanzas of the poem:

> From now on my poetry
> shall be like Thomas Hardy's—
> I shall write about ponds

and about dying trees

and the sadness that creeps
into love, over time
and that life is absurd
and death sublime.

Soon, though, Belz speaks of the differences he plans on cultivating vis-à-vis his great English model. "But I shall not grow / a broad mustache / and wax it each day," he writes, "or wear a starchy shirt." Nor, he adds, at the poem's end,

shall I bother

to refer to myself as "the tank engine."
People already know
I'm a tank engine.

It's not just the incongruity of the juxtaposition—the tragic author set against the plucky animated train engine from the beloved children's show—that matters here. That certainly plays a big role in the poem's comedy, as does the preposterous suggestion that Hardy called himself "the tank engine." There's also the notion that Belz himself is somehow known as the tank engine—something tough, something unstoppable, but, in the context of Thomas the Tank Engine, something childish and lovable, too. He's as familiar with pain as Hardy (the bitterness and failure Belz jokes about in "Team" are real; the book ends with a poignant evocation of a loss, in which "the last words she spoke" haunt "like a bell / whose peal continues to echo down dreams"). But Belz's characteristic move is to warp the kind of sadness and tragic absurdity that obsess Hardy into something else, something odd and funny, and in so doing give himself a way to endure, if not transcend. If we've been reading Belz's poetry for a while, what he says in this poem rings true: we've seen him depict himself as he chugs on stoically or with a brave smile through various kinds of disappointment and adversity, and in that sense we do already know he's a tank engine.

The divided self haunts the poems of *Glitter Bomb*, a figure both amused and choked with morbid sorrow, a figure in search of some kind of redemption, often an absurd one. This is what we see, for example, in "Song of Myself":

> As usual, I dined alone.
> I went to pay the bill
> and saw a printed sign:
> "We don't split checks."
>
> I told the woman at the till
> that the sad and happy
> parts of me wanted to
> go Dutch today,
> and could she make an exception?
>
> She suggested, "Perhaps
> the happy part could treat."
> I said, "He's broke."
>
> She seemed to understand
> but still refused to split
> the check. I stole
> the toothpick dispenser.

Walt Whitman may be large and contain multitudes, but Belz's psyche only seats two, the happy and the sad man. There's a kind of Groucho Marx charm to the line "he's broke," but what interests me more here is the final sentence: an act of pointless revenge against the universe, an attempt to make things right, to redeem them through misguided external aggression while the real problem goes unaddressed: in his low-key way Belz is giving us the drama of the angry spirit flailing, helpless and petty, no closer to wholeness and happiness than a character of Thomas Hardy's.

It is in the poem "Your Objective" that we see most clearly the nature of the divided self in Belz's poetry, and his sense of the comic as redemptive. It is here, too, that we see how he differs from Bergson about the nature of the comic:

> In a given situation
> Your objective should be
> To act as much like yourself
> As possible. Just imagine
> How you would act
> And act that way.
> A good rule of thumb
> Is, try to be similar
> To who you really are.
> But keep in mind
> That there's no way
> To perfectly replicate
> Yourself at all times.

The comedy here seems Bergsonian enough: the mechanical imposition of something upon life. The imposition, in this case, is of the strict rule to behave as you yourself would, for Belz to impose Belzian actions upon Belz; or for Archambeau to foist Archambeau-identity upon Archambeau, and for the concerned party to police against deviation. The tragedy behind the comedy lies in how we are never able to simply be ourselves, how we fall short of self-identity. And the fall has to do with self-consciousness: when we try to think of what we would do, we are seeing an image of ourselves separate from ourselves, and that very act divides us, makes us non-identical with ourselves. It's an old trope, at least as old as Romanticism's psychologizing of the old myth of the fall when, after eating from the tree of knowledge, Adam and Eve suddenly discover their nakedness, and with it their self-consciousness. So we continue, fallen, self-conscious and divided, unable to "perfectly replicate" ourselves. For Belz, the redeeming quality of comedy has to do with the reuniting of the self—its "ever-elusive *telos*," as he argued in *Something Mechanical*, being the perfect union of our earthly bodies and our eternal souls. Comedy's redemptive dimension lies in exposing division of these things and implying—purely by virtue of the portrayal of the division as ridiculous—that some higher reunion is possible, or at least desirable, to be striven for. Division is (according Belz's logic and Belz's Bergson) beneath us, something to be ridiculed—therefore unity hovers above us, and is something to which we might aspire.

Bergson, of course, saw it otherwise. "A really living life should never repeat itself," he avers, and we are laughable exactly inasmuch as we are imitable. To be ourselves, then, is not so much to achieve unity or self-identity as it is to unfold in ever-evolving diversity. Here lies the misapprehension of Bergson in Belz's critical writing. But if the idiosyncratic reading of Bergson in *Something Mechanical* helped Belz create the sorrow and laughter of *Glitter Bomb*, we're better off for the idiosyncrasy. After all, a poet's criticism is a funny kind of art.

Camping Modernism:
Timothy Yu's Chinese Silences

How does one go about being an Asian-American poet? Surely there are as many answers as there are Asian-Americans who write poetry. But Timothy Yu's answer—in the form of the poems collected in *100 Chinese Silences*—is a particularly powerful one, because it simultaneously involves an embrace of, and a distancing from, the Anglo-American poetic tradition from modernism on. The double gesture of closeness and distance amounts to a form of *camp*, that ambiguous aesthetic category traditionally associated with homosexual responses to popular culture. Indeed, Yu doesn't just show us one possibility for the Asian-American poet's relation to poetic tradition: he shows us a wider sense of camp than we are likely to have known.

An Exile's Letter

Yu's "Chinese Silence #92," from *100 Chinese Silences*, is a rewriting of Ezra Pound's "Exile's Letter." Pound's poem, along with others in the collection *Cathay*, was adapted from the Chinese poetry manuscripts that came to Pound from the scholar Ernest Fenollosa—and like many other poems in *Cathay*, its dominant theme is loneliness, specifically the loneliness of the scholar-poet whose audience consists of his scattered friends, strewn throughout an empire by powerful elites they serve but do not love. It's easy enough to see why Pound was attracted to the Fenollosa manuscripts: he could find, in the circumstances of ancient Chinese literati, enough parallels with his own situation and that of his friends to sense, or perhaps to manufacture, a kind of kinship. Modernist poets, after all, tended to be peripatetic, often expatriated, figures, meeting and parting with their few sympathetic peers, and existing either on crumbs of subsidy and hackwork from the literary establishment or (like Stevens and Eliot) working in some capacity for the materialist financial elites they quietly resented.

One of the things the Fenollosa manuscripts allowed Pound to do was to wax deeply sentimental about his own circumstances as a marginal literary figure far from home, loving art and beauty, meeting and parting from an international and constantly wandering group of the likeminded. He'd been trying to find a way out of the strictures of Imagism, which seemed to have taken him about as far as they could. But how to make broad, sentimental gestures when one has preached austerity, when one has made commitments to the hard, cold world of the image? One way that he'd already explored was the poetic persona, speaking in the voice of another, and the Fenollosa manuscripts gave him a new way to do this. So we get an opening like this:

> So-Kin of Rakuho, ancient friend, I now remember
> That you built me a special tavern,
> By the south side of the bridge at Ten-Shin.
> With yellow gold and white jewels
>   we paid for the songs and laughter,
> And we were drunk for month after month,
>   forgetting the kings and princes.
> Intelligent men came drifting in, from the sea
>   and from the west border,
> And with them, and with you especially,
>   there was nothing at cross-purpose;
> And they made nothing of sea-crossing
>   or of mountain-crossing,
> If only they could be of that fellowship.
> And we all spoke out our hearts and minds ...
>   and without regret.
> And then I was sent off to South Wei,
>   smothered in laurel groves,
> And you to the north of Raku-hoku,
> Till we had nothing but thoughts and memories between us.

There's a gushing of sentiment here that would have embarrassed the man who wrote something as terse as "The apparition of these faces in a crowd; / Petals on a wet, black bough." In the parts that follow there's also a celebration of both friendship and aesthetic delight that certainly resonated with Pound's lived experience, but rarely found straightforward expression:

> And when separation had come to its worst
> We met, and travelled together into Sen-Go
> Through all the thirty-six folds of the turning and twisting waters;
> Into a valley of a thousand bright flowers …
>   that was the first valley,
> And on into ten thousand valleys
>   full of voices and pine-winds.
> With silver harness and reins of gold,
>   prostrating themselves on the ground,
> Out came the East-of-Kan foreman and his company;
> And there came also the "True-man" of Shi-yo to meet me,
> Playing on a jewelled mouth-organ.
> In the storied houses of San-Ko they gave us
>   more Sennin music;
> Many instruments, like the sound of young phœnix broods.
> And the foreman of Kan-Chu, drunk,
> Danced because his long sleeves
> Wouldn't keep still, with that music playing.
> And I, wrapped in brocade, went to sleep with my head on his lap,
>
> And my spirit so high that it was all over the heavens.

In addition to granting Pound license to be publicly sentimental about the things he really was sentimental about, the Chinese persona allowed Pound to defamiliarize the experience of the scholar-poet, the world in which he lived. He could clothe it all in unfamiliar names and places and exotic garb. The kind of experience may have been familiar to those for whom Pound wrote (other modernist poets, a few artists and connoisseurs) but the Chinese context allowed Pound to filter the known through the unknown, and have it come back in

Inventions of a Barbarous Age

a shimmering aura—he could, to paraphrase his pal Eliot, know his circumstances again, as if for the first time.

Timothy Yu Defamiliarizes the Defamiliarization

> To Tom S. of Missouri, possum friend, clerk at Lloyd's.
> Now I remember that you rang a silent bell
> By the foot of the bridge at the River "Thames."
> With dull roots and dried tubers, you wrote poems and laments
> And grew more English month on month, bowing to kings and princes.
> Americans came drifting in from the sea and from the west border,
> And with them, and with me especially
> Everything was pig-headed,
> And I made hay from poppycock and painted adjectives,
> Just so we could start a new fellowship,
> And we all escaped our personalities, without expressing them.
> And then I was sent off to Rapallo,
>   trailed by children,
> And you to your desk at Faber-Faber,
> Till we had nothing but China and silence in common.
> And then, when modernism had come to its worst,
> We wrote, and published in Po-Etry,
> Through all the one hundred kinds of shy and whispering silence,
> Into a poem of a thousand blank pages,
> That was the first heave ...

So begins Timothy Yu's "Chinese Silence #92." What Yu has done, of course, is to transpose Pound's poem, written in the persona of a Chinese scholar-poet, onto Pound's life. So-Kin of Rakuho, the imperial official, becomes T.S. Eliot of Lloyd's bank, Ten-Shin becomes the Thames, and so on. But it's all much more interesting than that. Firstly, there's the matter of the original context from which Pound's poem came. Since "Exile's Letter" was already a transposing of the experiences of Pound and his expat poet friends onto ancient China, Yu's poem isn't just a turning of the text to a new context, it's a returning of the text to its original context. What had been an indirect treatment of Pound's life filtered through the exotic glamor of orientalism becomes, in Yu's poem, a direct treatment of Pound's life, with the orientalism still intact. But the orientalism now seems alien to its subject matter. In leaving the glamorous orientalist style intact while taking away the premise that what we're talking about are ancient Chinese poets, Yu draws attention to the style, to the defamiliarizing moves of "Exile's Letter." He shows us that the poem really is a take on Pound's own life, but a specific kind of take, and he directs our attention to the artifice of glamor.

Yu's spellings "Po-Etry" for *Poetry*, "Faber-Faber" for "Faber and Faber," and later "Ben-it-to" for "Benito Mussolini" emphasize the orientalist artifice of Pound's poem. Chinese names, after all, didn't matter too much to Pound's audience as specific people or places—few could tell you their history and associations. In "Exile's Letter" the names are there as local color, as a kind of intensifier for the artificial Chinese-ness of the poem. And when Yu spells *Poetry*'s name "Po-Etry," he's not really defamiliarizing the grand old literary magazine: he's defamiliarizing Pound's act of defamiliarization. "Chinese Silences #92" is a way of showing us, as if for the first time, the way Pound showed himself and his peers their own circumstances as if for the first time.

But what to make of what Yu hath wrought? What, even, to call the sort of thing we have in "Chinese Silence #92"?

Pastiche, Parody, and Camp

The easiest label to hang on "Chinese Silence #92" is that of pastiche. It is, after all, a brilliant move-for-move replay of the kind of orientalist-modernist persona poem Pound perfected in Cathay. If we look at Fredric Jameson's famous definition of pastiche in *Postmodernism, or, The Cultural Logic of Late Capitalism*, we seem at first to be dealing with exactly the sort of thing represented by Yu's poem: "pastiche," writes Jameson, "is, like parody, the imitation of a peculiar or unique, idiosyncratic style, the wearing of a linguistic mask, speech in a dead language." But then there's this, Jameson's critique of pastiche as apolitical: "But it is a neutral practice of such mimicry, without any of parody's ulterior motives, amputated of the satiric impulse, devoid of laughter." Indeed, for Jameson the proliferation of pastiche in the postmodern period represents nothing more than "the play of random stylistic allusion."

If pastiche is devoid of laughter, if its choice of old styles is random, and if pastiche is devoid of ulterior motives, especially political ones, then Timothy Yu's poem is no kind of pastiche. But should we, then, call it parody? Not in the simplest sense of that word, as a mocking imitation intended to undermine or delegitimate something—but perhaps in the subtler sense outlined by Yu's former colleague Linda Hutcheon in *The Politics of Postmodernism*. There, Hutcheon tells us that a certain kind of postmodern parody "both legitimizes and subverts that which it parodies." This captures much of what Yu's poem attempts. The subversion we understand—but what about the legitimation? Consider this: Yu's poem doesn't set out to re-ground Chinese-American writing in a tradition untainted by orientalism. It isn't an Asian-American version of, say, *négritude*, the African and African-diasporic movement to build a culture based not on Eurocentric models but on African traditions. Instead, Yu attacks the orientalism of modernism from within, reworking a modernist poem until we see it from a different angle. The poem doesn't set out to dislodge Pound and Eliot from the canon—if anything, "Chinese Silence #92"'s focus on the minutia of the lives and works of those poets re-enforces the reader's sense that he or she ought to know about them, if only to be in on the joke. When Hutcheon wrote that postmodern parody "manages to install and reinforce as much as undermine and subvert the conventions and presuppositions it appears to challenge" she might as well have been writing about Yu. And when Hutcheon tells us that a primary trope of postmodernism is to "de-naturalize some of the dominant features of our way of life; to point out that those entities that we unthinkingly experience as 'natural' … are in fact 'cultural'" her words could describe Yu's goal in foregrounding the way Pound invents a kind of sentimental Chinese identity as a way of expressing his own circumstances with an aura of exotic glamor—Yu won't let us forget that Pound hadn't tapped into the essence of Chinese writing so much as he'd concocted a formula useful for his own (Western) purposes.

Hutcheon's notion of postmodern parody doesn't fully capture the relation to Pound's modernism that we find in "Chinese Silence #92," though. One thing the dynamic of reinforcing/undermining she outlines doesn't really address, for example, is the question of affection. And as powerful as Yu's poem is in unmasking the artifice or orientalism, it is also a poem with a great deal of overt affection for modernism (an affection, needless to say, intertwined with critique).

Consider the loving piling up of modernist minutia. Yu's poem shows a tremendous intimacy, even an obsession, with the lives, the poetry, the prose, and the milieu of Pound and Eliot—and the intimacy isn't motivated by malice. The two are shown as capable of the virtue of friendship, for example, and while Yu is rightly unsparing about Pound's politics, the Pound that emerges in "Chinese Silence #92" is not so much a demon as a figure of pathos, even when being judged for his actions in the war:

> And our Roosevelt, who was brave as a rodent,
> Was president in Washing Town, and let in the usurious rabble.
> And one May he sent the soldiers for me,
>   despite the long distance.
> And what with broken idols and so on, I won't say it wasn't hard going,
> Over roads twisted like my brain's folds.
> And I was still going, late in the war,
>   with defeat blowing in from the North,
> Not guessing how little I knew of the cost,
>   and how soon I would be paying it.
> And what a reception:
> Steel cages, two books set on a packing-crate table,

And I was caught, and had no hope of escaping.

The image of Pound's twisted brain gives us a figure driven mad by events and ambient cultural hatreds, a lost and damaged figure caught and caged—and the poem ends with a similarly pathetic figure:

> I went up to the court for prosecution,
> Tried standing mute, offered a madman's song,
> And got no conviction,
>   and went back to Saint Elizabeths
>   Committed.
> And once again, later, you stood at the foot of my bed,
> And then the visit ended, you went back to Bloomsbury,
> And if you ask if I recall that parting:
> It is like the hair falling from my hieratic head,
>   Confused ... Whirl! Centripetal! Mate!
> What is the use of talking, until I end my song,
> I end my song in the dark.
> I call in the nurse,
> Hold the pill in my hand
>   As she says, "Take this,"
>
> And swallow it down, silent.

It's not an endorsement of Pound—far from it—but the gaze with which Yu looks at Pound and Eliot is as much affectionate as it is distanced and judging. And that kind of combination is best described not so much as parodic but as camp—especially when, as in Yu's poem, it is accompanied by a foregrounding of mannered style.

Christopher Isherwood's *The World in the Evening* is the *locus classicus* for the theory of camp, and the attitude it describes seems to coincide exactly with Yu's attitude toward modernism:

> High camp always has an underlying seriousness. You can't camp about something you don't take seriously. You're not making fun

of it; you're making fun out of it. You're expressing what's basically serious to you in terms of fun and artifice and elegance.

Yu isn't mocking Pound in the sense of making fun of him—the poem is too humane for that, and the pathos of some of the passages indicates that something other than simple mockery is at play. But the poem is certainly making fun *out of* Pound and his poem. Camp's classic queer form, drag, allows people to both participate in an identity and distance themselves from it, to have affection for that identity while also drawing attention to the artifice involved in creating the identity, and Yu's poem can be seen as a camp take on modernist orientalism—taking part in, but also drawing attention to the artifice of, its style and discursive movements.

It's no wonder that Timothy Yu has a complex relationship to Pound's "Exile's Letter." His identity as Chinese American, and as a professor of Asian-American studies, puts him at an odd angle to the poem's presentation of Chinese identity, and draws his attention to the artifice by which Pound constructs, rather than discovers, that identity. At the same time, though, Yu is himself a poet-scholar, one who has led a peripatetic life in several countries, one who travels for reunions with likeminded scholar-poets and reaches out to them by correspondence. He is certainly someone who, as a state employee in the reactionary Governor Scott Walker's Wisconsin, feels at odds with the power elites with whom he is nevertheless connected in complex and subordinated ways. He is, in short, both distanced from and intimately close to the attitudes and experiences embodied in "Exile's Letter." What else to do with that old modernist poem, then, but to camp it up—as Yu does brilliantly?

Ambiguous Pronouns Are Hot:
On Rae Armantrout

> They're sexy
> because they're needy,
> which degrades them.

So begins "Soft Money," one of the best poems in Rae Armantrout's *Money Shot*. It's representative of many other poems in the book for several reasons: it connects to sex and the body, it connects to money (the "money shot" of the title refers to the male orgasm in pornography) and it can be a bit slippery about just what it refers to in the world.

One of the more impressive things about "Soft Money" is the way it exploits the ambiguity of reference. Who, one wonders, are "they," those sexy, needy people? It's easy to read the poem as a piece of gender politics, with the "they" as either men yearning, sexually, for women, or as women, yearning to be noticed by the male gaze. In either case, the poem seems to say that there's something nasty going on: either it's women looking on men's neediness as pleasing because it puts women in a position of power, or it's men looking on the way women deck themselves out for the male gaze and settling smugly into a position of superiority, as the catered-to gender. And these are just the hetero- readings. So already we've got a kind of broad statement about how the field of sexual attraction is a place where desire is bound up with power, and people are more than willing to enjoy their positions of superiority over the self-degrading other. It's a nasty view of the world, hard and cold, but it's delivered with a kind of abstractness and deadpan matter-of-factness that makes it read very differently than, say, the works of the Marquis de Sade.

The poem continues by working variations on the theme announced in the opening stanza:

> They're sexy because
> they don't need you.
>
> They're sexy because they pretend
> not to need you,
>
> but they're lying,
> which degrades them.
>
> They're beneath you
> and it's hot.

The first proposition here takes the sexualization of power that we saw in the opening stanza and reverses it: those who turn away from us are sexy, because they're so above us. We seek them out because, we think, their lack of neediness for us indicates that they're something special. Desire is inflamed, Petrarch-style, by inaccessibility. Interestingly, this is just as plausible as the opposed proposition of the opening stanza. But just as we're about to settle into this new version of events, Armantrout undermines it: they only pretend not to need us, these ambiguous people (women? men?). And their "I don't need you" act is a sign of how much they really do need us, how they're trying to intrigue us. Which means they're in some sense beneath us—and once again Armantrout uses the strong term "degrades" to indicate this beneathness, and suggests that we're attracted to people when they make us feel like we're in the superior position. It's all a bit like the old Hegelian master-slave dialectic, with its co-dependency of the slave, who fears and labors for the master, and the master, who needs the recognition of the slave to maintain his sense of himself as an empowered agent in the world.

The title of the poem both re-enforces and undermines readings of the text that present it as concerned with the politics of sexual desire. The poem's title, "Soft Money" re-enforces that meaning best when we read it against the title of the book, *Money Shot*. If the money shot of the book's title indicates masculine sexual performance, "Soft Money" would seem to imply a kind of failure of that kind of potency—a masculine disempowerment that plays into reading the referent for the word "they" as "men" (who are, in this reading, desiring but disempowered—which would make the speaker of the poem a bit of a power-tripping misandrist figure, whether female or male). Such a reading is certainly available, but the poem can't be reduced to just that. The title-based reading is suggestive rather than definitive. One could still read the speaker as a smug male figure gloating over the power of the male gaze to make women objectify themselves.

But even these readings, in tandem, are too limited—because soft money is also something specific in the realm of politics. It's the common term for the unlimited monetary donations rich people and corporations can make to American political parties (as opposed to individual candidates). And this opens up a whole new way to read the poem. Suddenly, we can read the needy people as the political class, and the speaker as the corporate class, the loose affiliation of millionaires and billionaires (to borrow Paul Simon's phrase) that buys the deference and loyalty of politicians from both major parties. And now the smug speaker looks on the politicians as sexy because needy—a kind of condescending attraction. And when we read the degradation of that ambiguous "they" as the degradation of the elected officials of what is nominally a republic, we feel the degradation as a betrayal of what the politicians should be—representatives of the people.

The middle of the poem introduces something new:

> They're across the border,
> rhymes with dancer —
>
>
> they don't need
> to understand.

I like these lines, in part because of the rhyme, in part because they can be read as a kind of comment on the interpretive possibilities the poem has already laid out for us: "border" is a political term, "dancer" is more connected with eros and desire, and the two "rhyme" conceptually—that is, in the context of this poem, they've got some deep similarities. The political and erotic readings are both available, and the poem shows us the kind of smug attitudes that can come with being empowered in either realm. As for "they don't need / to understand"—well, that's got a double edge to it. On the one hand, it could be read as an expression of the (politically? erotically?) empowered person condescending to the disempowered people. On the other hand, it could be read as something like "they don't go around needing us as a rational thing, as a means of understanding—it's all more primal than that."

The next part riffs on the old Archibald MacLeish poem "Ars Poetica," with its famous contention that "a poem should not mean but be":

> They're content to be
> (not mean),
>
> which degrades them
> and is sweet.

Read in terms of the "this is a poem about eros and power" paradigm, these lines seem to say something about the disempowered people in the equation being mere objects, not subjects who have opinions and might "mean" something. That sort of lines the poem up with a male speaker, looking on "them" as self-objectified women, the kind of people who'd hang around high-status men and be ornamental, rather than being full participants in a conversation. But when we come to the next stanza, where the disempowered people are described as "sweet," the speaker's idiom is more feminine—"sweet" is a word some women apply to men who do things for them to ingratiate themselves without much hope of any kind of reciprocation. So the ambiguity of who "they" are continues to allow us to see the speaker as either a smug male or a smug female in a position of erotic superiority. But there's also the political way of reading the lines, the "soft money" paradigm for reading the poem. Looked at this way, the lines can be read as a condescending statement from those in the realm of economic power toward their political subordinates, who are happy to walk around being people with titles like "Senator," but who defer to their funders in matters of opinion and policy and don't mean to have any opinions of their own.

The next lines work with some Kantian or Sartrean philosophical language:

> They want to be
> the thing-in-itself
>
> and the thing-for-you —
>
> Miss Thing —
>
> but can't.

The disempowered people (men? women? politicians beholden to moneyed interests?) want contradictory things, here. They want to be independent ("the thing-in-itself") but they also want something from the erotically or financially empowered, and want it so badly they would change who they are to get it (becoming the "thing for you"). Those dashes—the most ambiguous form of punctuation—are great, because they allow "Miss Thing" to function in two different ways. "Miss Thing," a slang expression for the sexually provocative and desired woman, can be the person the disempowered people, men, want: they become the thing-for-you, with you being "Miss Thing." But "Miss Thing" could also be the disempowered woman, the self-objectifying person, the one who became a "thing-for-you."

And then we come to the ending:

> They want to be you
> but can't,

Robert Archambeau

>which is so hot.

The disempowered want to be the empowered, but can't, and this pleases the empowered, because they get to experience themselves as in an enviable position, a position they find arousing. I love that the final line echoes Paris Hilton's characteristic phrase, since it comes off as nasty, shallow, self-indulgent, and privileged—which works well for any of the myriad interpretations the poem proposes. Which is hot.

If I Were A Freudian This Essay Would Be Called "The Mother's Penis":

A Note on Daisy Fried

Of all the contemporary poets I've never met, I feel closest to Daisy Fried. I've been reading her forever, and we both spend too much time hanging out on Facebook. One reason I feel closer to her than I do to many of the poets I read is that we both have small daughters, and post about them with some frequency. Actually, the fact that we're both on Facebook so often, rather than dizzily pouring ourselves off some barstool somewhere, or climbing to Machu Picchu, is also probably a parent thing. So it was with particular delight that I read a poem of hers about parenting, "The Girl Grew and Grew, Her Mother Couldn't Stop It." In the end, though, it's a poem about more than parenting: it's an intervention into a world of symbols and motifs that disempowers daughters, and an attempt, in its small way, to make things right.

The poem's first line captures something very true about being a parent: "The girl grew and grew," writes Fried, "her mother couldn't stop it; it terrorized." The phrasing seems like something out of a horror story—where some kind of Frankenstein's monster grows too strong for its master and runs amok. But the terror here is subtler: it is the primal terror of losing one's small child to adulthood, which is also the inevitable result of successful parenting. They grow up, these children, and they grow away from you—and you, acutely aware of their vulnerability, let them go.

What follows is, for a time, a nicely-drawn and keenly observed catalog of children's experience, a world of play and crafts and school projects, behind which we sense the child's ravenous acquisition of skills and symbolic codes—geometry, biology, systems of writing, fine motor skills, and the like:

> What would the finger-dance do? Kindergarten art a buffet
> of markers

> gluings of stuffs to seasonally-keyed paper, Elmer's pools drying clear.
>   A stapling and testing of cylinders versus spheres versus cubes
> for kinetic and entropic possibilities, stuffing balled newspaper
>   into paper dragons, two sweet silver elephants with heads too small
> and trunks too long, situated off-center, snuffling flowers. And silver rain.
>   And 16 silver hearts stacked vertically and strips of masking tape, colored
> in reverse rainbow. Unnamable tendrils diffusing to scribbles. A bird.
>   Another bird, more rain, peace signs, a horse with sideways-flowing mane ...

All quite interesting, but one wonders, reading this, where the poem might go, how, if at all, the poem will turn. And then we find this:

> and knowledge: that the sky's full of blackstruck Ms and Ws, drifting
>   clouds; that her kitty cats watch sunsets; sky doesn't reach down to meet the earth;

We get a bit of a generalization, after all those particulars ("knowledge"), and we get a sense of the child's difference from the adult: the sky isn't represented according to the canons of adult realism.

The real volta, though, is yet to come. It arrives only at the poem's conclusion, with an end-word that turns the poem so sharply in a new direction that I'm surprised the page doesn't emit an audible shriek of squealing tires:

> mother shrinks to the size of a penis.

What to do with this? There is, of course, a literal dimension to consider: we're dealing with a child drawing something, and in that drawing the mother could indeed be the size of a penis. We are also invited to think about the diminishing importance mothers play in a child's life as that child grows up—the same diminishment that was so terrorizing at the beginning of the poem. But one could have said "doll" or "crayon" or, for that matter, "vagina." Why say "penis"? It is an incongruously masculine word to apply to the diminishing role of the mother.

Surely one thing that's at play is simply surprise and novelty: it's an incongruous image, by virtue of being so masculine in a poem about motherhood, but there's a rightness in it too, in scale and in having to do with reproduction and therefore parenthood. There is, too, the powerful sense of disempowerment that you wouldn't get, at least not in the same way, with another image. The penis is so connected to connotations of power that whole schools of psychology, from Freud to Lacan, use the term "phallus" to mean something like "empowerment" and "castration" to mean "disempowerment." We get a sense of the mother's disempowerment as the child, through all of the innocent and sweet seeming play and craft-making detailed in the poem, grows beyond the mother's control—and putting the word "shrinks" near the word "penis" gives us a sense of the detumescent loss of power or potency.

There's more than this, too: there is also the simple fact that the penis, here, becomes not just another iteration of the traditional symbol of power and potency: it becomes an image of smallness and disempowerment. There's something feminist in this, a reversal of the old Freudian model of masculinity as power and femininity as disempowerment. In a way, then, the poem isn't just a mother's lament for her loss of authority in the life of her growing child. It's that same mother's intervention in the realm of symbolism, aiming to undo some of the patriarchal imagery that still contributes to the disempowerment of women. It's a mother's attempt—as her daughter gains independence—to make the world that daughter will enter into a place less hostile to her. The mother works hard to help the daughter grow into strength and knowledge and independence—and, in the end, she also works to make the world itself a place better fit to receive that daughter.

Poetics of Embodiment

Quick, what do these things have in common? A Mexican man sewn into a car seat as a way to confound American border guards; the published prison memoirs of leftist German revolutionaries; the destruction of ancient statues in Iraq. Most people would struggle to find the connection, and the task of linking disparate things would only be compounded if we threw in the nine tracks of a Joy Division concert recording; the packaging of that recording and its bootleg copies; the rubble where two great statues of the Buddha once stood in Afghanistan; and Andy Warhol's interminable, experimental film *Sleep*. But the connections between these things are clear enough to Karl Larsson: they all provide rich material for meditating on embodiment, on the way bodies, artworks and texts enter the material world and maintain or lose a presence there.

It shouldn't surprise us, given these concerns with spatial experience, that Larsson is both a poet and a visual artist. As a sculptor and installation artist he has exhibited extensively in Europe, especially in his native Sweden, and taken a keen interest in both the physicality of texts—the palimpsest, or erased and written-over piece of writing is a favorite theme—and the way bodies interact with environments. One piece from a 2012 show consists of a bronze human head half-submerged in the gallery floor, evoking both a drowning person and a monument in the process of being unearthed. Like Marcel Broodthaers, the Belgian poet and artist who died in 1976, a year before Larsson's birth, Larsson is also a great explorer of the institutions that mediate our experience of phenomena—especially the "paratext," or writing that accompanies the main text of a book or the objects in a gallery exhibition. ISBNs, publication information, explanatory notes, tables of contents, indexes, as well as the conventions of visual layout and display—all of these are important to Larsson, because they act as containers for words and objects, and affect the way those things are received in the world. "One usually distinguishes between base and statue / pedestal and bust," he writes, but he refuses to separate such things: text and context, object and environment, are always a single phenomenon to Larsson: the format of a book determines our relationship to the text just as surely as the pedestal determines where we stand relative to the sculpture.

FORM/FORCE, published in Swedish in 2007 and belatedly available in English, is the first of Larsson's five books of poetry, and makes for a strong introduction to his characteristic themes. "What Andreas Baader Said," the first of the book's four sections, begins with quotations from the memoirs of the Baader-Meinhof group, the far-left revolutionaries who terrorized Germany in the 1970s. Larsson shows us how the specific typography of their writing expressed their desire to convert words into force, to give form to themselves as a radical collective entity. Certain phrases in their writings are always capitalized ("THE PIGS," "THE STRUGGLE GOES ON") and when they wish to stress the importance of a word, they apply special spacing on the page ("w a r," "t o g e t h e r"). Their idiosyncratic textual conventions serve to unite them as a special group with a special way of communicating. But the group cannot control the way their writing enters the world. Larsson uses the paratext common in book catalogs to emphasize the way Andreas Baader's writing, embodied in a book, leaves the context of revolution and becomes subjected to the rules of commerce:

> a book has a front, a back,
> spine, cover, pages
> or as the sales people write:
> rear board
> spine
> dust-jacket (dj)
> first free end paper (ffep)
> (purple) cloth binding
> etc.
>
> "spine clearly worn from reading.
> dj sunned, with tiny tears"

Larsson shows, too, how the embodiment of Baader's words in a book makes them subject to the law, describing the destruction of Baader's publisher by lawsuits regarding his book's international copyright. Much like the revolutionaries themselves, who die in prison, possibly at their captor's hands, books come across as terrifyingly vulnerable by virtue of their embodiment as physical entities. All the while Larsson remains neutral on the specifics of Baader-Meinhof politics—a coolly objective writer, more of a curator of found text than one who emotes in words.

But I've simplified "What Andreas Baader Said" too much, because it does more than explore the capturing of the revolutionaries in their cells and of their ideas in the pages of a book. It cross-cuts the Baader-Meinhof material with documents and descriptions from two disconcerting incidents: a man forcing his body into the interior of a car seat to cross illegally the U.S.-Mexican border, and the looting and destruction of Mesopotamian antiquities following the American invasion of Iraq. The human body contorts itself to evade the forces of power, and the embodiment of an epoch's worth of human imaginative aspiration crumbles as the great tectonic plates of power shift around it. Again, we see the terrible vulnerability of embodiment, the fragility of all things in a world of careless power. We see how the force of borders, laws and economic need can give new, demeaning form to the human body; and we see how geopolitical force destroys aesthetic forms we may have mistakenly taken for permanent.

The musical performance is one of the aesthetic forms we don't tend to think of as permanent. What could be more transient than waves of sound passing through the air? In the second section of *FORM/FORCE*, "Documentation/Performance (1980)/Re-Listening (2007)," Larsson examines the idea of musical performance as both an embodiment of its moment and as something embedded in multiple kinds of commemoration: recordings, memoirs, online fan discussions, and so forth. Larsson takes *Licht und Blindheit*, a 1980 seven-inch vinyl limited release by the post-punk band Joy Division, as his source text. The record, something of a fetish object among fans, was made on April fourth, 1980, at one of the band's final live shows, and Larsson is at pains to show us what a recording can and cannot capture. *Licht und Blindheit* gives off many signs of authenticity, from the capturing of an unknown voice before the show starts muttering "*right, we all start when the drum machine kicks in, lads*" to an unpalatable shout of "*sieg heil*" from a fan at the end of the performance (showing how a performance can be kidnapped into a context unintended by the performers—like many punk-affiliated acts, Joy Division attracted an unwelcome fascist fringe element to its shows). The band itself, in Larsson's version of events, was setting out to document a moment, to give form to the transient:

> the group attempts
> to articulate four four
> nineteen hundred and eighty
>
> the material is so charged
> that it revolts within the document
> and appears as raw, white sound

The very force of the performance shatters the attempt to tie the moody, angry-sad performance to the Thatcherite moment in recession-ridden Manchester.

Larsson juxtaposes the band's attempt to make their performance into a document of their moment with later attempts to document the performance itself. He examines the extensive fan discourse about the concert, addressing those things that can't be preserved—the loudness of the event, the press of bodies—and those that can, such as the importance of the band to a generation of largely working-class youth ("joy division convinced me," said one fan in an online forum, "I could spit in the face of god"). Larsson examines, too, the elaborate packaging of the recording and the various bootlegs of that copied it, including one so accurate that it was only revealed as a fake when the low quality glue used in the originals began to destroy the sleeve—an occurrence that raises interesting questions about authenticity and archival endurance. What is the status of the performing arts in the age of mechanical reproduction? What to make of a fake that is, in a sense, truer to the original than the original itself? How to feel about a self-destructive flaw that is also the sign of originality?

There's a subtle analogy in "Documentation/Performance (1980)/Re-Listening (2007)" between the flawed authentic recording and Ian Curtis, Joy Division's singer, who suffered from epilepsy and depression, and who hanged himself mere weeks after the *Licht und Blindheit* recording. In both cases, a deficit of some sort became, for fans, a signifier of authenticity. Larsson goes on to contrast the kind of hanging that destroys people—Curtis' suicide, and the hangings of dissidents in Afghanistan's Mazar-i-Sharif and in Germany's Stammheim prison, where the bodies of members of the Baader-Meinhof group were found—with another kind of hanging, familiar from Larsson's own work as an installation artist:

> for an artist the word hanging
> has the significance of (to hang paintings)
> to install an exhibition
> and put everything in place, to complete

We're invited, here to think about the strange irony of the documentation of moments of all kinds, including artistic performances: to what degree are they admirable tributes that extend the life of the moment, and to what degree are they entombments and (possibly grotesque) distortions of that which was once alive?

The book's remaining sections, "Enemy/The Red Shadows/In the Valley" and "Awakened from *Sleep*," continue the investigation of context and embodiment. The first of these sections addresses the destruction of two giant, ancient Afghan statues of the Buddha by Taliban artillery. That sad story is, as Larsson tells it, really several stories: a tale of religious intolerance, certainly, but also a tale of the inevitable destruction of all bodies, be they flesh or stone. It is, too, the tale of a world as indifferent to human suffering as it was enraged by the destruction of artworks. Larsson is always attuned to the way ideas and beliefs become embodied, and the way those embodiments interact with different explanatory and discursive contexts—sometimes, as in the case of the Afghan Buddhas, destructively. In "Awakened from *Sleep*" Larsson examines a less tragic instance of the process, looking at the way Andy Warhol's ideas about media culture led to the filming of poet John Giorno's body as it slept, and at how the representation of Giorno's body on film became a touchstone for a whole series of aesthetic controversies.

Larsson collages documentation about migrant smuggling and Middle Eastern political violence throughout *FORM/FORCE*, showing how both of these things contort and destroy the fragile human body. The juxtaposition of these scenes with his other material underlines the importance of the question of how bodies interact with power. Like another book addressing similar themes in a more specific context, Claudia Rankine's *Citizen*, *FORM/FORCE* presents few conventionally beautiful or musical poetic phrases. Like *Citizen*, it takes the book as a whole, rather than the individual poem or prose poem, as the unit of composition. The force of this kind of writing works on us not in the individual detail, but in the accumulation and juxtaposition of incidents. This kind of writing—from Larsson, from Rankine, or in a book like Craig Santos Perez's *gumá*—has emerged as an important poetic medium for meditations on the vagaries of bodies, power, and dispossession.

V
On Criticism

Hating the Other Kind of Poetry

1. This is not a how-to guide

It isn't quite a how-not-to guide either, but I suppose that's closer.

2. "What you *should* be doing," or: the limits of disinterest

A few years ago, when the Conceptualist poet Kenneth Goldsmith was making big waves in the little demitasse cup of the American poetry world, I wrote an essay that tried to explain what his work had to offer and what it didn't. The email I received in response was gratifying in quantity, if bewildering in content. I'd tried merely to describe Goldsmith's work, but I found I was condemned for having praised him, praised for having condemned him, praised for having praised him, and condemned for having condemned him—all in roughly equal measure. The uniform distribution of responses on the chart of praise and blame gave me some reassurance that my attempt at mere description hadn't unintentionally become a clear act of advocacy or disapproval, but it also confirmed my suspicion that people were not particularly inclined to view as innocent an essay that did its best to remain neutral: an agenda, the thinking went, must lurk just below the surface. I am not so naïve as to believe that truly disinterested inquiry is possible, but the notion that we may approach disinterest asymptotically—like a curving line that comes ever closer to another line without ever touching it—was clearly alien to a literary audience that had been through several decades of the hermeneutics of suspicion. Only M, a critic from whom I had learned a great deal over the years, and who had always been kind to me, saw the essay for what it was, or tried to be—and she didn't like it. "What you *should* be doing," she told me, "is making a strong case for the poetry you believe in, and against the poetry you don't." She'd been doing exactly that for decades, and I knew people who revered her for it. I also knew people who all but spat when they said her name.

3. "That never works," or: pluralism and failure

It wasn't the first time I'd been told something like that. Back in the final decade of the last century, when I was starting up a little magazine devoted to poetry, I received much helpful advice from K, a poet and critic who, like M, had long championed the more experimental wing of poetry. I was young and dewy-eyed, and had the usual delusions about what a little magazine might accomplish. "What I really want to do," I said, over coffee in some dingy university café, "is make a space for different kinds of poets to come together and talk to one another." "Yeah," said K, my senior by a decade and a grizzled veteran of the long march of experimental poetry from the wilderness into the academy, "that never works."

Years later, long after the fate of my magazine had proved K right, I was in touch with him again, this time after the early death of another poet, a tremendously charming American who'd moved to London and written formal verse in traditional rhyme and meter. He and K had been friends in their grad school days—"dope-smoking buddies, mostly," as K put it—but had, despite a few joyous reunions when all arguments were put aside, fallen out over poetry. They hadn't seen each other in years, and the news of the poet's death hit K hard. "I always thought there'd come a time when all these poetry wars would be behind us, and we'd be friends again" he told me. I didn't know what to say.

4. "I find your paper irritating," or: looking at the back of your own head

I don't remember what I said, and that's not what's important anyway: what's important is the aftermath. I was standing rather smugly before an audience at an academic conference where I'd just delivered a paper on a poet of some repute, fielding questions along with the other panelists, when I saw the formidable white mane of C rise above the crowd. A scholar whose elegant suits and forceful manner gave him an aura closer to that of a Mafioso than one would have thought possible for a professor of literature, C did not look happy, and he was looking at me. "I find your paper irritating," he said. "Don't misunderstand: I liked the other papers more, but didn't find them interesting enough to be irritating. Come to think of it, I didn't find your paper interesting either—it's the nature of my irritation with it that's interesting."

In the well-crafted spoken paragraphs that followed, C took my paper apart, but he did much more than that: he also disassembled his own reaction to my paper, pulled out the assumptions behind that reaction, held them up to the sunlight and saw what was beautiful and meaningful in those assumptions, and what was narrow and even cruel. It was magnificent. With the possible exception of the time an esteemed English editor took a cricket bat to some of my prose and beat it into a wet pulp from which he then formed a proper essay, C's takedown of my paper remains my favorite literary chastening. It also showed me something one could do with a text that wasn't advocacy (it was about as far from advocacy of what I'd said as one could get) and wasn't simply condemnation either. Nor was it disinterested or neutral explanation, of the sort I'd tried to supply in my essay on Goldsmith, and it certainly wasn't any sort of pluralistic live-and-let-live move, either. In the encounter with an irritating text, C had taken a step back and seen not only the irksome text in front of him, but seen himself looking at it. It was as if he stood behind himself, looking at the back of his own head. *Ekstasis*, the ancient Greeks called it—standing outside oneself. It was C's interpretive ecstasy, and we watched in wonder.

5. "That fucking Merwin," or: the back of Creeley's head

I know a lot of people who loved Robert Creeley, who saw the old sage of Black Mountain and Buffalo as a generous mentor and friend, and he certainly was that. He may turn out to have meant more to more younger poets than any other figure of his generation. But if you read his letters, you see that he had as large a capacity for hatred as he had for paternal or avuncular love. He despises Theodore Roethke and Louis Simpson, hurls abuse at Helen Vendler, spews bile in the direction of Louise Glück and Charles Wright, dismisses Kenneth Koch as a lightweight, and talks about cutting Frank O'Hara (the editors of the letters work hard, in a footnote, to explain this away as metaphorical, and may be right). "Fuck him," he says of Kenneth Patchen, and he tells us how "that fucking Merwin" is a "a symbol of rot." He clearly sees battle lines drawn between a kind of poetry he admires and the kinds he does not, and he takes exception when the people who should be on his side appear to cross the line and embrace the enemy. "I will never forget this," he writes to Kenneth Rexroth, when the older poet treasonously supported Roethke; and when William Carlos Williams spoke approvingly of W.H. Auden, Creeley demanded to know whether someone had held a gun to Williams' back. Academics have a special place in Creeley's inferno—even after so many of them had come to accept his views about who the important poets were. In 1985, he tells us that academics wouldn't deign to write about Williams or Olson—and does so with such vehemence that I wouldn't want to have been the one to tell him of the half dozen prominent academic articles on Olson that year alone, or the three dozen on Williams, or of the professor who'd just edited the sixth volume of Creeley's correspondence with Olson. Resentment outlives its occasion, and those who harbor it don't want to be reminded of the fact.

When I've mentioned this vituperative side of Creeley to his old friends and allies, they've been quick to point out that Creeley and the poets he supported were for a long time—and in some quarters are even now—the subject of a disdain every bit as strong as that which we find in Creeley's letters. They're not wrong, these friends of Creeley. You won't find as much invective about Creeley and his peers in the letters of those about whom he snarled, except perhaps in recent years, but that's simply because silence is the snarling of the powerful.

What, I wonder, would Creeley have seen if he'd looked, not at those he despised, but at himself looking at them? What if, like C, he had seen himself from outside himself? I suppose he'd have seen a man in something like the condition Pierre Bourdieu describes when he discusses what happens to an art when it is no longer playing for stakes beyond art itself in any meaningful way—when there are few significant financial, political, or ecclesiastical rewards at stake, when it operates at the margins of money and power. Under these conditions, it is the practitioners of the art itself who hand out the rewards, and while those rewards may be in some minimal sense matters of money or power or hierarchical position, they are primarily matters or recognition. No one's been made a lord for poetry since Tennyson, and no one hoping for riches nowadays would present a poem to a head of state, as Edmund Spenser did—successfully—to Elizabeth I. Bourdieu tells us that when the practitioners of an art become the primary decision makers about who gets the (largely symbolic) rewards, we see a phenomenon called "the social aging of art." This is a process in which one group—generally marginal, young, or both—seeks to discredit those who practice the art differently. One doesn't compete for money in a commercial market, but for prestige in a symbolic market, and the way to do that isn't to woo customers, but to discredit the other guys. It's no accident that the proliferation of manifestos and aesthetic dogmas came about at the moment when complex developments in mass education, publishing, and communications rendered poetry unviable as a market commodity. Freed from external demands—another way of saying "left to fend for themselves"—the poets proliferated styles and frequently looked with disdain at those whose work took a different path than their own. "That fucking Merwin," one might utter of another.

6. Conquistadors and anthropologists

The Polish philosopher Leszek Kołakowski once wrote with apparent sympathy of a group of people who believed fervently in their own ideals and disdained those of others, saying:

> A few years ago I visited the pre-Columbian monuments in Mexico and was lucky enough, while there, to find myself in the company

of a well-known Mexican writer, thoroughly versed in the history of the Indian peoples of the region. Often in the course of explaining to me the significance of many things I would not have understood without him, he stressed the barbarity of the Spanish soldiers who had ground the Aztec statues into dust and melted down the exquisite gold figurines to strike with the image of the Emperor. I said to him, 'you think these people were barbarians; but were they not, perhaps, true Europeans, indeed the last true Europeans? They took their Christian and Latin civilization seriously; and it is because they took it seriously that they saw no reason to safeguard pagan idols; or to bring the curiosity and aesthetic detachment of archeologists into their consideration of things imbued with a different, and therefore hostile religious significance. If we are outraged at their behavior it is because we are indifferent, both to their civilization, and to our own.'

Kołakowski was, however, playing devil's advocate—since, for him, the better angels of European civilization were not the conquistadors, but the anthropologists. "The anthropologist," Kołakowski writes,

must suspend his own norms, his judgments, his mental, moral, and aesthetic habits in order to penetrate as far as possible into the viewpoint of another and assimilate his way of perceiving the world. And even though no one, perhaps, would claim to have achieved total success in this effort, even though total success would presuppose an epistemological impossibility—to enter entirely into the mind of the object of inquiry while maintaining the distance and objectivity of the scientist—the effort is not in vain. We cannot completely achieve the position of an observer seeing himself from the outside, but we may do so partially.

Like the scholar C after he heard my irritating paper at the conference years ago, when confronted with that which is alien to our sensibilities we may make the attempt to stand outside ourselves, and in doing so see something other than an object of disdain. Indeed, we may get a kind of doubled or even tripled vision: we'll know the thing we're looking at—a poem, say—on something like it's own terms, as well as on ours. Moreover, we might discover something about our own assumptions—our assumptions and, one hopes, ourselves.

7. The potter's wheel and the back of my own head

When I wrote "one hopes" in the previous sentence, I suppose what I really meant was "I hope." But why hope for this kind of approach to poetry, as opposed to the naked partisanship of M or of K? Perhaps the explanation is generational: both M and K are older than I am, and I'm deeper into middle age than I care to admit. The names I recognized among those who wrote to praise or blame me for my article on Goldsmith belonged to an older set, too.

Perhaps as the memory of the exclusion of one sort of poet from the privileged world of academe becomes less a living thing, and more a matter of history, the rhetoric of partisanship will fade. Creeley could still feel marginal even after he was a Chancellor of the Academy of American Poets and a leading figure in the best-funded poetry program in the country, but that was because his formative experiences were those of a truly marginalized outcast. Nowadays, when I read screeds against the Poetry Foundation by full professors at top MFA programs, I suspect what I'm seeing are the last embers of the old fires of outsider resentment. The revolution of the young against the old and the new against the outmoded described by Pierre Bourdieu—the revolution that launched a thousand manifestoes and set anthologists at one another's throats—was the product of a climate of resource scarcity. When there were virtually no external rewards for poets, or when the few rewards (steady teaching jobs, say) are monopolized by a single group (let's call them the poets associated with the New Criticism), partisanship could rage, resentments flare, and those who wrote poetry different from one's own could very easily be cursed as lightweights and symbols of rot. But when academe has long since made room for poets as diverse as Rae Armantrout ,Billy Collins, Claudia Rankine, and Kenneth Goldsmith, it's harder to rage convincingly against a monolithic establishment. At least it is for the moment: perhaps the crumbling of the academic humanities will give us a renewed outbreak of heartfelt resentment.

Maybe, though, it's not generational: maybe it's just me. When I ask myself why I resist M's injunction to fight for the kind of poetry I find appealing, and against those kinds to which I am not immediately drawn, the first thing I think of is not my generation, or those coming after me. The first thing I think of is my father, bent over his potter's wheel. Dad is a ceramic artist, and I spent my pre-teen years as an art-school brat of the 1970s—or, to be more precise, as a *provincial* art-school brat of the 1970s, dad being a professor at the deeply rusticated University of Manitoba. What this means is simple: I saw a lot of abstract painters, earthwork sculptors, conceptual artists, installation artists, photorealists and post-minimalists jockeying around for fame and position, hoping like hell to get themselves off the Canadian prairies and back to the American east coast or at the very least to L.A., the kind of cultural centers from whence they'd come. My father had made the opposite move, leaving the faculty of the prestigious Rhode Island School of Design for the boondocks, in part because, like all ceramic artists (and unlike those post-minimalists and conceptualists), he harbored no illusions about becoming any kind of art star. Outside of Japan and a few other Asian cultures, there's simply no prestige to pottery, and no amount of raging or resentment will change that. Creeley could go from the outside in, railing at his enemies all the way, but there's a notable lack of revolutionary rhetoric among ceramicists, who experience the climate of non-recognition as a permanent condition, not as an injustice to be combatted. Most of our attitudes are absorbed from our environment without much conscious reflection on our part, and I imagine my distaste for battles about aesthetic recognition and campaigns against forms of art different from one's own comes less from all those grad school hours reading Bourdieu and Adorno than from seeing my dad roll his eyes at the rhetoric and ambitious yearnings of his colleagues.

Whether the resistance to partisan polemic is a matter of generational and institutional change, or simply a matter of my own peculiar formation, I don't know. I do know that my own resistance to polemic is strong enough that I don't even want this essay to be an advocacy of one approach to poetry over another, although at some level I suppose it inevitably is. What I want this essay to be is less a program than an examination—an attempt to look directly (and impossibly) at the back of my own head.

The Work of Criticism in the Age of Mechanical Recommendation

1. What is a critic for?

And do we need them (anymore)?

2. Your recommendations ...

When I go to online to buy a book, Amazon is quite good at providing me with recommendations, with no critic required. They do it using algorithms based on what I've already purchased and rated, and on other things people who also purchased those books bought and rated highly. Right now it suggests Rebecca Makkai's short-story collection *Music for Wartime* (which I want to read); McKenzie Wark's *Molecular Red: Theory for the Anthropocene* (which I want to read); Juliana Spahr's poetry collection *This Connection of Everyone with Lungs* (which I have read and admired), and the final book in Dav Pilkey's Captain Underpants saga (which I want to read—to my daughter). The accuracy with which they can predict my buying habits, if not exactly my taste, testifies that when we consider the act of criticism, we must now consider the work of criticism in the age of mechanical recommendations.

Sentimental attachments to the ideal of criticism aside, if the critic can't do more than tell us "you'll probably like this," the critic is likely out of a job.

3. "Is it good?" vs. "will you like it?"

Of course critics have long predicated their authority on the idea of answering questions larger than "will you like this?" In the eighteenth century David Hume drew a distinction between what he called "the argument of sentiment" and the question of taste. The argument of sentiment, he wrote, took as a given that discussions of taste were simply discussions of individual preference. You like Milton, I like

Marlowe, and that's the end of it. But what we're really discussing, then, aren't the qualities of *Paradise Lost* or "The Passionate Shepherd to His Love"—we're discussing ourselves, and our individual affinities and distastes. If you believe in the argument of sentiment, you can't really say whether one book is better than another. But if you know someone's predilections, you can predict, with some confidence, what that person might enjoy. "This is good" is beyond you, unless you're simply using it as shorthand for "I know a thing or two about you, and think you'll like this."

Amazon's algorithms are great aficionados of the argument of sentiment. But for Hume, the real critic doesn't rely on this way of judging. A proper critic really does want to say something about the object in question, rather than about the subject who will like or dislike it. The critic matters, because his or her (well, *his*, for Hume) judgment comes from due consideration of the aesthetic object, from sensitivity of perception, and from familiarity with many other objects of the same kind. How do you get to be a Humean critic? Practice, practice, practice. The sensitive, experienced critic knows what good art is because he knows how to judge, and has earned that authority. This is still the principal upon which many critics base their authority: "I've been reading poems carefully every day since you were in diapers, kid, so trust me: this is a good one, and if you're not feeling it, that's because you're missing something I'm not. Try harder."

Kant comes at things a little differently, but ultimately his game is the same as Hume's: he'll tell you we can distinguish the beautiful from the ugly not through some specific formula (the regularity or irregularity of a poem's meter, the ratio of one drawn line to another) but because we can figure out which acts of judgment are better than others. If we're letting our moral sense interfere with our judgment, we're not making a good one (the pyramids may have been built through the exploitation of slaves, but that doesn't make them failed monuments, for Kant—and *Triumph of the Will*, while an evil film, doesn't necessarily make it devoid of beauty). If we admire a poem because we're in love with the person who wrote it, we're also making an impure judgment. Only to the degree that we screen out personal connections, moral evaluations, and a sense of whether the art in question will work good or ill in the world, are we truly making a judgment of beauty. For Kant, the screening out of all these impure elements makes for a proper judgment of whether something is truly beautiful, and we can hypothetically (and perhaps only hypothetically), arrive at such pure judgments.

Beauty, though, isn't necessarily the standard by which things ought to be judged, at least not to many thinkers of our own time. Fredric Jameson, for example, distinguishes between taste (which is personal), analysis (which links a work's formal qualities to its historical moment) and evaluation (which "interrogates the quality of social life itself by way of the text or individual work of art"). The best critic, for Jameson, moves beyond individual preference and beyond scholarship. The critic sees the artwork as a symptom of the social system that gave rise to it, and makes an evaluation of the justice or injustice of that system based on the evidence of the artwork. Thus the aesthetic critic becomes the social critic, a creature we may find, for better and for worse, in many a faculty lounge across the land.

The experienced critic; the pure-minded critic; the politicized critic: each of these does something different, and something more, than saying "you might like this." But so do the machines, nowadays, at least a little.

4. The critics and the audience

When you go online to see if a movie has been well-received, the sites you are most likely to visit will break down the reaction into two categories: the reactions of critics and the reactions of audiences. You'll see the percentage of critics who thought highly of a movie, and the percentage of audience members who responded positively. Often the two numbers are similar, but at times they are at variance: sometimes you see a movie that was the critic's darling despised by general audiences, or vice-versa. The machines that assemble and present this system of dual ratings are making a distinction between the different types of appeal movies can have. Pierre Bourdieu, who measured reactions to artworks in much the same way that online algorithms do—by counting them—understood well the phenomenon of people appreciating different art for different reasons. He draws a distinction between "the pure gaze" that looks primarily at style, formal elements, and composition, and appreciates novelty; and its opposite, "the popular aesthetic," which wants want to participate in the artwork, to identify with its protagonists emotionally, to hate what the work hates and love what it loves and revel in the victory of truth and love in the final chapter of the book or the final scene of the movie. Bourdieu wasn't interested in saying one way of appreciating art was better than another, but he was interested in who looked at things what way. And what he found, after years of empirical study, was something very like the online movie rating systems division of the critics and the audience.

What do we get from Bourdieu's studies, or from the online movie sites? Not the critic's traditional "this is good, trust me." Nor simply "you might like this." We get something like "this movie is good for this way of looking at things, but not for that way of looking at things." If you're wanting a critic's pure gaze experience, this movie may let you down, but if you want what the popular aesthetic wants, break out the popcorn. We've moved to some kind of third ground beyond "this is objectively good" and "this is something you will like." Now we're looking at "this is good *for x*, but not so good *for y*."

5. To criticize the critic

One thing a critic can do in the age of mechanical recommendation, other than insist on the pure or practiced nature of his or her judgments, or the acuity of his or her political evaluation of the artwork, is this: the critic can do a better and subtler job of understanding what a particular piece of art or writing is good at, and what it doesn't do so well.

For this task, the critic needs to turn not to the qualities of the artwork itself, or not only to those, but to the way the artwork interacts with the critic's own sensibilities. When you, as a critic, react well or poorly to the work of art, you can go beyond recording this, and listing the pleasing or displeasing qualities of the object—you can take your own positive or negative reaction *as the text to consider.* When you analyze the whole phenomenon of the meeting of you and your circumstances with the object, you interrogate the result of that meeting: what was it about my expectations and standards that was delighted or disappointed by the work, and what does that tell me—not only about the work, but about the limits and significance of my habitual responses? Sometimes, if this is your practice, the works you find insignificant, ugly, offensive, or banal can be the most revealing, in that they expose the frontiers of your own sympathy, and can perhaps help in expanding them. The critic will understand, as well as judge, and will be able to say "the work is good at affirming these sorts of values, and not good at affirming those other values—and my judgment does the converse." This gives the reader more than mechanical recommendations can currently give us, except in the crudest and most rudimentary form. And it has the potential to liberate the critics from the tyranny of their own tastes. When we follow this path—which is not the only path, to be sure—the critic's sensibility (practiced, pure, political, or otherwise) becomes an object of analysis, rather than an iron law.

The Avant-Garde in Babel

The critic Per Bäckström begins his essay "One Earth, Four or Five Words: The Notion of the Avant-Garde Problematized" by telling us that theoretical terminology wears out and needs, periodically, to be regenerated. This is fitting, because the idea of linguistic entropy is one of the core notions of Renato Poggioli's treatise *The Theory of the Avant-Garde*, the misinterpretation of which serves to illustrate Bäckström's point about the degeneration of our terminology for avant-garde art. Bäckström's essay points out the ways terms like modernism, postmodernism, and avant-gardism lose much of their precision as they circulate through different linguistic contexts. I'm happy to see him dispel much of the confusion wrought by different national uses of similar terms, and happy, too, to see that some of the apparent disagreements about avant-gardism have been little more than misunderstandings based on different definitions of terms. I'm not quite sure how to feel about how easily these different uses can be traced onto our existing map of national stereotypes, though. In Bäckström's convincing and well-documented exposition we find laid-back denizens of the Latin America and the Mediterranean countries, happily accommodating a wide range of aesthetic activity under the broadly catholic, easy-going and somewhat imprecise rubric of (variously) "avanguardia," "vanguarda," or "vanguardia." We also find uptight and precise Germans, Teutonically policing the firm boundary between high-culture modernism and utopian avant-gardism. And we find befuddled Americans with undeveloped political consciousness confounding modernism with avant-gardism (and sometimes with postmodernism), all the while bumbling through a world whose languages they can't be bothered to learn.

If I have anything of value to add to his analysis, it is by way of pointing to two or three areas where some refinement may be possible. Specifically, I would suggest further interrogation of what is meant by the idea of a politicized, utopian avant-garde, and an exploration of the complex relationship that has developed between avant-gardism and the institutions of art and literature. One could also broaden the scope of thinking beyond an analysis of the relationship between modernism/postmodernism/the avant-garde, on the one hand, and mass culture, on the other. There would be much merit, for example, in an exploration of the relationship between all of these and what I'll call traditional bourgeois high culture.

The Bäckström Schema

The four or five terms Bäckström refers to in his title are modernism, avant-gardism, vanguardia (and its variants in the different Romance languages), postmodernism, and the neo-avant-garde, which I take to be his fifth, and somewhat less emphasized, term. Bäckström sees modernism as a term used in the Germanic and Anglo-American traditions to indicate an aesthetically experimental kind of art that defines itself by its rejection of popular culture's kitschiness and clichés. The avant-garde, in the precise usage of German theorists like Peter Bürger, refers to a movement that combined aesthetic and political radicalism, seeking to regenerate life by eliminating the boundary between art and life. In this view the avant-garde is less worried about maintaining a distance from popular culture than is modernism. The neo-avant-garde, for its part, simply tries to extend the project of the avant-garde into different historical circumstances. Although there has been much ink spilled in arguing over the definition of postmodernism, Bäckström finds its most useful definition to be one based on its complex relationship to modernism and popular culture, a relationship we could perhaps best see as a dialectical progression beyond the thesis of pop culture and its antithetical negation by modernism, since postmodernism contains within itself the formal experimentalism of modernism, even as it refutes modernism's distaste for pop culture (Bäckström, I should point out, is above such simple Hegelian triads, but I am not, and I extrapolate this definition from his detailed exposition). Vanguardia and its variants are terms from the Romance languages that refer to a range of experimental literary and artistic activity, including both anti-pop-cultural forms and politicized forms.

One indicator of the precision of Bäckström's schema is the ease with which it can be visualized. One could construct a Cartesian coordinate system based on his schema, with the terms politics and pop culture are at one end of the X and Y axes respectively, and their negations at the other. The overall field depicted would be that of artistic experimentalism in general, and one could plot the coordinates of the movements designated by Bäckström's terms thusly:

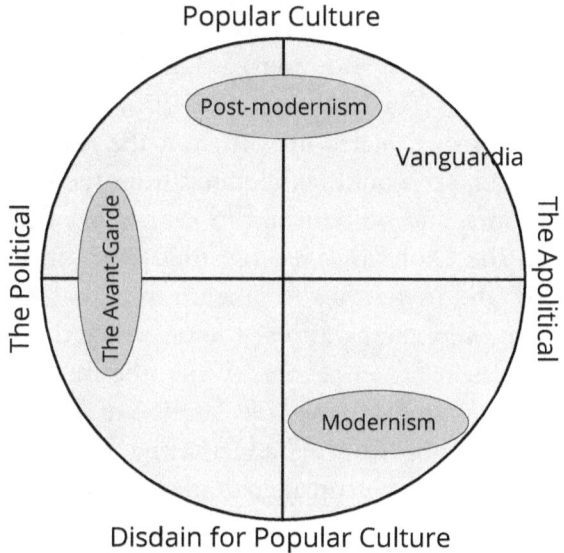

One could, of course, quibble about particular instances, or argue about areas of overlap. But you get the picture.

Art as Life, Art as Revolution, Art as Exhibit

It is right to insist on the Germanic tradition of maintaining a distinction between a primarily aesthetic and apolitical modernism, on the one hand, and a politicized avant-garde, on the other. But some further distinction between the kinds or degrees of political radicalism within the avant-garde seems desirable, especially since debate over the scope of the avant-garde's politics proved so divisive within the historical avant-garde itself. To assert that the avant-garde advocated a radical, utopian vision of the future is to mask the division between two forms of utopianism: one predicated on the belief in ending the division between art and life brought about by the institutions of art, and the other predicated on a the identification of the avant-garde project with political revolution.

Utopianism of the first kind is the subject of Peter Bürger's influential *Theory of the Avant-Garde*, in which he tells us that by the 1920s "the social subsystem that is art" has entered a phase of self-criticism, and rejected "the status of art in bourgeois society as defined by the concept of autonomy." The problems, in this view, were the institutions (such as art museums) and the discourses (such as literature) that walled art off from the rest of life. If these could be destroyed, art would be liberated from the stifling world of aesthetic autonomy, and be returned to the realm of life in general. In 1920, when the Dadaists exhibited their work in Cologne with hatchets nearby, and invitations to take up those hatchets to destroy the exhibits, they were taking aim at the reverence that shrouded art and set if over against life in general. When the Bureau of Surrealist Research issued its manifesto, the "Declaration of January 27, 1925," it boldly declared that Surrealism had "nothing to do with literature," and was certainly not to be considered anything so trivial or literary as a poetic form. There is a politics to this, and in some sense it does call for a revolutionizing of daily life. But this is a very different kind of politics from that advocated by the revolutionary parties whose specters stalked Europe in the early decades of the twentieth century.

The historical avant-garde of the 1920s was torn asunder by disputes about how closely they should identify their activities with those of political revolutionaries. André Breton, for example, asserted the inherent identity between surrealism and political revolution, and eventually he united with Paul Éluard and others in condemning Antonin Artaud for limiting his sense of revolution to the war against aesthetic institutions. Breton attacked Artaud for "seeing the Revolution as no more than a metamorphosis of the soul's inner conditions ..." and failing to understand its essential unity with projects of Marxist revolution. Examples of this kind are legion in the debates of the historical avant-garde, and can be found in postwar neo-avant-garde circles as well (one thinks of Situationism). Given the contentiousness within the historical avant-garde about whether the politics of the movement should be aimed at the problem of art and life, or extend to an identification with leftist political revolution, it is unfortunate that our descriptive terminology fails to reflect the division.

One wonders, too, if it might be unfortunate not to have a more precise understanding of the evolving historical relationship between avant-gardism and the institutions of culture. It is certainly true that institutions like museums, galleries, literary anthologies, academic departments of art and literature, and the like are still with us, having withstood the assaults of the avant-garde. And it is equally true that these institutions have absorbed the very avant-gardes that challenged them, to the point where Peter Bürger can complain "the demand that art be reintegrated in the praxis of life within the existing society can no longer be seriously made." There is a great irony in reading a statement like this, from the National Gallery of Art's archive commemorating their 2006 Dada exhibition:

> 448 works in a wide range of media, including collages, assemblages, photographs, prints, drawings, paintings, posters, films, and audio recordings were presented in this multimedia installation that traced the history of the Dada movement.... Audio recordings of sound poems by Hugo Ball, Kurt Schwitters, and Raoul Hausmann were played in listening chambers, and selected short Dadaist films were shown in a continuous loop in a special viewing area within the installation. An audio tour was narrated by National Gallery of Art director Earl A. Powell III and others.

The idea of a special viewing area is anathema to the movement that despised the institutional separation of art from the bustle of life, and unless Earl A. Powell III was present during his narration, and visitors were equipped with wet sponges to hurl at him, the spirit of the movement that invited viewers to take axes to artworks was deeply violated. Even such resolutely anti-institutional neo-avant-garde practices as Allan Kaprow's Happenings (and his later Activities) have fallen prey to the institutions of art they were designed to challenge and circumvent. These participatory and deliberately spontaneous and ephemeral entities have been filmed, documented, and embalmed by the Museum of Contemporary Art in Los Angeles, whose Kaprow exhibit is called (apparently without irony) "Art as Life."

One of Bäckström's most intriguing points is made only briefly and in passing, when he addresses Bürger's sorrow at the devouring of the avant-garde by the institutions of art. Noting that Bürger didn't seem to understand that the very idea of art had "imploded after the assault on art as an institution put forward by the historical avant-gardes and their 'inheritors' in the 1960s," Bäckström implies that in very the process of devouring the avant-garde, the institutions were changed by them. My sense is that this is entirely true, and that comparative research into the goals, structure, and function of the institutions of art would reveal that they were deeply changed through the encounter with, and absorption of, anti-art movements of the avant-garde. Research into this area—not only with regard to the visual arts, but with regard to such literary institutions as anthologies, academic syllabi, and the like—would be of immense interest, and would go a long way to showing us the different contexts and different functions of the prewar historical avant-garde and the postwar neo-avant-garde.

The Z Axis

I'll end with one more indication of how an analysis of the avant-garde could be extended. It seems to me, as I look at the chart I've drawn of his schema, that there's another axis, along with the axes denoting engagement with pop culture and politics, that could be drawn: an axis indicating the relationship between vanguard activity and the tradition of bourgeois high culture. It is certainly true that we can make some useful distinctions between, say, modernism and postmodernism based on their different relationships to popular culture; but it seems probable that we could find other, equally useful distinctions between and within such categories as modernism, postmodernism, avant-gardism, neo-avant-gardism and the like based on the relationships these movements have to the tradition of high culture inherited from the nineteenth century. Indeed, given Bäckström's deep familiarity with Andreas Huyssen's work on modernism, it is surprising that he doesn't follow up to any appreciable degree on Huyssen's observation that "both modernism and the avant-garde always defined their identity in relation to two cultural phenomena: traditional bourgeois high culture ... but also vernacular and pop culture." It is possible that the distinction will simply break down into a modernism that sought to preserve the bourgeois tradition (whether it be through a Poundian desire to make it new, or an Eliotic project of letting the dead poets of tradition speak through the contemporary work) and an avant-garde that sought to destroy that tradition (as in Marinetti's call for the immolation of Venice, and the desecration of its statuary). But one imagines significant national variations in this regard, possibly across the modernist/avant-gardist divide. How could, say, an educated German of the early twentieth century, raised with the idea of a redemptive Schillerian high culture as a birthright of his class, not differ from an American of similar background, raised in a culture saturated with liberal-utilitarian disdain for such culture? Wouldn't the relationship of such culture to fundamentally oppositional cultural formations such as the avant-garde appear different to them?

I am not prepared to offer the public a new schema of terms, be it of two, three, or some larger number of dimensions of Cartesian co-ordinates. But if you come across me in a bar or coffee house, you're likely to find me doodling many-dimensioned charts on whatever napkin or scrap of newsprint sits ready to hand. There is no end to the making of schemata.

Fanaticism! Intolerance! Disinterest!
Toward an Aesthetics of Camp

Camp remains one of our most poorly theorized aesthetic categories. It has a certain status in queer theory circles, to be sure, but is rarely a part of a more general discussion of aesthetics—in effect, it is a ghettoized term. The continued centrality of Susan Sontag's "Notes on Camp" shows how narrow the discussion of camp has been: her important but provisional notes remain the most authoritative poetics of camp we have. I don't propose to offer, here, an aesthetics or poetics of camp. But if I may use a term so ponderous and out of keeping with the lightness of camp that it practically comes out the other side as camp itself—I do hope to offer a prolegomenon to such an aesthetics or poetics. If camp calls for fun and elegance, I fear I will provide precious little of either—and, since I am confessing shortcomings, I suspect I will provide less by way of evidence and argumentative coherence than one might wish. What I do hope to offer, though, is a rationale for understanding aesthetic experience in terms of camp, and a sense of what is at stake in camp as a category of aesthetics. It is through an aesthetics of camp that we can go beyond a dichotomy that has long divided the aesthetic field into a dominant Kantian tradition based on dispassionate, Apollonian contemplation and disinterest, and a reactive counter-tradition based on (to take some words from Asger Jorn) "fanaticism," "intolerance," and a Dionysian disavowal of disinterest. Both the dominant tradition and its other lie open to forms of ethical and political criticism from which an unlikely hero—camp—promises deliverance.

The Liberal Vision: Aesthetics and the Habit of Disinterest

Among the inheritors of the Kantian tradition of aesthetics, which views aesthetic experience as a matter of disinterested contemplation, Schiller is the most explicit in describing the historical conditions that motivate the appeal of this kind of thinking to his generation, and among the greatest defenders of the tradition from a political or ethical standpoint. He composed the letters that made up *On the Aesthetic Education of Man* over several years in the mid-1790s, during the reign of terror and its aftermath in France, and to a great extent they are intended as a response to the challenges and pitfalls of republicanism and democracy. "Is it not at least unseasonable to be looking around for a code of laws for the aesthetic world, when the affairs of the moral world provide an interest that is so much keener?" he asks near the beginning of his inquiry. He provides an answer almost immediately, telling us that aesthetics are no mere frivolity in times of revolutionary bloodshed, because "we must indeed, if we are to solve that political problem in practice, follow the path of aesthetics, since it is through Beauty that we arrive at Freedom. Aesthetic disinterest, he goes on to argue, will aid us in the peaceful dispersion of political power.

In *On the Aesthetic Education of Man* Schiller approaches aesthetics through a theory of a two-sided human nature. The first part of our nature consists of what Schiller calls the *stofftrieb* or *sinnestrieb*, a kind of sense-oriented self-interest, a collection of appetites and desires. The second part of our nature is the *formtrieb*, something like our reason, but more specific: it is our drive to impose order on our experience, to create moral and conceptual systems. Neither of these parts of our nature should be allowed to dominate the other, lest we become imbalanced creatures. An excess of *stofftrieb* without *formtrieb* would either reduce us to mere appetites (think of Charles Dickens' image of the industrial workers of *Hard Times* as nothing but hands and stomachs), or turn us into monsters of self-interest, exerting a Nietzschean will to power over our rivals. For a creature of *stofftrieb* all is interest and nothing disinterest: something exists for him "only insofar as it secures existence for him; what neither gives to him nor takes from him, is to him simply not there." If we become creatures of *stofftrieb*, we may be curbed from dangerous behavior by the agents of law, but we will experience this law "only as fetters," neither understanding the law's rationale nor respecting its agents when we can avoid or overpower them.

The inverse situation, in which we have an excess of *formtrieb* without sufficient *stofftrieb*, is no better. Without an appreciation for the senses and the particularities of the material world, the man of *formtrieb* becomes "a stranger in the material world." Worshipping only his abstract system, he will be a figure as disconnected from quotidian existence as the scientists of Laputa in Swift's *Gulliver's Travels*, and a monster as ruthless as the Robespierre who so terrorized the opponents of his revolution during the years when Schiller composed *On the Aesthetic Education of Man*. One imagines Schiller may have had Robespierre and the other bloody-handed *philosophes* of France in mind when, describing the man in whom *formtrieb* triumphs over *stofftrieb*, he wrote that such an "abstract thinker very often has a cold heart."

For Schiller, human development follows a tripartite pattern, in which we leave our initial unselfconscious life as creatures of *stofftrieb*, pass through a phase when we are overly-governed by *formtrieb*, and finally become fully integrated creatures, in whom both urges are fully developed and fully reconciled. We are capable of such reconciliation only through the cultivation of a third drive, the *spieltreib* or play instinct. Man is "only Man when he is playing," writes Schiller, because it is only play that allows for a full recognition and engagement of both the senses and the urge for rules and order. The whole person is recognized and fulfilled in play. And play is most fully available to us through art, because the "cultivation of beauty" will "unite within itself" the "two contradictory qualities" of our nature. Art will, by its sensuous embodiment in its medium, "secure the sense faculty against the encroachments of its freedom" by the *formtrieb*'s desire to reduce everything to definitive order (anyone who has ever felt that a poem must not mean but be, or that a painting is not reducible to its description, has lived a Schillerian moment). Conversely, art will by virtue of its orderliness or engagement with pattern rescue us from "the power of sensation" alone. We will, in making or appreciating works of art, become for the first time our whole selves.

For art to function as the reconciler of our divided nature, we must approach it with disinterest. If we turn to art seeking to a particular moral or ideological point, or for some particular useful purpose—be it ecclesiastical, financial, didactic, or political—it cannot be the site where we reconcile our divided drives. "Beauty gives no individual result whatever ... it realizes no individual purpose, either intellectual or moral" writes Schiller, "it discovers no individual truth, helps us perform no individual duty" and when we have appreciated it, nothing specific has been accomplished except that the appreciator "has had completely restored to him the freedom to be what he ought to be," an integrated being. Content itself should be of no importance in the work of art, because

> In a truly beautiful work of art the content should do nothing, the form everything; for the wholeness of man [the *stofftrieb* and *formtreib* together] is affected by the form alone, and the individual powers by the content. However sublime and comprehensive it may be, the content always has a restrictive action upon the spirit, and only from the form is true aesthetic freedom to be expected.

It is in fact form that reforms man: the work of art's inner balance is more important than any specific goal, statement, or function. The disinterested, formalistic appreciation of an art autonomous of specific purpose gives us the opportunity to balance our drives, and so distances us from both cold reason and blind self-interest. When, therefore, we discover in a person "traces of a disinterested free appreciation of pure appearance," says Schiller, "we can infer some such revolution of his nature and the real beginnings in him of humanity."

The experience of the aesthetic is, in Schiller's view, of vital importance in making us fit for the modern world of liberal democracy. Aesthetic experience can prepare us to be citizens of a democratically reformed state because aesthetic experience is the surest means of enabling us to transcend the individual material self-interest represented by the *stofftrieb*. If he is to freely choose to enter into a democratic state, habituation to disinterested contemplation is absolutely necessary: it is the path for liberation from mere self-interest. "This much is certain" says Schiller, "only the predominance of such a character among a people can complete without harm the transformation of a State according to moral principles, and only such a character too can guarantee its perpetuation." Disinterested aesthetic experience, it turns out, makes for good liberal citizens. Or so the theory goes.

Excitement, Fanaticism, Intolerance: Rising from the Sepulcher of Disinterest

The tradition that runs from Kant through Schiller and beyond is not without dissent: Nietzsche, for example, represents a major force in a counter-tradition, rejecting unalloyed disinterest as an ideal of aesthetic contemplation. In *The Birth of Tragedy* Nietzsche presents what amounts to a case against both disinterest and, implicitly, the individualistic liberalism in which Schiller found its justification.

Apollonian experience, in Nietzsche's schema, is clearly a matter of disinterested aesthetic contemplation. The Apollonian experiences beauty from a distance, as a kind of vision that does not threaten to overwhelm him. "He observes," writes Nietzsche, "and enjoys his observations." He must maintain a calmness, a "freedom from all extravagant urges," and above all a sense of his individual integrity, for which Nietzsche takes an image from Schopenhauer's *The World as Will and Idea*:

> Even as on a raging sea, assailed by huge wave crests, a man sits in a little rowboat trusting his frail craft, so amidst the furious torments of this world, the individual sits tranquilly, supported by the *principium individuationis* and relying on it.

Apollo is the apotheosis of this principle of the individual, calm in a world he treats as distant spectacle rather than threat.

Rather than lauding the Apollonian ideal so precious to the Kantian tradition, Nietzsche points to its limitations, to how, when we allow experience to engulf us and shatter the *principium individuationis*, experience is transformed by the Dionysian rapture.

When this happens, "the individual forgets himself completely" and enters into a sense of solidarity with others unavailable to the Apollonian. Examples of Dionysian power include a plethora of collective experiences. Dionysian experience in medieval Germany, Nietzsche tells us,

> ... drove ever-increasing crowds of people singing and dancing from place to place; we recognize in these St. John's and St. Vitus' dancers the bacchic choruses of the Greeks, who had their precursors in Asia Minor and as far back as Babylon and the orgiastic Sacaea. There are people who, either from lack of experience or out of sheer stupidity, turn away from such phenomena, and, strong in the sense of their own sanity, label them either mockingly or pityingly as 'endemic diseases." These benighted souls have no idea how cadaverous and ghostly their "sanity" appears as the intense throng of Dionysiac revelers sweeps past them.

What is at stake here is something beyond the individual's distancing himself from self-interest: it is the individual's ability to lose self-identity and identify with the group—and, beyond that, with the whole, since "not only does the bond between man and man come to be forged once more by the magic of the Dionysian rite, but nature itself, long alienated or subjugated, rises again to celebrate the reconciliation with her prodigal son, man." Liberal individualism of the sort championed by Schiller, and to which his idea of aesthetic cultivation contributes, has proven weak at forming bonds of social solidarity. Indeed, the habit of disinterested aesthetic contemplation defined by Kant and advocated by Schiller can itself undermine social solidarity by becoming a class marker. As Pierre Bourdieu has shown in *Distinction: A Social Critique of the Judgment of Taste*, the "pure gaze" of the disinterested aesthete correlates with social and educational privilege, and serves as a means of justifying the superiority of the putatively "sensitive" aesthete over the insensitive mob. The distanced gaze of the individualistic Apollonian, so crucial to the liberal sense of self, has also proven weak at creating a solidarity with the earth, the kind of ecological ethic needed to sustain our continued existence. Nietzsche sees a possibility for the breaking of the Apollonian distance of the disinterested aesthete to bring about just such solidarities—to "redeem him through a mystical experience of the collective."

A more direct refutation of the aesthetics of disinterest can be found in the writings of the Asger Jorn. Jorn, a Dane whose intellectual formation lay in the Scandinavian left's resistance to the German occupation during the Second World War, and who remains relatively unread in the English-speaking world, was a key intelligence in the Situationist International, and his writings on aesthetics challenge the tradition of Kant and Schiller by championing interest over disinterest and the collective over the individual.

In *Magic and the Fine Arts*, Jorn argues that art is important not for distancing us from our passions and urges in a Schillerian fashion, but precisely because of its capacity for "agitation"—for creating "excitement, fanaticism, intolerance, enchantment." "To be enchanted means to enjoy something, and today," he asserts, "we have succeeded in defining aesthetic experience as disinterested enjoyment, or rather as darkened light. No wonder art is as grey as dirt." The realm of the aesthetic, for Jorn, is a place for the expression of interest. Institutions that encourage disinterested contemplation are the enemies of art: writing of New York's Guggenheim Museum in particular, and of museums more generally, Jorn tells us that the museum is "a place where works of art are directly placed in their sepulcher without ever having passed through a role in everyday life."

"Primitive peoples," Jorn writes, "do not relate to disinterest" such as one would find in a Kantian approach to art, or in scientific research, "but that does not mean that they have never done research—on the contrary—but their research has always been conducted out of an interest, an artistic or cultural desire to search for satisfaction." This research is conducted via aesthetic play, which itself has no preordained aim, but is the method through which we discover what our desires and interests are, or could be. As Jorn puts it, "the fundamental element in art" is "the unconscious active enjoyment of life through play with matter, with color, tones, clay, words, etc." This play "is not consciously directed to any goal but is a delight." When we are enchanted in the act of aesthetic play, we transform the world into that which is compatible with our desires—as Jorn's finest explicator, Graham Birtwistle, says "inspiration and enchantment mean for Jorn that external conditions are in tune with our physical and psychic needs." We therefore come, through the aesthetic, to concretize our needs, our interests, and desires, which may in fact prove different than what we had supposed. This is the vital function of the aesthetic, and the means by which it changes our habits of life. Aesthetic cultivation brings our lives into greater accord with our desires, needs, and our own interests. The interests at stake for Jorn, though, cannot be limited to self-interest, class-interest, or any other factional interest. The aesthetic is a form of play, and "play develops best in community" and the meaningful community is that of humanity as a whole—so the interests we discover via the aesthetic are not individual but collective: indeed, the aesthetic act takes us out of the realm of individual self-interest and into the realm of the general interest. Thus, only a socialist subjectivity can create the true aesthetic. The aesthetic becomes the arena of collective dreams, expressing them and inculcating them in others. If Schiller's is an Apollonian and liberal vision of the function of the aesthetic, Jorn's is a far more Dionysian and collectivist one. With Jorn, the human outcome of aesthetic experience is no longer the calm, disinterested individual judging the world while his own desires lie in abeyance and becomes, instead, the excited, enchanted, or enthralled community, fanatic about the realization of its collective desires.

Problems of the General Will

A useful distinction, in seeking to understand the collective interest expressed by the aesthetic in Jorn's thinking, is that between the 'will of all' and the 'general will,' concepts first articulated by Rousseau. The will of all, in Rousseau's *On the Social Contract*, is an aggregate or collection of individual wills, while the general will is the will of a community in which each member is thinking not of his or her self-interest, but the interest of the community as a whole. Jorn's idea of aesthetic experience is that it involves freeing us from individual self-interest—not through having us step away from it into disinterest, as in the Kantian tradition, but by bringing us into contact with the general interest of the human community. It is, in fact, a means for us to discover and experience the Rousseauian general will—if we add to the idea of the general will the heat of Jorn's "excitement, fanaticism, intolerance, enchantment."

The danger inherent in the idea of the general will is the danger of mistaking for general what is in fact partial or factional—mistaking self-interest or the interest of some relatively narrow group for the general interest. The liberal critique of Rousseau tends to be that his work tends toward despotism, to the tyranny of whatever agency claims to have apprehended the general will. And we can infer a similar critique of the idea of the general will, and the aesthetic as an embodiment of the general interest, from within the Western Marxist tradition as well. Consider the final meditation of Adorno's *Minima Moralia*, which begins:

> The only philosophy which can be responsibly practiced in the face of despair is the attempt to contemplate all things from the standpoint of redemption. Knowledge has no light but that shed on the world by redemption: all is reconstruction, mere technique. Perspectives must be fashioned that displace and estrange the world, reveal it to be, with its riffs and crevices, as indigent and distorted as it will appear one day in the messianic light. To gain such perspectives without velleity or violence, entirely from felt contact with its objects—this alone is the task of thought. It is the simplest of all things, because the situation calls imperatively for such knowledge, indeed because consummate negativity, once squarely faced, delineates the mirror-image of its opposite.

The general thrust of the passage is very much in accord with the kind of aesthetic explorations Jorn advocates. Adorno speaks of thought, and Jorn of aesthesis, but both yearn for a redemptive activity, one that would displace or negate the given, broken world with a vision of fulfillment, of the satisfaction of the general desire or will that amounts to redemption. But Adorno's meditation is not over, and the second part offers a dire warning of the calamity inherent in such visions:

> But it is also the utterly impossible thing, because it presupposes a standpoint removed, even though by a hair's breadth, from the scope of existence, whereas we well know that any possible knowledge must not only be first wrested from what is, if it shall hold good, but is also marked, for this very reason, by the same distortion and indigence which it seeks to escape. The most passionately thought denies its conditionality for the sake of the unconditional, the more unconsciously, and so calamitously, it is delivered up to the world. Even its own impossibility it must at last comprehend for the sake of the possible. But beside the demand thus placed on thought, the question of the reality or unreality of redemption itself hardly matters.

There is no point fully removed from self- or group interest, no unconditional or universal vantage point from which the general interest can be apprehended. The attempt to grasp it will be distorted—and passion in the service of distortion is a thing against which to be cautioned.

The Saving Contradictions of Camp

Exaggerated, mannered, and parodic—yet loving, a travesty that is also a tribute, camp is inherently contradictory. David Bergman tells us the term itself is drawn from the French *camper*, meaning "to pose, to strike an attitude," and the most plausible origin for the term in something like its contemporary sense is the life of the French military camp of the nineteenth century, where the exaggerated gestures of military ritual—mannered forms of walking, rituals such as the salute, and so forth—appear as simultaneously absurd and deadly serious. The contradictory nature of camp performance, which allows both participation in an identity and distance from it, has been one of its main powers in queering gender: it has been an essential vehicle, for example, for one gender wishing to embody characteristics of another without fully becoming that other, or for women wishing to participate in but not reduce themselves to forms of female sexuality created by the male gaze. Another form of contradiction camp embodies is that it creates a perspective that is at once interested and disinterested.

Camp, in the sense I intend it, is a kind of ludic and aestheticizing attitude that is also a kind of deep commitment. Christopher Isherwood, the first to use it in this sense, puts a good description of it into the mouth of a character in his novel *The World in the Evening*:

> High camp always has an underlying seriousness. You can't camp about something you don't take seriously. You're not making fun of it; you're making fun out of it. You're expressing what's basically serious to you in terms of fun and artifice and elegance.

Camp, seen this way, is a cousin of aesthetic autonomy, since it elevates play and beauty over utility and morality—an elevation well understood by Susan Sontag in her seminal "Notes on Camp" where she writes:

> To start very generally: Camp is a certain mode of aestheticism. It is one way of seeing the world as an aesthetic phenomenon. That way, the way of Camp, is not in terms of beauty, but in terms of the degree of artifice, of stylization.
>
> To emphasize style is to slight content, or to introduce an attitude which is neutral with respect to content. It goes without saying that the Camp sensibility is disengaged, depoliticized—or at least apolitical.

Sontag goes on to add:

> Camp is the consistently aesthetic experience of the world. It incarnates a victory of 'style' over 'content,' 'aesthetics' over 'morality'...

So far, Sontag has framed camp as a form of disinterest—involving an Apollonian distance from its object. Framed in these terms, it lies open to the same sorts of criticisms Nietzsche, Jorn, and others have leveled at the tradition of Kant and Schiller. But even as camp involves a kind of Apollonian aesthetic distancing, it also—contradictorily—embodies the Dionysian impulse to break down the barriers separating self and object. "Camp taste is a kind of love," writes Sontag, and it "identifies with what it is enjoying." The serious involvement of which Isherwood wrote is, in fact, an identification of self and object, a breaking down of the barriers of aesthetic distance, a Dionysian act of participation.

What camp offers, then, is Apollonian and Dionysian, disinterested yet interested. It breaks past the pallid individualism of the dominant tradition of aesthetics, but at the same time provides a kind of distancing from the potentially dangerous enthusiasms of those who seek in art and play an expression of the general will and general desire. This play of distance and identification has been best documented when camp addresses gender, but one can see it in broader terms as well: the camp misanthropy of a Philip Larkin or a Frederick Seidel, to the camp patriotism of Trey Parker and Matt Stone, and far beyond, camp creates a play of interest and disinterest that awaits its full analysis. Camp's pioneering theorist, Susan Sontag, ends the opening essay of the book that contains "Notes on Camp" with a call for an erotics of art. What aesthetics now cries out for is a poetics of camp.

The Abject Sublime, or:

Jean Genet's Vaseline

We critics don't do all of the things we once did, or at least we don't do them particularly well. In the eighteenth and nineteenth centuries, critics had a finely honed sense of the different shades and nuances of aesthetic experience, and deployed a rich vocabulary to discriminate between such categories as the charming, the beautiful, the sublime, and the picturesque, among others. Perhaps one reason for the failure to continue the project is the apparent shortcoming of the inherited categories when confronted with modern and postmodern art and writing. Some thinkers are bold enough to construe new categories—one thinks of Sianne Ngai's work on the cute, the zany, and the interesting, for example—but me, I'm content, for the moment, to see if the old aesthetic terms might be modified, retrofitted so as to bear on newer forms of expression. One term, among most venerable, certainly seems to have life left in it—the sublime. But some of the most exciting developments in the aesthetics of the past century combine sublimity with something one might think of as its opposite, abjection. One way to understand this is to consider a rolled-up tube of Vaseline as it appears in the writing of Jean Genet.

Like many people of my generation, I came to admire French theory in my graduate school years. One thing that puzzled me back in the early 1990s, when as a doctoral candidate in English lit I was happily chowing down on fricassée Foucault, bouillabaisse Baudrillard, and délice de Deleuze, was the relative lack of enthusiasm for these thinkers in American philosophy departments. Outside of the New School and Columbia—where the legacy of European émigrés was strong—and the Catholic universities—where theology kept philosophy wedded to continental traditions—the thinkers my friends and I found so congenial were often treated with suspicion by American professors of philosophy. Of course the question I should have been asking wasn't "why do the philosophy departments shun this stuff," but "why do we in English take to it so readily?" It is not obvious, after all, why a love of the poetry of Seamus Heaney should lead to an appreciation of Luce Irigaray. François Cusset traces the particulars of how the works of these thinkers traveled from France to the United States via various channels (notably French and comparative lit departments) in his wonderful study *French Theory*, but I think there's a core affinity between literary study and French theorists, something that lies behind the particulars of cultural transmission across the Atlantic. In the French tradition, theorists tend to arrive at their ideas by extrapolating from works of literature. That is, their concepts are, to a degree unmatched in Anglo-American philosophy, created from sorting through and regularizing the observations of poets, novelists, and playwrights: taking just the major works of Deleuze and Guattari as examples, we can point to their use of Artaud as the basis from which they elaborate the notion of the "body without organs" in *Anti-Oedipus*, and Karl Phillip Moritz as the basis of the idea of "animal-becoming" in *A Thousand Plateaus*. They begin where we begin, with a passage of literature, even though they tend to head in different, perhaps more ambitious, directions.

It should come as no surprise, then, to find Julia Kristeva basing her notion of abjection on the writings of Céline. In her classic book on the subject, *Powers of Horror*, Kristeva speaks of those who encounter the abject as feeling "a threat that seems to emanate from an exorbitant outside or inside, ejected beyond the scope of the possible, the tolerable, the thinkable." The abject thing—be it an object, an urge, a person, a class of people, a bodily function, what have you— is something we scapegoat, that we try to throw out as something we cannot accept and don't want to have any relationship with. But we inevitably have a relation to the abjected, despite what we'd like to think—and when we make something abject we still sense it as something "quite close" even though "it cannot be assimilated." It "fascinates desire, which, nevertheless, does not let itself be seduced." And our "desire turns aside; sickened." Our conscious minds cling to the (false) certainty the this abject thing is shameful and has nothing to do with us, even as unconsciously we are drawn toward the abject, which is "as tempting as it is condemned." The abject "has only one quality of the object—that of being opposed to I"—that is, to the ego's sense of itself. It is what we define as not-us, what we have subdued and expelled. "And yet," Kristeva continues, "from its place of banishment, the abject does not cease challenging its master." So what does this mean, specifically? I've seen enough people whose religious background has led them to reject and deny their own homosexuality to know that there are many people who turn their own sexual identity into something abject, and suffer a deep and unhealthy split between their conscious sense of who they are, their "I" or ego, and their rejected but ever-present sexuality—a version of the attraction-repulsion Kristeva describes. Or, moving to an even grimmer example, we could think of what the Nazis did to Jews (and others) as an extreme form of abjection: a casting-out of people, an assertion that there is no connection between them and us, and yet a fascination, an unconscious sense of kinship that needs constant denial, a lurking sense, constantly in need of being suppressed, that the dark qualities attributed by *us* to *them* might also belong to us. The core chapter of *Powers of Horror* is an analysis of Céline's writings, in which Kristeva notes that Céline presents himself as "the only authentic one" who recognizes that which society abjects, and who will guide us through the underworld of abjection in his *Journey to the End of Night*.

If I were betting on who would be elected to the laureateship of abjection, though, I wouldn't back Céline. I'd place my chips on the spot marked "Jean Genet," and I'll tell you why. He understands abjection from the inside: born to a prostitute, raised in foster homes, prone to petty theft, and homosexual in a hostile time and place, he lived abjection, and not as a voluntary tourist in the realm of the abject. What is more, he found something in abjection that Céline never found: a kind of sublimity. He turned rejection into a sign of strength and even glory. The best way to understand this is to take a look at a passage near the beginning of *The Thief's Journal*, where he writes about a tube of Vaseline.

Genet describes an early experience in Spain, where he'd been arrested. The police have him empty his pockets, and it is revealed that he was carrying a tube of Vaseline, which the police correctly understood as a sexual lubricant, and a sign of Genet's homosexuality.

> I was dismayed when, one evening, while searching me after a raid—I am speaking of a scene which preceded the one with which this book begins—the astonished detective took from my pocket, among other things, a tube of vaseline. We dared joke about it since it contained mentholated vaseline. The whole record-office, and I too at times, though painfully, writhed and laughed at the following:
> "You take it in the nose?"
> "Watch out you don't catch cold. You wouldn't want to give your guy whooping-cough."
> I translate but lamely, in the language of a Paris hustler, the malicious irony of the vivid and venomous Spanish phrases. It concerns a tube of vaseline, one of whose ends was partially rolled up. Which amounts to saying that it had been put to use. Amidst the elegant objects taken from the pockets of the men who had been picked up in the raid, it was the very sign of abjection, of that which is concealed with the greatest of care, but yet the sign of a secret grace which was soon to save me from contempt. When I was locked up in a cell, and as soon as I had sufficiently regained my spirits to rise above the misfortune of my arrest, the image of the tube of vaseline never left me. The policemen had shown it to me victoriously, since they could thereby flourish their revenge, their hatred, their contempt.

The object itself is neutral, of course: it is what the police do when they discover it that renders Genet abject: they need to re-enforce their own sense of difference and superiority, their brotherhood in the confraternity of the norm, by using the object a as a focus for revenge, hatred, and contempt. But watch the alchemy by which Genet redeems the despised object, and with it himself:

But lo and behold! this dirty, wretched object whose purpose seemed to the world—to that concentrated delegation of the world which is the police and, above all, that particular gathering of Spanish police, smelling of garlic, sweat and oil, but prosperous-looking, stout of muscle and strong in their moral assurance—utterly vile, became extremely precious to me. Unlike many objects to which my tenderness gives distinction, this one was not at all haloed; it lay on the table, a little grey leaden tube of vaseline, broken and livid, whose astonishing discreetness, and its essential correspondence with all the commonplace things in the record-office of a prison (the bench, the inkwell, the regulations, the scales, the odor), would, through the general indifference, have distressed me, had not the very content of the tube, perhaps because of its unctuous character, by bringing to mind an oil lamp, made me think of a night-light beside a coffin.

A night light beside a coffin! Great! And the description continues:

Lying on the table, it was a banner telling the invisible legions of my triumph over the police. I was in a cell. I knew that all night long my tube of vaseline would be exposed to the scorn—the contrary of a Perpetual Adoration—of a group of strong, handsome, husky, policemen. So strong that if the weakest of them barely squeezed his fingers together, there would shoot forth, first with a slight fart, brief and dirty, a ribbon of gum which would continue to emerge in a ridiculous silence. Nevertheless I was sure that this ridiculous and most humble object would hold its own against them....

There is a great deal one might say about this passage—including something about how the erotic way in which the police and the tube are depicted is a kind of revenge against aggressive heteronormativity. But the thing that I'd like to note is the resemblance between the passage and Kant's description of sublimity in *Critique of Judgment*.

It's uncanny how well Genet's passage maps onto Kant's notion of sublimity. For Kant, we get a sense of the sublime when we encounter something grand and vast, something that seems as though it could destroy us: a storm at sea, say, or a volcanic eruption, or a tornado near at hand towering above us into infinity. We experience these as sublime not because we are afraid of them (although we are certainly fearful) but because of something they call up within us. Such things, when we observe them and do not flee or faint, "raise the energies of the soul above their accustomed height and discover in us a faculty of resistance ... which gives us the courage to measure ourselves against the apparent almightiness of nature." We feel not only fear, but our own capacity to stand tall against the fearsome world, small though we may be. For Kant, this awareness of our own miraculous endurance in the face of vast powers is the essence of the sublime.

The despised, abjected tube (and the Genet who becomes despised and abjected by virtue of association with that tube) stands in relation to the police as the small but undaunted human stands in relation to the vast natural forces of which Kant speaks. It endures, in danger, and so gains a kind of dignity, a sublimity in its abjection—in fact, a sublimity by virtue of its enduring of abjection.

Soldiers have a certain sublimity for Kant, because they do not "yield to danger," but go forth "to face it vigorously with the fullest deliberation"—and it is significant, I think, that Genet turns to military language when, continuing his description of the Vaseline tube on the police station table, he says "I would like to hymn it with the newest words in the French language. But I would have also liked to fight for it, to organize massacres in its honor and bedeck a countryside at twilight with red bunting." Genet even adds, in a footnote, that he "would indeed rather have shed blood than repudiate that silly object." Genet would stand up for the tube of Vaseline just as it, on the police table, stands for him: defiantly there despite its abject status, despite its vulnerability. It asserts its being and resilience—and by extension, Genet's—in a world of powers that could easily destroy it. It is, in some profound sense, his comrade in arms. No one understands abjection as well as does Genet, perhaps because no one had to search within it so hard to find the dignity of the sublime.

VI
Afterword

Death of a Bookseller

This book is dedicated to Ron Ellingson, a bookseller who was every bit as important to my education as any professor. This essay is about him, and it's here because he would have argued with me over every sentence in this book, then defended them against anyone nearby who took his side.

If, like me, you can't pass a used bookshop without going in, to emerge at least an hour later with as many titles as you can carry shoved into your bag and your jacket pockets, then you'll know that such establishments come in two kinds: the carefully curated variety, with titles categorized precisely and books wrapped neatly in protective Mylar; and the other kind, where you wander among heaped mountains of books, ready at any time to be stunned by either a rare first edition or an avalanche. Chicago's Aspidistra Bookshop, which held down a spot on Clark Street for close to thirty years before closing in 1998, fell into the second category. And I should know: I had the honor of working there for a couple of years while I finished writing my doctoral dissertation. The place had two owners—Darrell Simmons, who only stopped in from time to time and who knew more about Yeats than anyone I've ever met (and I've met several Yeats scholars), and Ron Ellingson, with whom I worked. Yesterday I attended Ron's funeral, and I've been thinking about him and his bookshop all day.

A lot of people who came into Aspidistra asked about the name (on one occasion a woman told me she liked it so much she planned to name her daughter Aspidistra). The Aspidistra is a plant, but not just any plant: it's a plant you can abuse or ignore, but not kill. You can put your cigarette butts out in its soil and it will keep growing. You can put it in a coat closet for a month with no light and no water and it'll laugh the experience off. For Ron, it was an apt symbol not just for his bookshop, but for literary culture as a whole. Ron was also a big fan of George Orwell, whose *Keep the Aspidistra Flying* cast a hard, cynical gaze on the entire literary system, especially the world of bookshops. Only once did a customer come in and ask if Orwell had inspired the name—and Ron dropped the copy of Abbie Hoffman's *Steal This Book* he was putting into a locked glass case, strode around the counter, and kissed the man on both cheeks.

Ron grew up in Decatur, Illinois, where, as his wife Kathleen said at the funeral, no one wanted to talk about anything interesting except Ron, who was always reading and always wanted to talk about what he read. She married him and they talked for decades, and had a troop of children who talked books too, when they weren't hauling crates of them around Ron's Lincoln Park store, or to the second shop he briefly opened in Uptown, or to one of the many weird little attic or cellar book caches he had around Chicago. Like too many young men of his generation, Ron was sent off to Vietnam. A clerk in the Marine Corps, he never saw combat, but he had the unenviable task of shipping a great many dead bodies back to the U.S. "I like what they've done with the Vietnam memorial in D.C.," he once told me, "but there's no way I'm ever going—I'd cry until my eyes bled." He took an attitude toward authority that I've seen in a lot of veterans: it could go and fuck itself, in all its forms. That may be why his lawyer, a strange little guy who looked for all the world like Ron Jeremy in a cheap suit, was always coming by the shop with something to sign or be faxed. I don't think Ron and the tax system always played well together. Another time I remember an old-school Chicago ward politician coming by and telling (not asking) Ron to put up a poster for the mayor's chosen candidate for Alderman. That guy was lucky to get out without being hit on the head with a thick volume of the *Oxford English Dictionary*.

A bookshop is many things—at least a good one is. And Aspidistra, in its scruffy, scrappy way, was a very good bookshop, and served a number of functions. Firstly, it was a crucial part of my education. I was living a few blocks north of the store when I worked there, and taking the electric train out to South Bend, Indiana every week to meet with my doctoral advisors and take care of whatever grad school business I had to address. Grad school was very good to me, but doctoral study tends to make one narrow and deep—the logic guiding one's study is that of specialization in a field, and concentration on particular problems within that field (for me it was poetry, and questions of poetic influence). But Ron's bookstore was an exercise in intellectual breadth. You never knew what books would come in the door—anything from out-of-fashion historiography, philosophy, and literary criticism from the libraries of deceased academics to the books printed locally by the Chicago branch of the Surrealist movement to old Wobbly tracts to large collections of (shall we say) special-interest erotica. And Ron had an opinion about all of it. In a way, the exposure to the forgotten, the weird, and the academically untouchable has been a kind of secret weapon for me as a poet, critic, and writer—it's always been a kind of ballast against the winds of academic fashion.

Of course Aspidistra wasn't just about me and my education—though Ron certainly saw that as one of its functions. He was always asking me about how my dissertation was going, and I think he hired people largely on the basis of whether he thought it would be mutually beneficial to be in conversation with them. I remember my job interview: he saw that I studied British literature, and asked me to name three of the best English novelists writing. It was the mid-1990s, and I said "Martin Amis, Jeanette Winterson, and Julian Barnes." "Two out of three," Ron replied, with a grunt of disapproval (he would hold Barnes against me for the rest of his life). He also asked me to lift a very large cardboard box of books, and when I told him "that's too big—you can't lift it, and if you did the box would break" he said "you pass—you start tomorrow."

When I came back for work the next day, I discovered another of Aspidistra's great functions: as a kind of ongoing salon for the interestingly weird. I didn't see a lot of the old Aspidistra crowd at Ron's funeral—I think because a lot of them have passed on. Fred Burkhart, for example, has died—a giant of a man, an outsider printmaker and photographer who used to come by to hang out with his tiny young daughter, and who'd crash on hot days in air-conditioned comfort on the floor of one of the less-visited sections. As, I'm sure, has the man

I only knew as "Snowman," an ancient African-American gentleman from New Orleans who had been a reverend, a jazz musician, and filled every other conceivable sort of interesting role in the world (including, it was rumored, a cocaine dealer, the putative source of his nickname). I remember others who came by—art dealers, collectors of odd books, Situationists, left-over Black Panthers who'd pull Machiavelli off the shelves to argue over passages, a homeless man who had once been on the Existentialist Party ticket as a vice-presidential candidate, a tall astrologer and ladies' man called "Startouch," two old cross-dressers who were always pleased to be called "ma'am," a uniform fetishist (I once asked him which branch of the service he was in, since I couldn't quite tell, and got a lecture on each part of the hodgepodge of military gear in which he paraded around), and so on. One of Ron's sons told me at the funeral service that some of these people are still around, but fringy people are hard to get hold of, so they hadn't got the news about Ron's passing.

Once in a great while Ron would feel a sudden urge to throw a party in the store. "Let be be finale of seem!" he'd shout, quoting his favorite poem, Wallace Stevens' "The Emperor of Ice Cream," "I'm throwing a soirée!" I'd be sent out to lay in a supply of Guinness and fried chicken from the joint down the street, and he'd keep the doors open late for a gathering of all the regulars. It was always great.

I think what got me choked up at the service was the memory of those moments—it hit me hard when Ron's son Colin stood up next to the flag-draped casket and read "The Emperor of Ice Cream," just as Ron would have wanted. And then the service was over, and the music came on: "Crimson and Clover" by Tommy James and the Shondells. I remembered Ron putting that song on at one of his soirées, and could see him, Guinness in hand, dancing among the bookshelves among all his friends. It was a bit much for me, and I headed back to the cloak room, where I reached into the pocket of a jacket I hadn't worn for years and found a little Grove Press paperback of Brecht's *Threepenny Opera* that Ron had given me when he closed the store. I couldn't quite bring myself to go home after the funeral, and I was a bit too shaken up to stay and talk to the others who'd come. I spent the evening riding the El wherever it took me and reading the copy of Brecht that Ron had placed in my hands so long ago.

Acknowledgments

A critic writes for much the same reasons as he reads, talks, and listens: to have a conversation with the world. Those whom I have read, talked and listened to are sometimes also those about whom I have written. A partial list of the people whose words have meant a great deal to me during the writing of these essays would begin with my wife, Valerie, and include Michael Anania, Louis Armand, Sally Connolly, Joshua Corey, Joseph Donahue, Katy Evans-Bush, Lea Graham, R.S. Gwynn, Norman Finkelstein, Barbara Fisher, Johannes Göransson, John Matthias, Ben Mazer, Marjorie Perloff, Kevin Prufer, Michael Robbins, Mark Scroggins, Michael Gregory Stephens, Mike Theune, Marc Vincenz, John Wilkinson and Timothy Yu. These the companions ...

Many of the pieces published here first appeared elsewhere. "You Will Object: Four Futures of Poetry" was delivered as a talk at the Grolier Poetry Bookshop in Cambridge, Massachusetts; "Who is a Contemporary Poet?" and "The Future of Genius" appeared in *B O D Y*; "Charmless and Interesting: The Conceptual Moment in Poetry" was published as a special supplement to *Poetry*; "Inventions of a Barbarous Age: Contemporary Rhyme in Poetry" appeared in *Spoon River Poetry Review*; "Proud Men in their Studies: On Mark Scroggins" appeared in *Golden Handcuffs Review*; "So a Poet Walks into a Bar: Notes on Poetry Readings" was delivered as a talk for the Association of Literary Scholars, Critics, and Writers in Boston; part of "The Open Word: An Essay and a Letter for Peter O'Leary" first appeared in *Chicago Review*; and another part was delivered as a talk at the University of Louisville; parts of "A Scribe and His Ghosts: The Poetry of Norman Finkelstein" appeared in *The Offending Adam*; other parts were published in *Chicago Review*. "A Strange and Quiet Fullness: The Uncanny Charles Simic" and "Poetics of Embodiment" appeared in slightly different form in *Boston Review*. "John Crowe Ransom's Quarrel with God" was published in different form in *The Hudson Review*. "History, Totality, Silence" was delivered as a talk at the University of Maine, "An ABC of Gertrude Stein" appeared in *Lute and Drum*; "The American Poet as European, or Egon Schiele's Ladder" appeared in different form in *Pleiades*; "Poetry Ha Ha" was published by *At Length*; "Hating the Other Kind of Poetry" appeared in *Copper Nickel* and as the afterword to my book of poems *The Kafka Sutra*. "The Work of Criticism in the Age of Mechanical Recommendation" was published in *The Battersea Review*; "The Avant-Garde in Babel" appeared in *Action Yes!*; and "Fanaticism! Intolerance! Disinterest" was published in *VLAK*. Other essays here had their start, generally in less developed form, on the Samizdat Blog.

About the Author

ROBERT ARCHAMBEAU was born in Providence, Rhode Island in 1968, but his family moved to Canada before his first birthday—a strange kind of homecoming, given that his ancestors were among the first settlers of Quebec. Never quite at home as a Canadian or American, he came to inhabit what he describes as "the world's least interesting trans-national identity." He has vivid memories of his parents, at the end of the Nixon administration, considering putting an "America: Love It or Leave It" bumper sticker on their car, next to the Canadian license plate. He attended the University of Manitoba, where his father, a ceramic artist, taught, and where he had a fraught relationship with the regionalist poetic movement then in fashion among the poets associated with the university. Later, looking for a poetry that was concerned with regional identity but that was also attracted to the remote, the arcane, and the displaced, he discovered the work of the American poet John Matthias, whose work and background were as English as they were American. Archambeau went to study under Matthias at the University of Notre Dame, where he wrote a doctoral dissertation on the appropriation of Wordsworth's regionalist poetics by postcolonial writers, and where he accidentally blundered into an M.F.A. by hanging out in Matthias' living room, where the writing seminars were conducted, and writing poems.

A few regionalist poems made it into Archambeau's first collection of poems, *Home and Variations*, but what really came to fascinate him, as both poet and critic, were acts of creative appropriation and re-imagination. His chapbook *Citation Suite* consisted of a long poem composed only of quotations from various sources spliced into one another until they created a language of their own, and this pointed him in a direction his work was to follow. The present book and the chapbook *Slight Return: Remix and Ekphrasis* contain writing in this mode: an inhabiting and reworking of found text, generally literary in nature.

As a critic, Archambeau has been increasingly drawn to questions of the social position of poetry, of how it has functioned in different contexts. His first critical book, *Laureates and Heretics: Six Careers in American Poetry*, examined the reputations and career paths of six poets who studied at Stanford in the 1960s—including two, Robert Pinsky and Robert Hass, who went on to serve as poets laureate of the United States—with an eye toward understanding the intersection of aesthetic choices and poetic renown. A later study, *The Poet Resigns: Poetry in a Difficult World*, examines the question of the kinds of social conditions that make poetry popular or marginal. He has also edited several books, including *Word Play Place: Essays on the Poetry of John Matthias* and *Letters of Blood and Other English Writings of Göran Printz-Påhlson*. He taught for a time at Lund University in Sweden and is now professor of English at Lake Forest College, where he teaches Romanticism, literary theory and, occasionally, creative writing.

Other Books by Robert Archambeau

The Kafka Sutra

The Poet Resigns: Poetry in a Difficult World

Laureates and Heretics: Six Careers in American Poetry

Home and Variations: Poems

    As editor:

Letters of Blood and Other English Works of Göran Printz-Påhlson

The &NOW Awards: The Best Innovative Writing

Word Play Place: Essays on the Poetry of John Matthias

www.ingramcontent.com/pod-product-compliance
Lightning Source LLC
Chambersburg PA
CBHW020325170426
43200CB00006B/277